T0373713

# LIVE, WORK AND PLAY

## A CENTENARY HISTORY OF WELWYN GARDEN CITY

### MARK CLAPSON

The
History
Press

First published 2020

The History Press
97 St George's Place, Cheltenham,
Gloucestershire, GL50 3QB
www.thehistorypress.co.uk

British Library Cataloguing in Publication Data.
A catalogue record for this book is available from the British Library.

ISBN 978 0 7509 9401 9

Typesetting and origination by The History Press
Printed and bound in Great Britain by TJ International Ltd.

# CONTENTS

# ACKNOWLEDGEMENTS

I am grateful to the Welwyn Garden City Heritage Trust for choosing me to write the Centenary History of Welwyn Garden City. The Trust funded a buyout from teaching while I was at the University of Westminster, which was very welcome. Angela Eserin, Vanessa Godfrey, Lorraine Dewar and Tony Skottowe of the Trust were always prompt in replying to questions, supplying materials, and generally being supportive.

I'm also grateful to the staff of the Hertfordshire Archives and Library Services, based in Hertford, and to the staff of the British Library; thanks also to WGC Library for the use of their images. And at some remove I express gratitude to those who were interviewed by the Welwyn Garden City Heritage Trust, and of course to the interviewers, for their Where Do You Think We Played?, Where Do You Think We Lived? and Where Do You Think We Worked? projects. A quarter of all references in this book are to WGCHT materials.

# ABBREVIATIONS

| | |
|---|---|
| **AE** | Angela Eserin |
| **AIA** | American Institute of Architects |
| **ARP** | Air Raid Precautions |
| **ATC** | Air Training Corps |
| **CNT** | Commission for the New Towns |
| **CPRE** | Campaign for the Preservation of Rural England |
| **FJO** | Frederic James Osborn |
| **HALS** | Hertfordshire Archives and Library Services |
| **HCC** | Hertfordshire County Council |
| **HUD** | Department of Housing and Urban Development (US) |
| **ICI** | Imperial Chemical Industries |
| **LDV** | Local Defence Volunteers |
| **LNS** | Land Nationalisation Society |
| **MTCP** | Ministry of Town and Country Planning |
| **NCSS** | National Council of Social Service |
| **NLS** | Nationalisation of Labour Society |
| **OU** | Open University |
| **RDC** | Rural District Council |
| **RFC** | Rugby Football Club |
| **RPAA** | Regional Planning Association of America |
| **RTPI** | Royal Town Planning Institute |
| **SHM** | Special Housing Mission |
| **SME** | Small to Medium Enterprise |
| **SOE** | Special Operations Executive |
| **TCPA** | Town and Country Planning Association |
| **TPI** | Town Planning Institute |

| | |
|---|---|
| **TS** | Tony Skottowe |
| **UDC** | Urban District Council |
| **WDYTWP** | Where Do You Think We Played? |
| **WDYTWW** | Where Do You Think We Worked? |
| **WGC** | Welwyn Garden City |
| **WGCCC** | Welwyn Garden City Cricket Club |
| **WGCDC** | Welwyn Garden City Development Corporation |
| **WGCFC** | Welwyn Garden City Football Club |
| **WGCL** | Welwyn Garden City Ltd |
| **WGCHT** | Welwyn Garden City Heritage Trust |
| **WGCUDC** | Welwyn Garden City Urban District Council |
| **WHDC** | Welwyn and Hatfield District Council |
| **WVS** | Women's Voluntary Service |

# TIMELINES

## Antecedents to Welwyn Garden City

**1776**  Cromford housing opened for Sir Richard Arkwright's employees in Derbyshire
**1776**  New Lanark village initiated by David Dale in Scotland; later improved upon by Robert Owen
**1853**  Copley textile village opened built in Halifax, Yorkshire, by Edward Ackroyd
**1860**  Ackroydon workers' village founded in Halifax
**1869**  'Garden City' opened in Long Island, New York
**1871**  Ebenezer Howard moves to USA
**1875**  Bedford Park begun in London
**1887**  Port Sunlight founded in Cheshire
**1893**  Bournville village initiated by Cadbury in Birmingham
**1898**  Ebenezer Howard's *Tomorrow: A Peaceful Path to Reform* published
**1899**  Garden Cities Association founded
**1901**  New Earswick founded by Rowntree in York
**1903**  Letchworth Garden City initiated by Ebenezer Howard
**1905**  Hampstead Garden Suburb founded in London
**1906**  Brentham Garden Suburb founded in London
**1914**  Outbreak of First World War leads to cessation of house building
**1917**  The New Townsmen formed
**1918**  *New Towns After the War* first published
**1918**  Prime Minister David Lloyd George makes 'Home for Heroes' speech

| 1918 | Tudor Walters Report recommends improved housing standards |
| 1918 | Ebenezer Howard and colleagues visit land near Hatfield Hyde |
| 1919 | Housing and Town Planning Act introduces nationwide council housing |

## Key Milestones in the Growth of Welwyn Garden City

| 1919 | Welwyn Garden City (WGC) initiated by Ebenezer Howard |
| 1920 | Welwyn Garden City Ltd (WGCL) formed |
| 1920 | Louis de Soissons Plan for WGC adopted |
| 1920 | Temporary construction workers' homes and WGCL offices open on Campus |
| 1920 | First homes available at Handside Lane |
| 1921 | A Civil Parish for Welwyn Garden City formed |
| 1921 | *Welwyn News* begins publication |
| 1921 | First members of Welwyn Garden City Ltd elected to Rural District Council |
| 1921 | The first temporary branch of Welwyn Stores opens |
| 1922 | Welwyn Rural District Council build first houses |
| 1922 | *Daily Mail* model village built and opened by Earl Haig |
| 1923 | Handside School opened, the first new school in WGC |
| 1925 | The White Bridge spanning the Luton to Dunstable railway line opens |
| 1926 | Railway station opened by Neville Chamberlain |
| 1927 | First election to the new Urban District Council |
| 1928 | Charles Purdom removed from WGCL |
| 1928 | Ebenezer Howard dies |
| 1933 | First Town and Country Planning Summer School held at WGC |
| 1936 | Frederic James Osborn leaves WGCL |
| 1936 | Co-operative Stores begin trading in WGC |
| 1937 | Council offices open on Campus |
| 1937 | Ten new shops open on Howardsgate |
| 1939 | New Welwyn Stores officially opened |
| 1940 | *Life and Work in Welwyn Garden City* published |
| 1942 | *New Towns After the War* republished |
| 1943 | Ministry of Town and Planning formed |
| 1943 | WGC Post-War Committee established |

| | |
|---|---|
| **1945** | Silver Jubilee Celebrations for WGC |
| **1946** | The first New Towns Act in Britain |
| **1946** | Green Belt established between WGC and Hatfield |
| **1947** | Town and Country Planning Act |
| **1948** | Public Enquiry into New Town designation |
| **1948** | Welwyn Garden City and Hatfield designated as new towns |
| **1948** | Welwyn Garden City and Hatfield Development Corporations established |
| **1948** | Reg Gosling appointed Chair of WGC Development Corporation |
| **1949** | WGCL winds up; assets transferred to WGC Development Corporation |
| **1952** | Harold Macmillan, Minister for Housing, visits WGC |
| **1957** | Sir Theodore Chambers dies |
| **1958** | Reg Gosling dies |
| **1959** | Death of Richard Reiss |
| **1961** | The Commission for the New Towns (CNT) established |
| **1962** | Louis de Soissons dies |
| **1963** | Queen Elizabeth opens QEII hospital |
| **1964** | A new Howard Memorial unveiled in Howardsgate |
| **1965** | The New Towns Act of 1965 creates a further phase of UK new towns |
| **1965** | C.B. Purdom dies |
| **1966** | CNT begins work at WGC |
| **1970** | Anniversary celebrations to mark fifty years of Welwyn Garden City |
| **1970** | Pre-war WGC west of railway line designated a conservation area |
| **1973** | Welwyn Hatfield District Council (WHDC) formed |
| **1974** | WHDC takes over |
| **1978** | Death of Sir Frederic Osborn |
| **1981** | Initial plans for major town centre redevelopment (the Howard Centre) published |
| **1983** | More assets transferred from CNT to WHDC |
| **1987** | Howard Centre plans published |
| **1987** | Redevelopment of Cherry Tree site announced |
| **1990** | Howard Centre and multi-storey car park opens |
| **1990** | Seventy-fifth Anniversary of Welwyn Garden City |
| **2020** | Anniversary celebrations to mark 100 years of Welwyn Garden City |

## Key Industries and Places of Employment in Welwyn Garden City

| | |
|---|---|
| 1921 | Digswell Nurseries established; a subsidiary of WGCL |
| 1921 | Welwyn Builders Ltd established; a subsidiary of WGCL |
| 1921 | Welwyn Brickworks Ltd established; a subsidiary of WGCL |
| 1921 | Welwyn Stores Ltd first opened; a subsidiary of WGCL |
| 1921 | Midland Bank opens |
| 1922 | A.D. Dawney and Sons Ltd, steelworks, established |
| 1922 | Barclays Bank opens |
| 1925 | Herts, Gravel and Brickworks Ltd established; a subsidiary of WGCL |
| 1925 | Shredded Wheat Co. Ltd factory opens |
| 1927 | Barcley Corsets Ltd factory opens |
| 1928 | British Instructional Films Studios begins production |
| 1928 | Nabisco takes over Shredded Wheat |
| 1929 | Bickiepegs Ltd established |
| 1929 | Captain H.R.G. Birkin car engine research establishment opens, developing the 'Bentley Blower' |
| 1929 | Cresta Silks Ltd clothing manufacturers established |
| 1929 | Murphy Radio Ltd established |
| 1930 | Andrew Buchanan and Sons Ltd confectionary makers established |
| 1930 | Norton Grinding Wheel Co. opens |
| 1931 | Pure Extracts Co. Ltd opens, food production |
| 1932 | Murphy Radio moves to purpose-built premises |
| 1932 | Beiersdorf Ltd pharmaceuticals opens factory |
| 1934 | Studio Lisa photographic studios open |
| 1935 | Neosid Ltd opens, making electrical components for radios |
| 1935 | Welwyn Studios Ltd opens, filmmakers |
| 1936 | Catomance Processing Ltd opens, making chemicals for textiles |
| 1936 | Lacre Lorries Ltd begins production |
| 1936 | John A. Weir Ltd, car bodies and sliding roof manufacturer opens |
| 1936 | Roche Ltd begins production in WGC |
| 1937 | ICI Ltd begins operations at WGC |
| 1937 | Atomised Food Products Ltd begins production at WGC |
| 1937 | Celtis Ltd opens |
| 1947 | Eylure Ltd begins operations in WGC |

**1951** Smith and Nephew buy Herts Pharmaceuticals

**1959** Smith, Kline and French opens at WGC

**1969** *The Guardian* reports twenty-one new companies added to WGC since 1948

**1976** Small and medium-sized workshops opened

**1982** Smith and Nephew leave WGC

**1982** ICI closes most of its operations in WGC

**1983** John Lewis acquires Welwyn Department Stores

**1985** Hi-tech employment park first mooted

**2008** Shredded Wheat ceases production after seventy-three years in WGC

## Living and Playing: Key Dates in Sport, Leisure, Religion and Politics in WGC

**1921** Welwyn Garden City Cricket Club formed

**1921** Welwyn Garden City Football Club formed

**1921** Welwyn Garden City Theatre Society formed

**1921** Welwyn Garden City Arts Club formed

**1921** Welwyn Garden City Book Club formed

**1921** Welwyn Garden City Music Society formed

**1921** Cherry Tree Restaurant opens

**1921** The Constitutional Club (Conservative) established

**1921** Welwyn Garden City Labour Party established

**1923** Golf course of nine holes opened by WGC Golf Club

**1925** Welwyn Garden City Rotary Club formed

**1926** Roman Catholic Church of St Bonaventure consecrated

**1927** Congregational Church built

**1927** Welwyn Harriers (Athletics) established

**1927** Golf course extended to eighteen holes

**1927** *Site Planning at Welwyn Garden City* shows many facilities were open or being built

**1928** Boys' Brigade established in GC

**1928** Welwyn Theatre opens in Parkway, also showing films

**1929** General Election returns Conservative MPs for WGC

**1929** The Free Church and St Michael's Church open

| 1930 | Success for Bentley at Le Mans |
| 1932 | The Barn Theatre opens |
| 193? | Handside Playing Fields open |
| 1933 | Lea Valley Swimming Pool opens |
| 1933 | Welwyn Garden City Swimming Club formed |
| 1933 | King George V Playing Fields taken over by Urban District Council |
| 1933 | *I Was a Spy* filmed in WGC |
| 1934 | Welwyn Town Band formed |
| 1935 | General Election returns Conservative MP for WGC |
| 1935 | WGC Welsh Male Voice Choir formed |
| 1935 | St Francis church consecrated |
| 1936 | Save the Woods Campaign initiated |
| 1937 | Welwyn Garden City Photographic Society formed |
| 1938 | Baptist and Congregational Church buildings completed |
| 1940 | *Life and Work in Welwyn Garden City* criticises some aspects of leisure provision in WGC |
| 1941 | Air Training Corps Squadron for WGC formed |
| 1942 | Welwyn Garden City Bowling Club formed |
| 1945 | General Election returns a Labour MP for WGC |
| 1948 | Many sports and cultural facilities are transferred from WGCL to WGCDC |
| 1952 | Great Britain Olympics Hockey team captained by leading WGC hockey player |
| 1953 | Welwyn Athletic Club formed |
| 1956 | Welwyn Garden Residents Association formed |
| 1957 | Welwyn Garden City Literary Society formed |
| 1959 | Gosling Stadium opened |
| 1960 | Welwyn Athletic Club represented at Rome Olympics |
| 1960 | Housewives Register established in WGC |
| 1964 | Cyclists from WGC race at Tokyo Olympics |
| 1965 | Ludwick Club Badminton Team tours Denmark |
| 1966 | Many sports and cultural facilities transferred from WGCDC to the CNT |
| 1970 | Stanborough Lakes Park opens |
| 1973 | Campus West completed |
| 1974 | Many sports and cultural facilities are transferred from CNT to WHDC |

## Welwyn Garden City and the Wider World

| | |
|---|---|
| **1925** | C.B. Purdom visits USA |
| **1933** | International Planning Conference held at WGC |
| **1936** | American green belt towns acknowledge influence of WGC |
| **1937** | Richard Reiss begins the first of three pre-war tours to the USA |
| **1938–39** | Jewish refugees arrive in WGC |
| **1939** | The Second World War begins |
| **1939–40** | Population of WGC increases by 21,000 |
| **1940** | The Blitz on London and other British cities begins |
| **1940** | The Blitz comes to WGC |
| **1945** | Jubilee Celebrations |
| **1946** | The Crown Prince of Sweden visits Welwyn Garden City |
| **1947** | Welwyn Garden City FC tour the Netherlands |
| **1952** | Athletes from WGC compete in the Olympic Games (Helsinki) |
| **1960** | Athletes from WGC compete in the Olympic Games (Rome) |
| **1964** | Athletes from WGC compete in the Olympic Games (Tokyo) |
| **1968** | Athletes from WGC compete in the Olympic Games (Mexico City) |
| **1965** | Frederic and Margaret Osborn visit Japan |
| **1970** | Silver Jubilee celebrations; Queen Mother visits WGC; many international visitors |
| **1990** | Seventy-fifth anniversary celebrations attract international visitors |
| **2020** | Centenary anniversary of Welwyn Garden City |

INTRODUCTION:

# A NEW HISTORY OF WELWYN GARDEN CITY

## The State of the Art

This book was commissioned by the Welwyn Garden City Heritage Trust to mark the centenary celebrations of one of the most influential English towns in the world. Although countless words have been written about the origins, development and significance of WGC, a new history is long overdue. Beyond the symbolic significance of the anniversary itself, WGC deserves a fresh historical appraisal. In this book, its social, cultural and economic history is intertwined with an account of its planning, origins and expansion since 1920.

Until recently, histories of WGC have fallen into three broad fields. The first might be termed the 'the insider histories' written by followers of the 'founding father' of the Garden City Movement Sir Ebenezer Howard. Frederic James Osborn (FJO), Richard Reiss and Charles Benjamin (C.B.) Purdom are notable here. Howard had provided the rationale and key planning principles of garden cities in his *Garden Cities of Tomorrow* (1898), later published as *Tomorrow: A Peaceful to Real Reform* (1902). The book was essentially a template for the garden city he initiated at Letchworth in Hertfordshire in 1903. And in 1919 Howard was proactive in getting Welwyn Garden City, the second garden city, off the ground. The town centre shopping mall, the Howard Centre, and the thoroughfare Howard's Gate, are both named after him.

A second and arguably more objective field comprises the town planning histories of WGC, undertaken largely by academic historians of town planning, and some scholars of urban development. While only a couple of academic planning history books exclusively examine the history of WGC itself, it features prominently in a number of scholarly works on the garden cities of the twentieth century. The significance of WGC in town planning history is evidenced, furthermore, in its place in many general academic histories of British town planning, and in evaluations of the international impact of the Garden City Movement during the twentieth century.

And the third pool of WGC histories might happily be summarised as 'local history and heritage'. Many enthusiastic local historians, activists in heritage organisations, and oral and visual historians have been keen to document and promote the social history of WGC, particularly from the point of view of those who have lived there.

This book aims to embrace all three approaches, to provide a wellresearched and scholarly account of the social and planning history of WGC, drawing upon a wide range of sources: official reports; academic histories, local histories; oral histories; newspapers and journals. It is hoped that the book will be of interest not only to an academic but also to a popular readership, which will hopefully include many citizens of the Garden City itself, whether they are long-established residents or more recent migrants.

## The 'Insider Histories'

Most people living in Welwyn Garden City have heard of Frederic Osborn, or 'FJO' as he called himself and as he was often referred to by his contemporaries. He has both a school and a major road near the railway station named after him. As we will see, he was a major player in the development of WGC, serving as Secretary to Welwyn Garden City Ltd for many years. On the national and international stages, he was also a key mover in professional town planning organisations, an adviser to British political parties and governments, and possibly the most influential exponent of the Garden City Movement during the twentieth century. Osborn moved from Letchworth to Welwyn Garden City soon after WGC was designated in 1919. He lived at Guessens Road, in the opulent heart of town, just down the street from Howard, who died in 1928. During his long lifetime, most of it spent in WGC, Osborn wrote a number of histories of the town. His *Genesis of Welwyn Garden City* (1970) covers the earlier days of the garden city and Welwyn Garden City Ltd, to its transition to a new town after the Second World War, and its near-completion as a planned entity by 1970. And in his co-written book *New Towns: Their Origins and Achievements* (1970) Osborn assessed the national and overseas impact and legacy of the Garden City Movement, and gave a summary history of WGC. As both activist in and chronicler of the British Garden City Movement at home and abroad, Osborn always placed his experiences at WGC at the centre of his work. His transatlantic correspondence with his friend Lewis Mumford also provides much information on how FJO evaluated life and the built environment in WGC, and interpreted social and economic change between the 1930s and the '70s.

In the Woodhall area of WGC a couple of culs-de-sac are named after other leaders in the development of WGC. One is Chambers Grove, named after Sir Theodore Chambers, who became Chairman of Welwyn Garden City Ltd in 1920. Chambers also has a footpath named after him – Sir Theodore's Way – in the shopping area, and a monument to him in Parkway. There is another little street in Woodhall called Purdom Road, named after C.B. Purdom. It is a modest little street compared with Osborn Way, a spatial expression of the pecking order in the movers and shakers that made Welwyn Garden City. As we will see, Osborn and Purdom were allies for many years, both followers of Howard and enthusiasts for the WGC that they were building. Purdom was an advocate of planned new 'satellite cities' to be designed along the Garden City model, writing a book on this, *The Building of Satellite Towns*, during the 1920s. He viewed WGC as a key exemplar of both. But as early as 1928, just eight years after the beginnings of the town, Purdom was out of favour with many of his elite colleagues. He would later write a somewhat jaundiced autobiography, *Life over Again* (1951), which also acts as a partial history of WGC. Purdom updated his analysis of WGC as a satellite town during the wartime debates on the future of housing and town planning in Britain. Following the destruction and losses to property caused by the Blitz and other air raids, WGC would play a major role in the emergent new towns programme following the New Towns Act of 1946, becoming a new town itself in 1948.

The memoir to Captain Richard L. Reiss, written by his wife Celia, also provides invaluable information about life in Welwyn Garden City. A politician, housing reformer, humanitarian and a leading member of Welwyn Garden City Ltd, Reiss played an important role not only in managing the growth of the Garden City, but in his patronage of sports and leisure clubs. He also spread the word about WGC to the wider world. Osborn, Purdom and Reiss figure prominently in this book.

## Town Planning Histories of Welwyn Garden City

The most recent, readable and thorough history of WGC is to be found in Stephen V. Ward's *The Peaceful Path: The Hertfordshire New Towns* (2016). His book takes its title from Howard's *Tomorrow: A Peaceful Path to Real Reform*. WGC is viewed as at least as important as its predecessor, Letchworth, and the significance of the actions and writings of Frederic Osborn are given their due weight. In addition to his work on WGC, Osborn was a leading national campaigner for garden cities, and during the Second World War, as head of the Town and Country Planning Association, he fought tirelessly for both a new towns programme, and a more systematic national town planning apparatus. Osborn could, and did, claim some credit for the formation of the Ministry of Town and Country Planning in 1943, and the New Towns Act of 1946.

Osborn personifies the link between the Garden City Movement and the new towns. WGC has been viewed both by Ward and by this writer as the metaphorical umbilical link between the British garden cities of the first half of the twentieth century, and the new towns programme after the Second World War. Unlike Letchworth, WGC was redesignated as a new town in 1948, gaining a second phase of planned growth. This history is also examined in Frank Schaffer, *The New Town Story* (1972), a book that almost but not quite qualifies as an insider history. Schaffer was a founder member of the Ministry of Town and Country Planning, established in 1943, and from 1965 became the Secretary for the Commission for the New Towns. The Commission took over the management of WGC from the Development Corporation in 1966. Schaffer was also a leading light in the Town and Country Planning Association, and known to Osborn. As an advocate of the post-war new towns programme, Schaffer pointed to the achievement of the new towns in providing a new and more prosperous life for millions of people, and he defended them, including WGC, from unfair criticisms that they were more 'soulless' or prone to social problems than older urban cities and towns.

One of the leading planning historians was Gordon E. Cherry, whose studies of British town planning during the twentieth century have contributed much to our understanding of Howard, Letchworth and WGC as influencers on the nature and trajectory of new community planning. However, Cherry's *The Evolution of British Town Planning* (1974) and *Town Planning in Britain Since 1945* (1996) suffer from a sometimes simplistic account of the rise of British town planning, and of the influence of Howard and his followers within it. Dennis Hardy's *Garden Cities to New Towns* (1992) underplays the importance of WGC in the history of British new communities of the twentieth century.

Back during the 1970s, when the Open University (OU) was beginning to make a splash in distance learning across Britain, it provided a popular second level unit entitled 'Urban Development'. In *The Garden City* (1975) Stephen Bayley critically discussed the origins of planned new towns and garden cities, from the factory villages of the nineteenth century to the larger new towns of the last century. WGC was given a great deal of attention, not least because of the role of its influential architect Louis de Soissons, who was appointed Chief Architect by WGCL in April 1920. His synthesis of modern town planning with a Georgian-influenced architectural style was also much praised by Ray Thomas and Peter Cresswell, *The New Town Idea* (1975). It is pause for thought that these course units are among the most detailed and thought-provoking histories of WGC from garden city to new town. In establishing the national and international reputation of the OU in the new city Milton Keynes, the academics were drawing upon the histories of WGC and Letchworth and earlier planned new towns.

The importance of WGC is also explored in studies of the British Garden City Movement. The work of Anthony Alexander, Robert Beevers, Michael Hebbert and Standish Meacham, to take just four examples, has delved into the history of WGC from many different angles, demonstrating that there is not one agreed interpretation of the history and significance of the town. Alexander for example, in *Britain's New Towns: Garden Cities to Sustainable Communities* (2009), argues that the history of WGC from garden city to new town and now towards a more sustainable urban environment fulfils some key aspects of Howard's original intentions while demonstrating the town's adaptability to change. By contrast, in *Garden City Utopia: A Critical Biography of Ebenezer Howard* (1988), Robert Beevers shows how the original, perhaps naïve, idealism of Howard's thought was undermined by the actual process of building garden cities, and the constraints and political realities faced by their exponents. WGC is an obvious case in point. In *Regaining Paradise: Englishness and the Early Garden City Movement* (1999), Standish Meacham also analyses a process of dilution of Howard's ideals, arguing they relied on romantic notions of past living that would find a difficult fit into the twentieth century. In a number of scholarly contributions to books on the Garden City Movement, for example, 'The British Garden City: Metamorphosis' (1992), Michael Hebbert also demonstrates some key mismatches between the original template of Howard and developments in Letchworth, WGC and other experiments in garden cities during the twentieth century.

## Local and Heritage Histories of Welwyn Garden City

Among the most useful books to anyone, academic or otherwise, interested in WGC is Maurice de Soissons' *Welwyn Garden City: A Town Designed for Healthy Living* (1988). Maurice was the son of Louis, yet his history of WGC, whilst properly noting its achievements and successes, also draws attention to some of the problems in the town's history, from internal divisions in Welwyn Garden City Ltd, to local opposition to both the garden city and the new town, tensions between local political organisations, social problems between the wars and since, and also difficulties in meeting demand with the supply of materials and services. It is a skilful book, moreover, blending a corporate and planning history of WGC with its social, economic and political development. The current book has been quite dependent upon it.

The work of the Welwyn Garden City Heritage Trust (WGCHT), funded by successful applications to the Heritage Lottery Fund, makes the most significant contribution to *Live, Work and Play*. The Trust was begun in 2005 when a few people, who later became trustees, took up arms successfully against a planning application in the garden city. There followed a realisation that the town lacked a dedicated champion for its heritage and so the Trust was established as a charity and not-for-profit company in December 2006. Since then it has created an invaluable collection of oral testimonies and other materials. Of particular value to this book has been the collection of oral history interviews with Welwyn Garden City residents for Where Do You Think We Worked? and Where Do You Think We Played? Two publications carry the

same titles and draw upon those interviews. Another series of interviews was
Where Do You Think You Lived?, although these remain unpublished at the
time of writing. Oral history can be problematic, as people tend to remember
selectively, and often reinterpret the past in a positive light. This is known as
'retrospective contamination' by oral historians. But oral history also supplies
lively memories and personal experiences of life and work in twentieth-
century WGC that are often absent from the printed record.

The DVD *Welwyn Garden City: A Brave Vision* (1996) was the idea of the
WGC Society, who obtained sponsorship and practical help from Rank
Xerox to create the original film. It was issued to mark the seventy-fifth
anniversary of the town in 1995. The initial format was a cassette with copyright held by Hertfordshire County Council (HCC) but by 2006 this format
had been largely replaced by the DVD and sales had dried up. Recognising
the quality of the production, the Trust approached HCC with a view to
acquiring the copyright and converting the format to a DVD, which HCC
were happy to accept. The film was relaunched to celebrate the town's ninetieth anniversary, since when over 500 copies have been sold throughout the
UK and overseas. The ability of the Trust to gain funding for the promotion
of local history is a testament both to those who have worked for it, and also
to the 'can-do' culture that had been instilled in WGC since its earliest days.
The WGCHT web address is www.welwyngarden-heritage.org. The website contains many quotes from interviews, pictures and photographs, many
relevant to this present book.

Another example of an active and concerned citizenry is the aforementioned Welwyn Garden City Society, much of whose work is available online
at http://welwynhatfield.co.uk/wgc_society. The Society is dedicated to
preserving the character and qualities of the built environment and the
amenities of the town. In addition to publicising WGC, conserving its buildings, and promoting an engaged and well-informed civic culture, the Society
is now at the forefront in defending the Garden City from a new phase of
planned development and infill that threatens the very essence of the Garden
City principles that have served WGC so well over the past 100 years.

# 2

# DREAMERS AND DOERS: THE MAKING OF WELWYN GARDEN CITY

## Industrialisation, Urbanisation and the Search for Solutions

The County of Hertfordshire in south-east England is the home, some might say the cradle, of the world's earliest modern garden cities. Letchworth was the first, designated in 1903, but its successor, Welwyn Garden City, is just as well known in the county, the country and across the world as its slightly older sibling.

The story of Ebenezer Howard and his founding of Letchworth and Welwyn Garden Cities has been told extensively, but historical context is required in order to understand the antecedents of WGC, and the ideas and working examples that influenced Howard. The two Hertfordshire garden cities were the latest chapters in the story of planned industrial villages and model communities, a story stretching back to the Industrial Revolution that began during the later eighteenth century, and which continued to evolve throughout the nineteenth century.[1] These were the factory villages built for the working population, and some innovative garden suburb experiments. They were a fascinating part of the wider story of humanitarian interventions and progressive reforms to improve the social, cultural and economic conditions of the unplanned industrial towns and cities, particularly the poorest, overcrowded and insanitary districts.

## Factory Villages in Britain During the Industrial Revolution

Among the most famous British examples are the company housing experiments built by paternalistic employers for textile workers during the Industrial Revolution of the late eighteenth century. Two stand out: Cromford in Derbyshire, and New Lanark in Lanarkshire. Built during the 1770s, Cromford was a factory village for textile workers, financed by the paternalistic employer Richard Arkwright. In addition to the nearby mill, the houses for the workers were also accompanied by a church and a community hall, an early version of living, working and playing in a community setting.[2] Robert Owen, the utopian socialist, bought out David Dale, the founder of New Lanark, providing further recreational facilities such as schools and meeting places. Owen also established New Harmony, Indiana, in 1825, an early example of the international diffusion of idealistic planned new communities. These were practical empirical examples of utopian ideals made real, unlike the grand but unrealised schemes of French philosophers such as Proudhon and Saint-Simon.

The mature phase of the Industrial Revolution saw the birth of Copley in 1849, and Saltaire in 1850, named after its capitalist benefactor and employer Sir Titus Salt. And in 1860 the factory village of Ackroydon was begun in the industrial zone of Leeds and Bradford in Yorkshire, named after its industrialist benefactor Colonel Edward Ackroyd, who had also previously financed Copley. Another famous new community, founded during the 1870s, was the upscale suburb of Bedford Park in London. Influenced by a number of leading Victorian architects, including Richard Norman Shaw, it created Arts and Crafts residences for high-minded aesthetes who consciously rejected mass production.[3] The jam-making company Hartley's, based in Liverpool, developed a model village at Aintree from 1880 for its workers, while soon afterwards Port Sunlight was established on the Wirral, a model village established by the Lever Brothers for their workforce and named after 'Sunlight Soap'. William Hesketh Lever, a contemporary of Howard, brought into existence an aesthetically fine village, which was to influence the Garden City Movement as that movement emerged and saw its first expression at Letchworth. Its romantic Arts and Crafts domestic architecture was designed by the architect William Owen, and also bears the imprint of Richard Norman Shaw. As the respected architectural historian Stephen Bayley argues, 'No two blocks of cottages at Port Sunlight are the same':

… and although over 1,000 were eventually built, most of this took place in a short period of time for there was relatively little building activity after the First World War. There were two basic types of accommodation: the 'kitchen cottage' with kitchen, scullery and three bedrooms, and the 'parlour cottage', which differed in that it had the advantages of four bedrooms and an added parlour.[4]

Lever also funded the village of Thornton Hough in Cheshire, during the 1890s, and later during the 1920s, as WGC was being constructed, he funded the extensive new housing estate of Wythenshawe in Manchester. By then he was Viscount Leverhulme in recognition of his industrial and humanitarian achievements. The importance of Port Sunlight, however, was to introduce variety into cottage-style domestic architecture that influenced the Garden City Movement.

If Port Sunlight was fashioned from profits made from soap, two other important influences on the emerging Garden City Movement owed

much to revenue gained from the manufacturing of chocolate. These were also privately funded company villages. The Cadbury Co. began Bournville in the Midlands in 1898, the year that Howard's *Tomorrow: A Peaceful Path to Reform* was published. Following its first phase of construction, a second building campaign began in 1905, hence coterminous with Letchworth's early development.[5] The significance of Bournville for the twentieth-century design of garden cities was again in the cottage-style housing, with gardens, and the subsequent low-density residential development, but

Ebenezer Howard.

also in innovations in street planning, such as the 7m (20ft) setting back of houses from the street, allowing for a generous provision of front gardens.[6] This was a distinctive break from the terraced by-law houses of late Victorian Britain that were built following the Housing Act of 1875. With front doors opening out directly onto the street, and containing a toilet and a small backyard, by-law houses were a distinct improvement on the jerry-built back-to-backs and slums of the Victorian years.[7] Yet the types of homes being offered by Bournville were an improvement on by-law terraces, offering more outdoor space and better interior design.

In York, the Rowntree Co. began New Earswick in 1902, its development continuing in earnest with the establishment of the Joseph Rowntree Village Trust in 1904. Its significance to the Garden City Movement, alongside the fact it was initiated at almost the same time as Letchworth, is that its architects were Barry Parker and Raymond Unwin, who drew up the master plan for Letchworth, and also Hampstead Garden Suburb in north London. With its straight main roads, curved minor roads and culs-de-sac, New Earswick was an early expression, in miniature, of what was built in Letchworth. It also anticipated the street pattern at WGC, from 1920.[8]

## 'The Garden City Geyzer': Ebenezer Howard

Following an uninspiring clerical career in London, Howard spent the years from 1871 to 1876 in the United States of America, where in Nebraska he came to understand the importance of communal self-help in rural communities. His life as a farmer there did not go well, so he moved to Chicago where he witnessed many experiments in new community building in low-density suburbs and semi-rural areas, and mixed with leading American writers and reformers. As the writer Lewis Mumford observed, Howard's time in the USA provided him with the 'constant spectacle of new communities being laid out every year on new land, and he was impressed by the possibility of a new start'.[9] The sense of pioneering in the United States, of creating active new forward-looking communities some distance from the, as he saw it, moral degradations of the industrial city, was a powerful influence on Howard's developing utopianism. On his return to England, he gained employment as a shorthand writer working in the Houses of Parliament, where he mixed with people in positions of power. Howard took full advantage to promote his ideas as his real talents lay in imagining new planned communities, and he was fortunate enough to live in a historical context where many ideas and proposals to reimagine urban-industrial societies were forthcoming. This was the 'Progressive Era' in American and European social thinking and politics, lasting from 1880 to 1940. Howard would make his own unique contribution to the case of progressive social reform.

A key theme in the British radicalism during the eighteenth and nineteenth centuries was land reform. The English writer and utopian thinker Thomas Spence laid some of the ground for Howard's work by arguing in his lecture *The Rights of Man* in the 1770s that everyone deserved an equal right to land and liberty. Sometimes called 'the first English socialist', Spence envisaged utopian communities in 'Crusonia' and 'Spensonia', experiments in communal living and collective land ownership.[10] Howard was no socialist but he deserves to be viewed within the utopian-radical tradition of questioning industrial capitalism and its social and environmental consequences, and of proposing grand alternative visions.

Although he was no intellectual, Howard was incredibly open-minded, hungry for ideas and influences to mould his vision for a reinvigorated and optimistic urban future. Hence he drew upon an eclectic set of writers and thinkers. During the 1880s he read Edward Gibbon Wakefield's *The Art of Colonisation*, originally published in 1849, which called for a more systematic approach to the construction of new communities in the Empire.[11]

At much the same time as Wakefield was developing his ideas, the Christian radical utopian writer James Silk Buckingham saw his plan for a radical new model industrial community published in *National Evils and Practical Remedies* (1849). Calling for an end to unplanned and dangerous urbanisation, he proposed his vision for Victoria, 'a model industrial town laid out on rectilinear principles.'[12] The importance of self-containment, as well as of thinking big, is evident in Victoria.

A more contemporary and significant influence on Howard were the arguments of the influential American political economist Henry George. George was exercised by the great paradox of urban-industrial societies, and particularly in his own country, that as increasing levels of wealth and prosperity were generated by the economy, growing levels of inequality and poverty accompanied the material achievements of the nineteenth century.

His book *Progress and Poverty* (1879) called for the producers of wealth to keep the value of what their labour had created. He also argued that the economic values based on land should belong to each and every member of society, and that the state should compulsorily acquire the land, rather than private interests and *rentier* capitalists.

Howard acknowledged that George's *Progress and Poverty* was an eloquent and inspiring call for land reform, but he refrained from the negative caricatures of landlords as 'pirates and robbers' and was reluctant to countenance the forceful acquisition and nationalisation of land under the auspices of the state. Instead, Howard called for '"force of example" that is by setting up a better system, and by a little skill in the grouping of forces and the manipulation of ideas.'[13] These principles led Howard to argue that the land in his proposed garden cities would be in held in trust, and on lease, on behalf of all the citizens by the company that would manage the birth and development of the new town.

Howard did not completely reject the proactive role of the state in land for planned urban development, however. He was acutely aware that 'large areas of land must be obtained' for any major planned new community, and he argued that just as the Government had assisted in the purchase of private land to extend the railway network nationwide, so the state could involve itself in land purchase for an expanding network of 'social cities', or 'town clusters' each individually designed to 'a well-thought-out plan'.[14] This idea later eventuated in the British post-war new towns legislation.

Another, and in some ways more surprising, influence on Howard was the Russian anarchist Peter Kropotkin, who first visited London in 1881. Howard was not particularly enamoured of the revolutionary and libertarian components of anarchism, but derived from Kropotkin the significance of local economic initiative both on the land and in towns, and the importance of self-government by local people. As Beevers notes, Howard cited Kropotkin's *Fields, Factories and Workshops* in his second edition of *Tomorrow*.[15]

In 1888, a year of urban protest at poverty and unemployment in Britain, Howard organised a reprinting of the visionary book *Looking Backward*, by the American writer Edward Bellamy. A key argument that a future where land was in common ownership rather than at the mercy of private interests exercised a profound impact upon Howard, evidenced in his own efforts to publicise these arguments. In 1890 the Nationalisation of Labour Society (NLS) was established to promote Bellamy's ideas, and as Stephen Ward argues, the NLS provided Howard with one of his earliest opportunities to speak publicly about them.

During the early 1890s Howard used the term 'Rurisville' for his new settlement, but by 1896 he had begun to refer to 'garden city' instead.[16] He did not coin the term but Howard would become its most prolific exponent, and his name synonymous with it. The American writer and expert on urban history, Lewis Mumford, who came to know WGC very well, suggested that Howard may have taken the name 'garden city' from the eponymous 'Garden City' built on Long Island, New York, from 1869. Howard was also well acquainted with Chicago during his time in the US, which had once been known as 'the garden city'.[17] Other scholars of architecture and planned new communities have made the same point.[18]

A further important influence on Howard was the British economist Alfred Marshall, who in 1884 argued strongly for the decentralisation of manufacturing away from the overcrowded cities into factory villages located in rural settings. Here was another key theme – dispersal – that influenced Howard.[19]

Howard was aware of most of the important utopian proposals for new communities in Britain, Europe and the USA, and was versed in those experiments that had been realised, as discussed above. Howard's philosophy of garden city planning was explained extensively in his 1898 publication *Tomorrow: A Peaceful Path to Real Reform*, republished with the slightly catchier title of *Garden Cities of Tomorrow* in 1902. As Roberts and Taylor have argued, the second title was also more palatable to the conservative-minded Victorian capitalists to whom Howard was appealing for forward-funding for his projects.[20] It is widely acknowledged by planning historians that Howard was 'neither architect nor scholar' but more of an urban reformer and idealist.[21] The book was a synthesis of the influences on Howard, and an ambitious statement of his garden city vision. His key principles may be summarised as follows:

- *Self-sufficiency*: the garden city was to harness agriculture and industry within the local economy, providing local employment and cutting down on the need for commuting to other towns for work, and on the long-distance transfer of goods. Local services, shops, and leisure facilities would enable every citizen to be able to live, work and play in a garden city.

- *Self-containment*: spatial limits of growth were to be constrained by a green belt upon which development would not be permitted in order to prevent the much-detested suburban sprawl of which Howard, in common with many writers, artists and reformers, was critical.
- *Zoning*: as a considered reaction to the mixed-use, noisy often squalid and overcrowded streets of the town centre, Howard proposed a separation between residential areas and those containing industrial and commercial activities. Homes were to be upwind from industrial pollution and smog.
- *Collective land-ownership*: the land upon which the garden city was built should not be privately owned but held in trust by a development company. (However, changes of governance and land ownership in the history of WGC, and the rise of private owner occupation, undermined this aspiration.)
- *Decentralisation*: the planned new community drew upon a dispersed population from the existing industrial city, and from the more remote rural areas where there was little opportunity for employment. The garden city was thus intended to prevent urban growth by rural to urban migration, and provide an improved environment for those from the town or country. This was the magnet, the attraction of the garden city as the best of both urban and rural. And this was evident in the final principle:
- *A balance of town and country*: the perils of rural isolation on the one hand, and of overcrowded and insanitary city life on the other, would be solved by the harmonious environment of the planned new community.[22]

Howard's Garden City diagrams portray the town centre with a Central Park and a Crystal Palace for shopping and socialising. Grand boulevards radiate out from the centre, dividing the town into distinct areas, or 'wards'. The ward was to be within easy access of the centre, but also to contain its own retail and social facilities. As Osborn argued in his preface to Howard's republished *Garden Cities of Tomorrow* (1965), the ward idea prioritised 'the need for local facilities for local life and popularised in Britain the theory, familiar for many years in America, of the "neighbourhood unit."'[23] Mervyn Miller, an architectural expert and historian, agrees that the ward was 'the forerunner of the neighbourhood unit'.[24] The neighbourhood unit was a planning concept finessed in the USA and applied to British new towns, including WGC, after the Second World War, which is discussed later in the book.

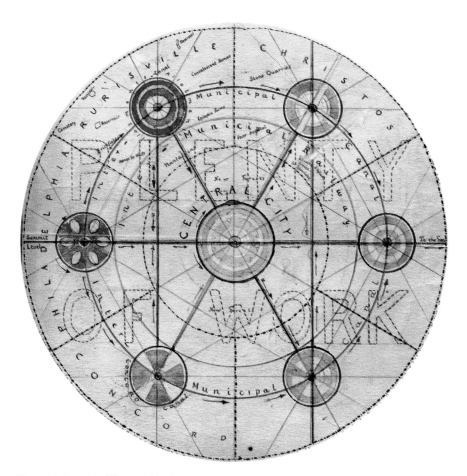

Howard drawing, 'Central city'.

After 'garden city', the term that most succinctly crystallises Howard's vision is 'social city'. All of the above came together to produce what he hoped would become living new communities, socially engaged, culturally progressive, and economically self-sustaining. Each garden city would be a social city, a place where people could live, work and play all their lives.

For all his achievements and the grandness of his vision, Howard remained essentially a modest man, living a modest life. His home in Guessens Road, WGC, during the 1920s was a medium-sized, semi-detached house, where he lived with his second wife. One man recorded by the Welwyn Garden City Heritage Trust (WGCHT) who moved to Guessens Road as a young boy in 1924 lived just across the street from Howard, and recalled him as a kind and quiet gentleman.[25]

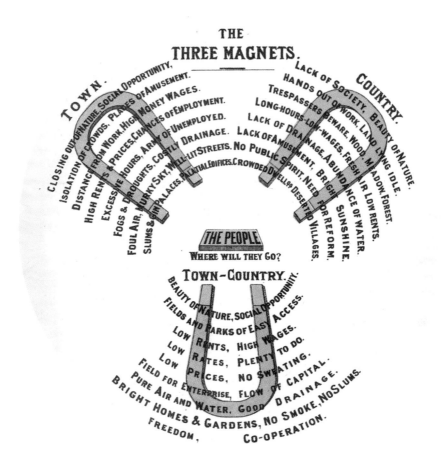

Howard drawing, 'Three magnets'.

There is an old saying that it is the quiet ones you should watch. *Tomorrow: A Peaceful Path to Real Reform* marked 'a turning point in British planning history'.[26] In the year following its publication, the Garden Cities Association (GCA) was formed, renamed in 1909 as the Garden Cities and Town Planning Association (GCTPA). In both guises, the association was at the heart of a progressive network of intellectuals, social reformers, writers and politicians.

The first Secretary of the GCA was a Scots surveyor, Thomas Adams. Relatively young and ambitious, he played a key role in promoting the garden city idea in principle and practice; for example, organising a national conference at Bournville in September 1901. George Cadbury provided not only financial assistance to the conference but also accommodation.

Speakers included George Bernard Shaw, Ebenezer Howard and a number of advocates of planned developments.[27]

According to Beevers, Shaw went down much more positively than Howard, partly because he was more charismatic, more famous, and a better speaker. It is worth noting here that Shaw was ambivalent towards 'the heroic simpleton' Howard, whom he called 'the garden city geyzer', adding that the planner was 'a fountain of benevolent mud'. Yet Shaw was a supporter of the garden city idea, and even called, in *John Bull's Other Island*, for garden cities to be built in Ireland. In Britain, Shaw invested 'sizeable sums of money' in both the companies at Letchworth and WGC.[28] He lived in the Hertfordshire village of Ayot St Lawrence, just a few miles from the second garden city.

The dream of building new communities was inextricably connected to the urban surgery required for the older unplanned cities brought about by the Industrial Revolution or by haphazard growth over the course of many centuries. And the nearest large city to Hertfordshire, expanding into its southern fields and woodlands, was London. Rapidly urbanising with little guidance from Government, London was by 1900 the largest metropolis in the world, a behemoth where the paradox that exercised Henry George was extensively played out. For London contained individuals of great wealth, a burgeoning middle class, but also large pockets of working-class poverty, as well as areas where streets of wealth were closely proximate to slums and poor housing areas.

Victorian London was in urgent need of radical improvement, and there was much evidence to prove it. General William Booth of the Salvation Army had written his powerful tract *In Darkest England and the Way Out* (1883), which likened the poorest and most degraded areas of the city to the terrible conditions in many parts of Africa. The monumental survey of Charles Booth, *Life and Labour of the People in London*, undertaken between 1886 and 1903, produced detailed data on insanitary, overcrowded and impoverished slums or poor housing areas, all of which continued to generate social problems while more affluent working-class, lower-middle-class and middle-class Londoners enjoyed increasingly comfortable homes and lifestyles, often in the burgeoning suburbs of the capital city. Those who could afford to were getting out of inferior housing, voluntarily removing themselves from the poorest places.[29] Charles Booth was part businessman, part social investigator and reformer, and, like Howard, a religious nonconformist. He was one of many opinion formers who observed the dispersive forces in the capital city as wealthier sections of society left poorer inner districts for more comfortable suburbs, hence relieving the pressure on poorer urban areas.[30] Decentralisation soon became a reality. From the 1890s the London County Council (LCC), established in 1889, began to build large new social housing estates to rehouse people from slums. This was also a process of dispersal, planned by a local authority.[31] Howard was a reformer and visionary within this late-Victorian to Edwardian context, but he was also a practical realist. He was one of many forward thinkers getting to grips with the legacy of the past century.[32] The plight of urban-industrial cities, thrown up hastily and haphazardly since the late eighteenth century, was one of the most pressing large-scale problems in one of the world's wealthiest countries. In his chapter 'The Future of London' in *Garden Cities of Tomorrow*, Howard clearly viewed decentralisation to rural Hertfordshire as the solution to London's problems.[33]

The first experiment at Letchworth has been extensively studied by town planning historians, urban historians, social historians, architectural historians and geographers. Initiated in 1903, it was the hugely influential Edwardian exemplar of the twentieth-century garden city. The origins of WGC cannot be fully grasped without acknowledgment of its important predecessor. It was a truly pioneering community established on the principle elaborated by Howard, who settled there along with leading members of the Garden City Movement in the years leading up to the First World War.

As Maurice de Soissons noted, the experience of Letchworth was 'vital' for Welwyn Garden City. The initial development of the first garden city suffered from practical difficulties in land use and planning, financial problems and also 'architectural conformity', which Welwyn Garden City assiduously sought to avoid. And, of course, the administrators of Letchworth, notably Osborn and Purdom, went on to become the most effective champions of WGC and the Garden City Movement in general.[34]

Before coming on to WGC, it is important to note that Letchworth inspired a number of contemporaneous garden-city-style housing schemes that are more accurately termed garden suburbs, notably Wavertree Garden Suburb, Oldham Garden Suburb, and most famously of all Hampstead Garden Suburb in north London.[35] Begun in 1905, and also planned by Parker and Unwin, it owed a great deal to the efforts of Henrietta Barnett, whose husband, Canon Barnett, was a reformer concerned with urban poverty and decay.

The crucial difference between garden suburbs and garden cities, however, is a fundamental one. Garden suburbs were simply planned extensions of towns or cities, often superior in amenity to unplanned suburban sprawl. But they were all about housing, whereas the garden city was a synthesis of residential, economic and social planning, and the creation of a complete urban environment. As the early twentieth century progressed there were increasing tensions between the garden city and garden suburb movements. Furthermore, many suburban council estates built by local authorities owed much to housing styles pioneered at Letchworth and Hampstead.[36]

The Garden City Movement played a nuanced role during the First World War. Letchworth became associated with the controversial 'conscientious objectors' such as Ramsay MacDonald, the Labour leader, Herbert Morrison, a London Labour politician, and Osborn himself. Fear for one's own life was not the basis of objecting to the war, nor can objectors always be viewed as unpatriotic, for they undertook war work on the Home Front. Morrison, for example, was ordered by the Conscientious Objector's Tribunal to take up 'land work', so he went to Letchworth and worked for a market gardener, an employer who Morrison observed was favourably inclined towards socialism.[37] The conflict was viewed by its socialist critics as essentially a class war, tragically wasteful of young men's lives. Yet for those who lost relatives – sons, brothers, husbands – in the trenches and at sea, those who refused to fight were branded as cowards. Letchworth took a long time to shake off this unpopular image.

Yet the so-called Great War was also the catalyst for the second garden city at WGC. Many of the leading advocates for garden cities who had settled in Letchworth during the relatively calm Edwardian years viewed the war and its consequences as an opportunity for domestic reform in general and for a second garden city in particular. As the conflict took its terrible toll in the trenches of northern France and Belgium, and as aircraft and airships dropped bombs on British and European cities for the first time, prominent 'New Townsmen', namely Ebenezer Howard, Frederic Osborn, Charles Benjamin (C.B.) Purdom and Captain Richard L. Reiss, looked beyond the immediate and tragic impacts of war to the years beyond the ceasefire. Another casualty of the First World War was the moratorium on most housing construction between August 1914 and November 1918. As the slums grew worse, and with the prospect of hundreds of thousands of servicemen

Frederic Osborn.

returning from the battlefields, the case for planned urban dispersal to relieve the overcrowded city centres was powerfully strengthened.

Herbert Morrison remained in contact with Osborn for many years, and went on to become the leader of the London Labour Party during the 1930s. He remained a steadfast supporter of the principle of decentralisation, as well as of other town planning ideas, notably the green belt, an area surrounding a city or town protected from urban development.[38]

As the war drew slowly towards its end, FJO kept himself busy in the British Library writing his important *New Towns After the War*. Published on behalf of the New Townsmen, it called for a new phase of decentralisation, for planned new communities to enable those dispersed from the urban centres to live in an ostensibly self-contained garden city. (The term 'New Townsmen' is also unwitting testimony of the simple fact that the emerging profession of town planning was almost completely male dominated. Yet, as we will see, women made a vital contribution to planned urban development and the social experience at WGC.)

The timing of publication was fortuitous. During the General Election of 1918, held while the war was still being waged, the Liberal Prime Minister David Lloyd George understood that the key to gaining votes was social reform. In his famous 'Homes Fit for Heroes' to live in promise to the electorate, he cleverly tied in improved housing for the working classes with the sacrifices they made during the war years.[39] Following the victory of the Liberal–Conservative National Government, in 1919 the first nationwide

Housing (Town Planning) Act was passed, steered through Parliament by the Liberal MP Christopher Addison. The 1919 Act initiated the era of social housing, then called 'council housing' because local authorities (councils) were subsidised from Central Government to build homes for rent from the councils. Most of these were intended for slum dwellers. Yet by 1922 it had been deemed insufficient to deal with the national housing crisis by Addison himself, due to the cutbacks to government expenditure caused by the economic downturn from 1921.[40] Nonetheless, the 1919 Act and subsequent Acts during the 1920s led to council house building in most towns and cities, including Welwyn Garden City.

Welwyn was the one and only garden city to eventuate in Britain following the Armistice. In *Garden Cities of Tomorrow,* Howard had argued that where the state was unable or unwilling to become involved in the development of planned new towns, some private land purchases could occur from estate owners.[41] In 1918, before the First World War had ended, and as the 'Homes Fit for Heroes' atmosphere intensified, Howard took Osborn and Purdom to the tract of land within the Panshanger Estate near Hatfield Hyde. It was the area he had been considering for his second garden city. They walked from Hatfield Hyde to what became the centre of the second garden city. As Howard's first biographer noted, WGC 'was one of the beauty spots of Hertfordshire': 'the land was well wooded, there was sand and gravel in places, a stream borders the estate, the site was only twenty miles from London, and there was a railway station already on the north end of the estate.'[42]

Howard independently asked the Marquis of Salisbury, then President of the GCTPA, whether a large area of his Hatfield estate might be made available for his second garden city, but was informed that much of the land was owned not by the Marquis of Salisbury but by Lord Desborough. However, Howard's initial disappointment turned to rejoicing when Desborough suddenly announced in the early summer of 1919 that a large proportion of his estate was now up for purchase, to be auctioned at the Panshanger sale.[43] Death duties had forced Desborough's hand.[44]

Without informing his fellow New Townsmen, Howard single-handedly purchased 2,300 acres (931 hectares) in the auction (there is another study to be made of the role of the aristocracy and large landowners in facilitating changing land uses for new community planning). The importance of securing investment for land purchase was paramount. Howard had to plead and cajole his friends to assist him with the task of getting enough capital. As he recalled:

> I knew that the reserve price was to be £30,000, and a few days before the sale I had only £1,000 in sight. That had been promised if I made a second effort to build a Garden City. I got busy on the telephone and by ten o'clock I had another £2,000 promised, two offers of £500 and one of a thousand. That was 10 per cent on the purchase price, enough to pay the deposit. So I went to the sale, made my bid, and secured the site of the Second Garden City.[45]

As Paul Roberts and Isabelle Taylor have argued, when Howard first set about creating 'his second privately funded garden city the idea was met with a mixture of ridicule, indifference, even hostility'.[46] Nonetheless, and even in the face of some bemusement from his fellow New Townsmen, including Osborn, Howard was successful, despite some financial issues during the process of land purchase.

The land purchased from Lord Desborough included Digswell House, which stood in a park of about 100 acres (40 hectares) with a further adjacent 190 acres (77 hectares). Soon after the first auction other areas of Desborough's estate were put up for sale, including a local beauty spot known as Sherrardspark Wood. Land owned by the Marquis of Salisbury at Ludwick and Hatfield Hyde was later added to the total area designated for Welwyn Garden City.[47] A quiet area in a mostly rural county was about to become the site of the second experiment of the British Garden City Movement.

There was certainly some opposition from those living within or adjacent to the designated area. Osborn noted the 'chilly' attitude of the 'county' society of Hertfordshire, the wealthy rural middle class and smaller landowners fearful of the intrusion of urbanisation into their gently rolling and attractive countryside.[48] Some members of the Rural District Council (RDC) were also wary of urbanisation, and of course jealous at the potential loss of powers to WGCL over the designated area. Rural conservative opposition to urban encroachment has a long history, of which WGC is simply one chapter. Yet as we will see in later chapters, WGC was increasingly influenced by Conservatism during the twentieth century.

Born of eighteenth- and nineteenth-century responses to the chaos of urban-industrial capitalism, WGC was a child of the twentieth century. While Howard and his Garden City Movement drew upon ideas from Europe, the Anglo-American connection was particularly important, and would remain so throughout the course of the last century. WGC would become the embodiment of modern town planning for new communities and new towns in Britain and across the world. Although it was not the first of Howard's garden cities, those who moved there would help to make WGC a success. As the following chapters argue, they helped to forge its identity as a living and working garden city with exceptional qualities in its social life, its economy, and its built environment.

# 3

# EXPANSION, CRITICISM AND CONTROVERSY: WELWYN GARDEN CITY BETWEEN THE WARS

Although Howard had unilaterally gone ahead with the land purchase required for his second garden city, the establishment of this new community and its early development would require a strong and determined collective effort by Howard and his fellow town planners. Optimism for the future was a defining characteristic of the first days of any garden city, but a host of practical difficulties lay ahead. This chapter charts those problems and demonstrates that, despite some significant problems facing those tasked to develop WGC, an impressive degree of success had been achieved by the time the Second World War broke out. Yet the *esprit de corps* required to complete the task sometimes broke down, while WGC developed a number of social problems that would tarnish its reputation, both with the wider public and also with politicians who had the power to determine the fortunes of the garden city.

# The New Company

In 1919 the Second Garden City Ltd was established, and renamed Welwyn Garden City Ltd (WGCL) the following year. The estate purchased now became the freehold property of the Company. Chief executives and officials of WGCL exhibited a powerful continuation of personnel with Letchworth, namely Frederic Osborn, who became Secretary of WGCL until 1936. His old comrade Charles Purdom took up the role as financial adviser until the difficult year of 1928.

In 1913, Purdom had written a tenth anniversary history of Letchworth Garden City in which he extolled its intrinsic virtues as a civilised and well-balanced place to live, but he would move to WGC from Letchworth in order to play an active role in making the second garden city. Purdom has tended to play second or even third fiddle to Howard and Osborn in the history of the British Garden City Movement, but his 1913 study of Letchworth and its lessons for town planning as a whole has been acknowledged as an influential work. It was republished in the USA in 1985 as one of 'thirty-five important titles documenting [the] major transformation', namely 'the rise of urban Britain'.[49] Yet Purdom had and still has something of a mixed reputation. According to one biographical account, he was 'simultaneously didactic, imperious, tactless, zealous, intelligent and eloquent' and not always a team player. Some of his colleagues respected him, others less so.[50]

Richard Reiss became Vice Chairman of the Company. In his younger years, Reiss was essentially an Edwardian Liberal, and stood as a Liberal candidate for Chichester, Sussex, in the General Election of 1909. He was an interventionist in the field of housing, and a friend of the Rowntree family that had built New Earswick. Reiss fought and was wounded during the Mesopotamia Campaign in 1917.[51] Following his discharge due to his war wound, Reiss served in the Ministry of Reconstruction in 1917–18, where he was involved in survey work on

Charles Purdom.

Richard Reiss.

the housing problem. During the so-called 'Coupon Election' of 1918, Reiss also stood and lost as a Liberal candidate for East St Pancras in Central London. He also worked on the Unhealthy Areas Committee of 1919–20, under the chairmanship of the Conservative coalitionist Neville Chamberlain, which advocated a programme of satellite towns. It is perhaps no coincidence that Chamberlain, as prime minister, in 1937 established the Barlow Commission to research the rationale and possibilities for a decentralisation policy. Reiss also served on the Tudor Walters Committee in 1918, alongside Raymond Unwin, whose report called for higher standards of housing for the masses. It argued that every house should have at least three rooms on the ground floor, namely a living room, parlour and scullery (a now mostly unused word for kitchen), with three bedrooms, a larder (cool food cupboard), and an internal toilet and bathroom. This became a key text in the 'Homes Fit for Heroes' campaign during the Coupon Election.

Hence Reiss's housing and town planning experience, and by extension his garden city credentials, were pretty impressive.[52] In 1918 he grasped the public and political mood for a new housing programme with his book *The Home I Want*, which also understood that most people desired a traditional-looking house with pitched roofs, and a garden. In the same year he was invited by the executive of the Garden Cities and Town Planning Association to become its chairman. A long-standing acquaintance of Henrietta Barnett of Hampstead Garden Suburb, in 1922 he was elected onto the Board of the Hampstead Garden Suburb Trust, a position he held into the post-Second

World War years.[53] During the early 1920s he was impressed by the 'jolly good lot' of the Labour Party, possibly because of his close acquaintance with Osborn in WGC, and became a Labour Party member, worked in the Fabian Society, and later joined the Independent Labour Party (ILP).[54]

Finally, Theodore Gervase Chambers became the Chairman of WGCL in 1920, holding that position throughout the life of the Company. A surveyor known for his business acumen, he had enjoyed a successful career in the City of London, and during the Great War he was appointed controller of the National Savings Scheme, which raised money from the public to assist the financing of the war effort. Possessing estate management experience, Chambers also held official roles elsewhere in the expanding interwar planning culture.[55] He served on the Departmental Committee for Garden Cities and Satellite Towns, otherwise known as the Marley Committee, established in 1932. This was further proof that the notion of planned decentralisation of people and resources from older urban centres was gaining ground in political circles between the wars.

The key Board members were joined by J.R. Farquharson, an industrialist who had supplied Howard with much of the initial deposit, Francis

Fremantle MP, Walter H. Layton, later Lord Layton, and Bolton Smart. The New Townsmen on the Board knew that estate management was essential to the start-up of WGC, so they invited Sir John Mann, a well-known accountant, onto the team.[56] Following some informal enquiries by Theodore Chambers to professional architects, Louis de Soissons was recommended by word of mouth and appointed town planner and architect, alongside Captain W.E. James as engineer, and C.W. Care as accountant.[57] The task ahead was daunting for this all-male team:

Theodore Chambers.

When the land was acquired there was no railway station between Hatfield and Welwyn North. There was no water supply, main drainage, electricity or gas. There were a few farm houses and cottages, 'The Waggoners', 'The Beehive' and 'The Woodman' were small public houses.[58]

About 400 people lived in the designated area. There were only six roads, all of which were country lanes, including Handside Lane, Woodhall Lane and Peartree Lane, which would give their names to three of the districts of the garden city. Woodhall was a particularly large area that was incorporated into the plan. This predominantly rural part of Hertfordshire was now on the cusp of major change, and many living in the designated area were opposed to that.

## The New Political Culture at WGC

Unsurprisingly, the existing Rural District Council feared a de facto loss of governance over the designated area. In October 1921 a new civil parish was established to incorporate the Company's estate, and was brought into Welwyn Rural District Council. Conversely, the planners at WGC would find allies in the locality, notably in the powerful firm of solicitors Longmores, 'of which the head Sir Charles Longmore, was clerk'.[59] His son, Elton Longmore, was clerk of the Rural District Council, and proved along with his father to be a warm supporter of the garden city and useful advisers 'in matters of local government reorganisation, education, highways, housing and other public services'.[60]

As Reiss recalled, 'a parish meeting was held' and the first parish councillors elected represented the ascendant power of WGCL: (Sir) Ebenezer Howard (33 votes); Sir Theodore Chambers (29); W.C. Horn (24); A.J. Squire (24). Sir Theodore Chambers was elected Chairman, and W.C. Horn (who had been farming the land before the acquisition) was elected Vice Chairman. F.J. Osborn was appointed clerk.[61]

Captain Reiss did not appear on the early RDC but he was an active member of the Labour Party, standing as a Labour candidate in General Elections in Suffolk, between the wars.

In 1923 the membership of the Parish Council was increased to twelve, and Welwyn Garden City gained three additional seats on the RDC. Yet the powers of the RDC were soon to be swept aside to a large degree. In 1926 a special meeting of the Parish Council applied to create an Urban District Council (UDC), which was formed the following year. The political composition of the UDC reflected the continuing ascendancy of the Company interest, but also revealed the predominance of independent councillors and the emergence of the local Labour Party in WGC during the 1920s. Thirteen Independents were elected, including Chambers and Horn, and three Labour councillors. The new UDC 'decided to have joint officers with the Company as a measure of efficiency and economy'. This further solidified the Company's power, as Osborn, a Labour activist, was appointed clerk, while W.E. James and C.W. Care were also elected to the UDC.[62] Unlike Osborn, however, Care was a Conservative. Just as Osborn was instrumental in establishing the Labour Party in WGC, Care was a key mover in the local Welwyn Garden City Conservative Party. Living in Handside Lane, he was the Honorary Organising Secretary, and his wife was a member of the local Conservative Party's committee during the earliest years of the garden city.[63]

The President of Welwyn Garden City Ltd was Lieutenant-Colonel Sir Francis Edward Fremantle. In 1919 he had been elected as a councillor on the LCC representing the Municipal Reform Party, the name of the Conservative Party in London politics. He stood as the Conservative candidate in General Elections from 1923 to 1935, and was elected each time, despite national political transitions between minority Labour Governments, and Conservative or the Conservative-dominated National Government of the 1930s.

The relationship between the UDC and WGCL was a very useful base from which to develop WGC, and one strengthened in the case of shared membership between the two. The UDC was a democratically elected body with the same functions and responsibilities as any urban council in England and Wales. The Company, however, was the sole landowner for the UDC administrative area, making for a relatively straightforward, if not always conflict-free, planning process. In most towns and cities many landowners meant many competing interests and less unity of purpose in delivering planning goals. In WGC, each and every planning application by the Company was scrutinised and approved, or not, by the Council as the statutory planning authority for the urban district. While there was sometimes discord between the UDC emphasis upon the public interest versus the planning prerogatives of the

Company, dovetailing of personnel and the simpler pattern of land ownership and control made for relatively smooth urban development from 1927.[64]

The first decades of WGC must be viewed as a whole, so it is important to emphasise that the political influence of the Company was aimed almost completely at getting the garden city built to Howard's guiding principles, and to deliver to the shareholders an acceptable level of dividend, an income for which they would have to wait patiently. Housing, shops, industry and employment, and the provision of social and cultural facilities, would all be firmly established between the wars, in the face of a number of issues.

## Rhetoric and Realities: the Earliest Years of Welwyn Garden City

The ambitious plans of WGCL were summarised in its *Prospectus of an Investment in a New Town in Hertfordshire*, published during the early 1920s and aimed at potential investors in the planned new community. Welwyn Garden City would be a second exemplar of integrated planning, good housing, new educational establishments, places of worship, indoor and outdoor leisure amenities, medical facilities and the preservation of natural beauty. All of this would combine to create a happy, healthy urban population. And this population was promised a dynamic local economy, where industrial growth, agricultural bounty and good communications were organised. The business-like nature of the enterprise was obviously emphasised to attract investors.

One of the first groups of investors approached by the WGCL Board was a number of 'old Balliol men', after the Oxford University College, where three Board members had been educated before the First World War. Although this appears as elite networking, which in many ways it was, the forthcoming garden city was presented not as a paragon of upper-middle-class living but as a mixed community, which offered construction jobs to demobilised ex-servicemen, and a promise that any division between capital and labour would become insignificant as the new garden city grew.

The idealistic and optimistic vision for WGC is crisply summarised in this oft-quoted statement that enshrines a top-down 'live, work and play' approach that infused the social planning of the garden city with land ownership and management:

A town designed for healthy living and industry of a size that makes possible a full measure of social life but not larger, surrounded by a rural belt;
the whole of the land being in public ownership, or held in trust for the
community.[65]

To live in WGC, of course, housing was required and early site work and
construction of homes began before the formal plan was drawn up by de
Soissons during the early 1920s.

## Housing in Interwar WGC

At the beginning of 1920, a camp of huts was constructed on the area that
now houses The Campus, to accommodate building workers, whose numbers were augmented by ex-soldiers.[66] Ex-army huts were used as a makeshift
company office and meeting room. One woman recalled how her father had
moved from London after the First World War to look for construction work
in WGC, and was inadvertently involved in the type of class-mixing favoured
by Howard:

> It was just after the First World War, and my father was looking for work
> and he came from Woodford, which was his original home, and he came to
> Welwyn Garden City – well, he went to Stevenage actually and lived with
> his mother-in-law. And they tried to get work and in the end he cycled
> from Stevenage to WGC and he got a job helping with the building, and
> he used to sit in the cabins on The Campus, with the architects and people
> like that …[67]

In the spring of 1920 housing construction began in Handside and
Brockswood Lanes, the first houses being ready for occupation in December.[68]
The earliest housing and street layouts in the designated area were designed
by the architect Courtenay Crickmer. Crickmer was a resident and pro-
ponent of Letchworth and the initial housing, built in Handside Lane, was
reminiscent of the cottage-style domestic architecture there.[69] By 1923 Louis
de Soissons and his associate architect A. W. Kenyon had added another set
of cottages, with open forecourts, to the road.[70] Today in Handside Lane the

Handside Lane under construction c.1920.

resident, and of course the visitor, can witness the juxtaposition between the more Arts and Crafts cottages of Crickmer and the later neo-Georgian styles that came to dominate the domestic architecture of Welwyn Garden City.

Moreover, the Housing and Town Planning Act of 1919 initiated a nation-wide programme of council estates intended, true to the spirit of 'Homes Fit for Heroes', to relieve the slums. Steered through Parliament by Christopher Addison, the Liberal Housing Minister, the results of the 1919 Act were disappointing, as Addison himself acknowledged in his angry booklet *The Betrayal of the Slums* (1922). Public expenditure cuts undermined the target numbers of local authority housing, unwittingly adding to the failure of interwar governments to solve the housing problem and thus providing longer-term justification for a programme of large-scale, garden-city-inspired new towns from the 1940s. At WGC, the Rural District Council commenced construction of the first council houses in the town in Applecroft Road and Elm Gardens.[71] In 1922, the *Daily Mail* newspaper, which had begun to sponsor the 'Ideal Home' exhibitions in London, built a 'model village' on Meadow Green and its immediate environs. In 1925, a significant level of construction began in the Peartree District, leading to a growing number of houses and an influx of population. A shop, school, church and other community-focused buildings followed suit in Peartree.

Welwyn Garden City must also be viewed within the wider national context of housing programmes after the First World War. For example, a number of garden suburbs were constructed during the 1920s, notably Wythenshawe in Manchester and Becontree and Dagenham in East London. These were to a certain degree influenced by garden city planning principles, sharing some similar street layouts and styles in domestic architecture. Yet as Osborn, Purdom and other garden city advocates were keen to point out, they were not focused on maximising economic self-containment or the creation of socially mixed and balanced communities.[72] They became suburban extensions of major cities between the wars, and during the course of the twentieth century their social and economic evolution would compare relatively unfavourably with that of WGC.[73]

In his book *The Building of Satellite Towns*, Purdom defined their key characteristics, drawing attention to the main difference between WGC and other interwar planned developments. 'By a satellite town is meant a town in the full sense of the word':

> … a distinct civic unit with its own local government and corporate life, possessing the economic, social and cultural characteristics of a town, and, while maintaining its identity, in some sort of relation of dependence upon a large town or city.

That large city was, of course, London, whose future Howard had been so concerned about in *Garden Cities of Tomorrow*. Purdom went on to emphasise that a satellite town 'should have a certain degree of completeness in itself' and a political and administrative apparatus for self-government that was independent of the city from which so many of its citizens and industries came. Highlighting that 'satellite towns in the sense in which we are considering them are garden cities', he invoked Howard's original characteristics of the garden city.[74]

As a self-conscious satellite town, WGC was within the orbit of London, and was more interdependent with the capital in terms of employment and commuting. This important fact remained a key difference with Letchworth, which lay further away from London. Yet it also meant that WGC was self-consciously different to a garden suburb, or any other type of suburb. In some of its earliest promotional materials WGCL was at pains to point out that

WGC was 'not a mere suburb': 'It is an entirely new town with an interesting character all its own, situated in the most beautiful part of Hertfordshire
and easily reached from London.'[75] As a satellite within the orbit of London,
however, WGC was always in danger of being deemed 'suburban'. Its advertising posters and other promotional literature sometimes unwittingly hinted
at what could be misinterpreted as middle-class 'suburban' characteristics.
A four-page publicity pamphlet for WGC issued by the estate agents Knight,
Frank and Rutley during the 1930s made much of both the attractiveness
and the privacy of the gardens in the garden city. 'People who come to see us
at Welwyn,' enthused one house-proud woman:

> see our garden before they see the house, and they can form a pretty good
> estimate of our taste. As well as the private garden or 'cabbage patch',
> which every house possesses at the back, there are open gardens in front, so
> arranged that they form one continuous garden or linear park the whole
> length of the road.[76]

The house with a garden was a key attraction of WGC. One woman
interviewed by the WGCHT, who had been born in the town in 1927,
remembered how their interwar home in Knella Road had not only 'lovely
gardens' but also a nearby area for growing vegetables. Both the flower garden
and the ability to grow fresh food 'were very important to our life'.[77]

Superficially, the image of a home and garden lent WGC a suburban
identity. Yet as noted, the Garden City Movement was an antidote to suburban sprawl. Nonetheless, an American historian of the British Garden City
Movement unfavourably compared the satellite status of WGC with its predecessor, alluding to supposedly dormitory suburban aspects of its nature:

> People had travelled to Letchworth in its early days to see the future. People
> travelled to WGC to eat their evening meal and sleep amid the tepid joys of
> a well-planned and aesthetically pleasing satellite suburbia.[78]

This judgement, while acknowledging the fine planning at WGC, shows
that the work of Purdom and others has not been fully understood by some
historians of town planning. As Lewis Mumford argued in his classic tome
*The City in History*, 'critics who should know better' often refer to the classic

De Soissons plan, 1920.

Louis de Soissons.

garden cities, or to the British new
towns of later vintage, as if they were
mere suburbs, because they were all
laid out in an open – perhaps too
open – framework.[79]

While Mumford was an enthu-
siast for garden cities, he favoured
slightly higher population densities
and closer building patterns than
Howard and his architect followers. And as we will see, despite the
judgement of such an authority as
Mumford, this perceived suburban
character of WGC would be used
as a stick to beat it with during the
onset of the new town after the
Second World War.

In microcosm, Handside Lane had
demonstrated that a number of the
general practices and principles in
the Garden City Movement that had informed the planning of Letchworth
would be applied to WGC. Ultimately, however, the master plan for WGC
would be also based upon a different vision to that of Parker and Unwin.
In 1920 WGCL commissioned the architect-planner Louis de Soissons, or
to give him his full name Louis Emanuel Jean Guy de Savoie-Carignan de
Soissons, as the Master Planner for WGC. Born in Montreal, Canada, his
family had moved to London during his childhood. The WGC commission
was his first major appointment, and the first draft of the plan was completed
by 11 June 1920 within six weeks of being appointed. The physical construction of the original plan for WGC up until 1927 was recorded in *Site
Planning in Practice at Welwyn Garden City* (first published in 1927) by Louis
de Soissons and his associate architect Arthur William Kenyon.

Before going on to look at the enactment of the plan, it must be noted
that the name A. W. Kenyon tends to be absent from many accounts of the

planning history of WGC, and in the beautiful reissue of *Site Planning in Practice*, the new introductions by various scholars have next to nothing to say about him. Yet, as Geoffrey Hollis has argued, his contribution has been somewhat overlooked.[80] Born in Sheffield in 1885, Kenyon had at least one other position before he began work with de Soissons at WGC during the early 1920s. His designs for houses at WGC were 'very much traditional hipped-roof designs, wavering between an Arts and Crafts idiom and the neo-Georgian'.[81] He was, therefore, a perfect partner in style with de Soissons, and as we will see went on to design a number of key housing developments with him in interwar WGC.

And who has heard, in the UK anyway, of Alfred John Brown? He is virtually ignored in the histories of WGC, including the otherwise comprehensive survey by Maurice de Soissons. Born in New Zealand, he became an associate of the Royal Institute of British Architects (RIBA) in 1919. The following year he was appointed as assistant architect to de Soissons. Impressed with the medium-to-low density residential areas and housing with abundant gardens, and the unpretentious 'Arts and Crafts' housing in some roads in WGC, he became an advocate of WGC in the professions of architecture and town planning in Australia, following his move there in 1930. He designed some houses in WGC, and was known to Osborn. His wife Doris Jocelyn Brown was enamoured of the attractive gardens she saw in WGC, and designed gardens in the English style in Australia.[82] This was one of many examples of the international influence of WGC, discussed in more detail in a later chapter.

In 1923 building regulations were introduced by the Company that gave de Soissons a great deal of power over building and landscape design. He 'approved everything' or rejected things he did not like. And in the face of slow growth and sometimes adverse financial circumstances he relentlessly pursued his vision.[83] In his introduction to the first edition of *Site Planning in Practice*, C.B. Purdom emphasised that in planning the residential areas, both the contours of the land and the initial funding shortages mean that 'the architectural effect that was aimed at had to be secured by strictly utilitarian means':

> There was no money for embellishments. The land had to be so laid out that the greatest amount of it could be developed at the lowest possible cost. The roads therefore follow the contours so far as that could be done while providing the main traffic routes.[84]

Example of a cul-de-sac c.1927.

Purdom also noted the well-wooded areas of large parts of the site, the careful conservation of most of the trees, particularly oaks, and the reflection of the arboreal beauties of the area in the planting of a variety of trees including beech, chestnut and lime trees on most of the new roads. He was also keen to highlight an 'interesting characteristic feature of the WGC layout', namely 'closes' or 'culs-de-sac roads'. And here he drew attention to a unique aspect of garden city planning: the rejection of smaller secondary through roads where possible, to preserve the residential character of the streets, and the inclusion of both straight roads and curves to provide variety in the streetscape. This enabled a more attractive mixture of houses with gardens, and buildings, than in less-well-planned or unimaginative developments.[85] Yet in praising the variety of homes built for purchase, Purdom unwittingly drew attention to what would become a problem for WGC during the interwar years:

> The houses that have been built in the town range from £600 to about £3,000, so that the component parts of the street effects are small detached or semi-detached houses, and a satisfactory result depends on right placing

of the buildings, flexible use of the building line, and particularly the maintenance of a cornice line throughout the street, both sides of the street being considered together.[86]

Most working-class citizens of WGC, however, could not afford these properties. They were, moreover, mostly built around the centre to the west of railway line. This would later become part of a significant and much commented-upon social division in WGC, discussed below.

Purdom was a strong advocate for the garden city so he was perfectly entitled to accentuate the positive. His views of the residential areas of WGC were later shared by the more objective evaluation of the architectural historian and critic Sir Nikolaus Pevsner. 'The residential layout is clearly derived from the Unwin ideas and patterns,' argued Pevsner:

Old trees are meticulously kept, straight roads are rare, and closes everywhere determine the pattern. The predominant style of the houses, however, has characteristically changed since Letchworth. It is now a quiet, comfortable neo-Georgian, no longer olde-worldly.[87]

De Soissons and Kenyon were responsible for designing more than half the residential units in interwar WGC. As noted, following some earlier Letchworth-style homes, the housing at WGC departed in architectural styles from the romantic model village experiments of the Garden City Movement, while the street pattern did bear the imprint of earlier innovations, for example in Bournville, New Earswick and relatively nearby Letchworth.

De Soissons designed almost all of the key community and public buildings in the garden city before 1940. These included the theatre (1928), Barclay's Bank (1929), the Free Church (1929), St Francis Church (1935) and Welwyn Stores (1939). The famous White Bridge that gives the classic beautiful view of Parkway, and Hunter's Bridge over the Great Eastern railway line were also designed by de Soissons. He was also responsible for some of the most important industrial architecture, not only in WGC but in Britain between the wars, notably the Shredded Wheat factory (1925) and the sectional factories, which hosted a variety of businesses on affordable rents.[88]

Pevsner was often highly critical in his appraisal of architecture and environmental compositions that were less explicitly modernist, and he hated

Parkway viewed from the White Bridge.

poorly expressed historicism or overly romantic building design. He was, however, broadly impressed with the composition of the town centre at WGC, arguing that the civic spaces mostly possessed 'a feeling of confidence, although the style of the buildings is in no way revolutionary':

> The earlier public buildings, including the station, are of brick, with stone dressings and some classical detail. This urban area is something that the Hampstead Garden Suburb lacks, and that Letchworth received only slowly and never adequately, owing to its arrested growth.[89]

Although Pevsner felt that the main town centre could have been rendered to a slightly more regular plan, his favourable comparison with two earlier iconic developments in English garden city planning was a significant compliment both to de Soissons and to WGC itself.

Later validation of de Soisson's composition came from an important local contributor to the *New Towns Record CD Rom* (2002). David Irving, who was appointed Principal Architect to WGC in 1976, Chief Architect in 1982, and later worked as Director of Environmental Services for Welwyn Hatfield District Council, argued that WGC was a more *beaux arts* style of architecture than other garden cities. He summarised the main principles of the composition thus:

> There is a great deal of symmetry and wide boulevards and so on, which you don't find in Letchworth to anything like the same extent. [De Soissons] also developed cul-de-sac design and most of the town was entirely built on a combination of wide tree-lined streets and the housing is actually in culs-de-sac off the streets, which gives you a much more intimate feel to each of them.
>
> And he went on to emphasise the strong design of the town centre, particularly the social and environmental prominence of the 'main boulevard', namely Parkway. Praising its width and inter-connectedness with adjacent roads and spaces, Irving argued 'everybody lives at Parkway'.[90]

Not everyone involved in architecture and town planning was impressed by Howard and his realised vision, however. Looking back on the era of reconstruction, the housing architect and planner Lionel Esher dismissed WGC as a mere dilution of the more successful experiment at Hampstead Garden Suburb, and lamented its influence on other new towns. He had more admiration for Parker and Unwin than the 'insipid' town centre design of de Soissons, and the neo-Georgian buildings that populated it, which he damned with faint praise.[91] The expert on architecture and urban affairs, Thomas Sharp, could not have been more contemptuous: 'Howard's new hope, new life, new civilisation, Town-Country is a hermaphrodite; sterile, imbecile, a monster; abhorrent and loathsome to the Nature which he worships.'[92]

Yet, as this writer has argued elsewhere, the majority of urban dwellers in England during the twentieth century wanted just that: a home with gardens that was not in the overcrowded city centre, nor in the remote countryside, but which offered the convenience of the town with the attractions of the nearby countryside.[93] The garden city was not 'suburban', but de Soissons was successful in achieving a synthesis of town and country in his design for the built environment. His plan also provided places for work and leisure in accordance with the principles laid down by Howard. First we will look at leisure and non-work social groups and associations, then the economic expansion of WGC.

## Living and Socialising in Welwyn Garden City

One of the most important keywords when understanding the subjectivity – the values and self-image of the earliest settlers of WGC – is 'pioneers'. Howard had been impressed with the pioneering spirit of those who settled the homesteads of the North American Frontier during the nineteenth century, and many of those earliest planners and community builders who moved to Letchworth during the Edwardian years viewed themselves as pioneers, moving into raw territory, a *tabula rasa* even, and converting it into a living entity.

Looking back after twenty-five years of Welwyn Garden City, the souvenir programme for a 'Pioneer's Party' dedicated to Sir Theodore Chambers addressed him thus:

> As a group of workers and citizens of those early days in the history of our town we consider that you and we were all pioneers; and that we shared together the joys and excitements, the discomforts and risks of that time. So also we feel that we have our part with you in whatever honour and renown has come to Welwyn Garden City.[94]

Many who moved to WGC during the early 1920s, or were young enough to remember that decade, identified as 'pioneers'. As John H. recalled, 'These are memories of WGC from the very early days,' and he hinted at the sociability that came with the sense of newness of WGC:

> My parents Wally and Edith H. came to Welwyn Garden City for work in 1922. As pioneers they lived for a while in Handside Farmhouse by the Barn Theatre. My father was the Water Works Engineer for the WGC Council … My mother was secretary to Arthur Howard the Chartered Surveyor/Estates Manager to the Welwyn Garden City Company from the beginning and worked for the company until December 1927 when my twin brother Michael and I were born on 22 December 1927 in the Cottage Hospital … Our first home was in Guessens Road, one of the first Council housing schemes in the town, and we moved to 39 Elm Gardens in about 1930. I remember a family garden party in 1935 to celebrate the Silver Jubilee of King George V.[95]

Barn Theatre programme cover
Charles Paine design, 1947.

In an essay on the pioneering 'personalities' of WGC, written when
it was barely six years old, Osborn
emphasised the obvious importance of the leading business people,
architects, planners, estate managers
and others within the Company,
but also those beyond who were
actively building up the social life of
the town. His account is fascinating
for a number of reasons:

> the personalities not directly con-
> cerned with the administration of
> the town are so interesting in their
> variety that any selection must
> appear unrepresentative. J.W. Bryce of the Shredded Wheat company is con-
> spicuous for the accents of transatlantic decidedness that he brings to local
> issues. W.H. Washington's activities as universal treasurer of every kind of vol-
> untary society almost submerge his importance as manager of Barclay's Bank.
> J.F. House, the stationmaster, is a very popular figure and is much in request
> as MC at social functions. J.W. Sault, editor of a local newspaper, has amused
> the town for years by alternating splenetic attacks on certain of the garden city
> institutions with religious prophesies and doggerel verses.
>
> The thought of the many well-marked individualities in the social and artis-
> tic life of the town, its actors, musicians, dancers, painters, craftsmen, writers; of
> the well-known faces and names in the stores and estate offices; of the religious
> leaders, doctors, dentists and other professional men; of the leading cricketers,
> footballers, golfers and tennis players – the very thought of these shows how
> invidious any selection, including the above, might be.[96]

The gnomic mention of Sault might have been because he had been critical
of many of the Company's actions. Sometimes he was a friendly critic, other

times more full-on in his judgements. He had edited *The Pilot* newspaper during the early 1920s, which in effect acted as a kind of alternative voice to the *Welwyn Garden City News*, later the *Welwyn Times*. Yet, Sault also seems to have had a higher regard for Theodore Chambers than Osborn, between whom there were growing tensions. Sault issued two slim editions of cartoons in 1928 entitled *Who's What in Welwyn: What Town Planners Ought to Know*. Interestingly, Osborn was ignored in them. Chambers was characterised as a strong man, looming above the tree-lined landscape of WGC. Purdom was affectionately caricatured as optimistic but naïve. Reiss was depicted in profile as a friend of Sault, a fan of *The Pilot*, and humorously described as 'wounded in the Great War and in a series of General Elections'.[97] The latter reference was to the fact that Reiss unsuccessfully stood as Labour candidate in Colchester, Essex, in General Elections following the First World War.

Of Sault and *The Pilot*, Purdom noted they 'had splendid targets in the Company and the stores, without which it could not have lived, and it played a part in the development of opinion'.[98] This rather grudging assessment may partly explain why Purdom was ejected from his managing role of Welwyn Stores, and from the Company, in 1928. He appears to have been very prickly when it came to criticism of his work, and of the Company's monopolistic trading culture.

In one important respect, however, Osborn was perfectly correct. As the commercial and public institutions in the town became more established and numerous, so the social life of WGC became more diverse and viable. There was a dynamic inter-relationship between them. And while admitting to the invidious act of selection in highlighting key individuals, he is somewhat hoisted by his own petard. The connection between leading commercial and public figures in the town and the culture of voluntarism is cast entirely as a male culture. A sense of the 'Great Man' approach to town making and community building pervades this account. The contribution of women is subsumed into the welter of people and groups who made up the social life of the garden city. For example, where was any mention of Sydney Mary Bushell? Here is another relatively neglected area of the social history of the Garden City Movement and of the new towns, namely the role of women in early housing management, and more widely, in raising housing issues and problems as they impacted upon women.

One of the members of the women's section of the Garden Cities and Town Planning Association, Bushell moved with her father to Welwyn

Garden City during the early 1920s. A sociologist and a follower of the Octavia Hill school of house visiting, Bushell was also a member of Women's Pioneer Housing, an association established in 1920 to provide accommodation for single women, many of whom had become more economically active and self-sufficient during the First World War. Bushell wrote and broadcast on the radio about women's issues in the domestic sphere. While at WGC she took an active interest in the role of labour-saving devices in the home, and became a relatively well-known figure. In a small but significant way, while at WGC she was a pioneer of social intervention on behalf of women.[99]

Moreover, a woman was at the forefront of establishing healthcare pro-vision in WGC, as we will soon see. Osborn was unconsciously reflecting the predominant patriarchy of the Garden City Movement. Debunking the attacks upon the garden city institutions, moreover, was a tactic frequently used by the Company when it felt unfairly criticised.

In his books *Greenbelt Cities: The British Contribution* (1946) and *The Genesis of Welwyn Garden City* (1970) Frederic Osborn emphasised the active contributions of the original pioneer settlers, which included himself, to forming associations, clubs, groups and societies, all of which reflected shared common interests and provided the building blocks of community and neighbouring in the new city. And as the term 'pioneer' also implicitly sug-gests, sectional differences and petty squabbles were, ostensibly at least, put to one side in order to create an optimistic sense of the present and the future. Pioneers were, of course, leaving an older way of life and an established home for the new opportunities offered by the garden city. Most of these opportunities reflected a culture of what the Victorians and Edwardians had termed 'rational recreation'. Essentially this meant leisure pursuits should improve the mind and body, and enable respectful sociability. Proponents of rational recreation were opposed to alcoholic consumption, gambling and forms of leisure that were seen to be unhealthy, socially toxic and economi-cally destructive to the incomes of the poor in particular.[100] Howard and other leaders in the Garden City Movement were staunch Victorian rational recreationalists when it came to leisure and leisure provision due to their nonconformist religious persuasions.[101] Letchworth had no licensed premises for many years after its birth, for example. WGC was allowed a few licensed houses, but God was more prominent than ale in the town centre.

## Welwyn Garden City at Worship

The accusation of religious puritanism associated with WGC did not really appreciate the diversity of places of worship and of religious practice there.[102] If the Society of Friends, the Quakers, and the Salvation Army are included there were fourteen religious establishments in WGC by 1940. One of the first church groups to be founded in the designated area was the Welwyn Garden City Free Church, the Presbyterian Church, and it is certainly true that nonconformist Presbyterians were associated with teetotalism.

The Free Church aimed to provide a place of worship for all denominations, and in 1927 became affiliated to the Presbyterian Church of England. After years of meeting in individuals' houses and temporary wooden buildings, a Free Church designed by Louis de Soissons was opened in Church Road in 1929. The church was the base for a Junior Church, a 'Fellowship of Youth' and a Women's Club.

Christchurch Baptist began life in 1928 in the Backhouse Room with a decision to separate from the Free Church. Their permanent building, sharing pride of place opposite St Bonaventure's at the southern end of Parkway, was dedicated in 1940. It ran one of the town's largest Sunday schools and hosted a number of women's groups, as well as a Young Wives Club and a Men's

Free Church, Church Road c.1930.

Contact Club. Christchurch Baptist also hosted film shows for children, possibly as an antidote to the growing number of films deemed unsuitable for young people as cinema swept across interwar Britain.

Nonconformity in WGC was also evidenced in the Congregational Church in Woodhall Lane, which ran the Boys' Brigade, Girls' Life Brigade, a Life Boys team, and a 'Woman's Own' Club. In 1933, a Council of Christian Congregations was established in WGC 'for the purpose of co-ordinating action on social and religious matters in the Town'.[103] It claimed to be one of the first in Britain to bring together Free Churchmen and Anglicans. The Quaker Society of Friends Meeting House in Handside Lane was a further reflection of the nonconformist conscience in WGC. By 1940 it had made its premises available to the United Synagogue Membership Group and the Jewish Communal Council. The 1930s witnessed an influx of Jewish people escaping from Nazism, and WGC was a key destination, as we will soon see. The Quakers would later donate land at Handside Lane for a purpose-built synagogue, opened in 1956.[104]

As one man recalled, his parents were Baptists who moved from London to WGC in the mid-1920s when he was a little boy. The popularity of nonconformity in WGC was an attraction for them:

> They had been Baptists but following the mass slaughters in the First World War they were attracted to the thinking of the Society of Friends – Quakers – and they joined the Society and I think that one of the attractions in the Garden City was that there was a new growing meeting and they also liked the idea of the Garden City.[105]

Appropriately, perhaps, given the time spent by Ebenezer Howard in the USA, the First Church of Christ, Scientist, was based in the Christian Science Reading Room on Howardsgate. An American nonconformist religion, begun during the 1940s, the WGC branch was seen as an offshoot of the 'Mother Church' in Boston, Massachusetts. In addition to its services, it also held a Sunday school 'to which visitors up to the age of 20 are welcome'.[106]

The Church of England was the religion of the majority in WGC, as it was in the rest of England. Worship was held in temporary premises for a long period of time due to lack of funds and it was May 1935 before the foundation stone of St Francis of Assisi, the parish Church in Parkway, was finally laid. Designed by Louis de Soissons, it was one of the most prominent places of worship in the garden city. In addition to regular church services and the rites of passage ceremonies for christenings, weddings and funerals, it hosted the St Francis Scouts, the St Francis Cubs, the Mother's Union and choir practices for adults and boys. Again film shows were all part of the offering, reflecting the enthusiasm for cinema as well as for Christ.

From early 1927, Church of England services were also held in the Peartree Clubhouse on the eastern side of the town. By mid-1930 the grow-ing congregation of Peartree had raised enough money for a substantial brick-built church hall, which was dedicated to St Michael and All Angels on 29 November 1930. This hall became a social centre for the Peartree area, and alongside its role as a place of worship was used for the Women's Fellowship. Girl Guides meetings, the Cubs, a Men's Fellowship, the Youth Fellowship, and a branch of the Mothers' Union that 'exists to maintain Christian stand-ards of Home and Family Life and the permanence of marriage'.[107] The hall was also a place where billiards, darts, and 'table games' were played, where a cricket team met, and, at a time when gaming as in playing cards for money was illegal, whist drives were held at 8 p.m. on a Tuesday. The slightly duplici-tous role of the church in condemning gambling while using such events for socialising or for fundraising did not go unnoticed.

The Roman Catholic Church also had its main place of worship on Parkway, namely St Bonaventure's. As more completed houses became avail-able for the increasing numbers of citizens in WGC, the Roman Catholic Diocese of Westminster realised that there would need to be provision made for the Catholics amongst this growing population. A community of Italian nuns wished to extend their influence to England. They were given permis-sion by the authorities of to set up in Welwyn Garden City. Three Canossian Sisters from Milan arrived on 3 November 1922 and took up residence in a house at No. 17 Meadow Green. The first resident priest of the new parish arrived on 3 October 1925. The size of the congregation numbered five to begin with, growing steadily to fifty by the time the new church was opened.

St Bonaventure's was the first church to be built in Welwyn Garden City. Designed by T.B. Scott, it was dedicated by Cardinal Bourne on 14 September 1926.

In common with other places of worship, St Bonaventure's became a site for organised behaviour for young people. Catechism was given to children in primary and secondary schools there, while parochial organisations reflected a key dynamic in religious social life: to indoctrinate children into Christianity. They included the Catholic Young Men's Society, St Bonaventure's Youth Group, and the Children of Mary. Other groups included the Catholic Women's League, and the 'Association for the Propagation of the Faith'. The Catholic Canossian Convent Chapel was also on Parkway, which could perhaps claim to contain more new church buildings than anywhere else in interwar Hertfordshire. Yet inculcating faith in the young was no monopoly of the Catholic Church. In addition to those youth groups just mentioned, the Gospel Room held at Peartree Boys' Club on Peartree Lane was offering a young people's meeting during the 1930s. This also indicated that providing for young people's leisure was an important aspect of the wider recreational facilities for WGC.

## Problems and Progress: Building a Viable Economy

The keystone of self-containment in the making of garden cities meant that from the very outset the creation of local employment was a priority. Unfortunately, the designation of Welwyn Garden City in 1920 coincided with the curtailing of the so-called restocking boom that followed the end of the First World War, and the onset of a downturn in the British economy. At the end of the 1920s, and casting its shadow long into the '30s, came a worldwide depression. Despite some often formidable structural problems in the national and global economy, Welwyn Garden City Ltd was able to establish an expanding economy between the wars, one that might justly be viewed as a working model for other subsequently planned new towns and garden cities. Diversity is a keyword when understanding the success of the emerging employment opportunities in WGC.

Between the wars more than 120 employers, some large-scale, others what would now be termed small–medium enterprises, moved to or were established in WGC. And that figure does not include many smaller traders and shops.[108] Welwyn Garden City Ltd led this growth. Under the business-minded direction of Theodore Chambers and his tireless team, it created a host of affiliated or subsidiary companies to build the infrastructure and develop the services required by the new town. In the words of one architectural and planning historian: 'This meant a monopolistic approach, but it was highly effective in getting the job done, and by 1926 the town had been built.'[109]

One of the first subsidiary companies to be established in 1921 was Welwyn Brickworks Ltd, an essential supply sector for the building of the new town. It was soon followed by Welwyn Builders Ltd, another subsidiary of WGCL, and Welwyn Stores Ltd, also opened in 1921, following numerous attempts to persuade an existing store to set up in the town. Selfridges and the Co-op were both approached but refused, presumably as they had no faith in the future of the town. WGCL opted to do it themselves, an approach that was increasingly used to create services but that became a means to increase income. This did not go unremarked upon by citizens of the garden city. A leading article in the short-lived but self-identifying 'bright and breezy' local newspaper *The Pilot* in January 1924 was entitled 'Yes we have no shops'. It attacked the 'monopoly' as a 'negation of democracy'. The article was written by the newspaper's editor J.W. Sault, who asked polemically, 'is democracy or autocracy ruling at present in this town?'[110]

Moreover, the building and supply companies operated by WGCL were the sole providers of construction materials and labour until further firms established themselves as WGC expanded during the mid-1920s, namely A.D. Dawney & Sons Ltd, who provided steel for construction and Frederick Palmer Ltd. Also involved were Herts Gravel and Brickworks Ltd, a further subsidiary of WGCL. Dawney was the first major manufacturing company established in WGC and in common with other businesses and so many individuals, it had relocated from London.[111] Many of the earliest working-class citizens of WGC were, unsurprisingly, construction workers, as infrastructure had to be laid before homes and social, commercial and industrial buildings were built.[112]

Digswell Nurseries also began in 1921, a subsidiary of WGCL and another essential sector in a garden city. The company was based on a site near Digswell Road, and among its chief activities were maintaining grass lawns and verges, roadside verges and open spaces, and the woodlands and trees that were not under the jurisdiction of the local council. The nursery grew many of the trees and other landscaping materials needed to complete the planting of the town, as they were in short supply after the First World War. Digswell also trained their own gardeners. Both Midland Bank and Barclays Bank established themselves in the first couple of years of the town's growth,

Shredded Wheat. *(Courtesy Cereal Partners UK)*

a reflection both of the confidence of the finance sector in WGC, and of the needs of the expanding population.

A number of major North American companies arrived in WGC between the wars, most famously of all Shredded Wheat in 1925, which was later incorporated into Nabisco. The company was partly attracted to the town by its clean surroundings that complemented the image of a healthy breakfast cereal.[113] Its iconic Shredded Wheat factory, designed by Louis de Soissons, made breakfast cereals for an increasingly health-conscious population in Britain. Soon after the factory opened, it was able to produce about 100 million Shredded Wheat breakfast biscuits per week, an impressive achievement, and a testament to American modern production processes based upon the working concept of F. W. Taylor.[114] The Quaker ownership of Nabisco was sympathetic to the pioneering nonconformity of Howard, and represented the importance of food manufacturing to both the local and the national economies.

Marion T. recalled how her father had moved to WGC to work at Shredded Wheat in 1926, thanks to word of mouth from her uncle, his brother, already an employee there. Her father worked 'on the outside', making deliveries on the railway service line, and other manual tasks. However, most workers were women, who made and packed the Shredded Wheat biscuits. Marion also took temporary summer work at 'the Wheat', and recalled how the women worked like 'silver lightning' to meet production targets, often spurred on by little incentives and treats. Her father worked for the company until he retired in 1968 after forty-two years there.[115]

Other food manufacturing establishments included Bickiepegs baby foods, Buchanan Toffees, Pure Extracts (established in WGC during the Great Depression) and Atomised Food Products. The latter company was a pioneer in making dried foods to which hot water was added prior to eating, namely soup powders and coffee. Atomised food was particularly useful for feeding troops during the Second World War.[116] And just prior to the outbreak of the Second World War, and possibly in anticipation of it, the Danish Bacon Co. moved from Smithfield Meat Market in Farringdon, London, to WGC. This continued to be a significant employer in the town.[117]

In addition to 'the Wheat', further American investment came with Barcley Corsets Ltd, housed in another modernist signature building, from 1927. The corset-makers Spirella had famously located in Letchworth, and now Barcley followed them into the second garden city. Given the product, Barcley's offered work mostly for women. A number of ex-employees of Barcley's recalled – and this is where we need to be careful with oral testimony – that there was always friendship and camaraderie between the women on the production line. They would listen to 'music while you worked', post photographs of their favourite movie stars on the walls, and socialise inside and outside of work. Some of the women started work aged 14, others were already at Barcley's. They also remembered a visit of the American Barcley family to the factory during the 1940s, but were unsure of the exact date.[118]

Between the coming of Shredded Wheat in 1925 and Barcley Corsets, a significant milestone in WGC's economic as well as social evolution came with the opening of the new railway station in 1926. As a satellite town, many workers in WGC commuted to and from London for their employment, so improved facilities enhanced the attraction of the town. The new station was opened by the Conservative Minster of Health, Neville Chamberlain, who stated in his speech that he had become 'convinced' of the rightness and viability of the proposals by WGCL for the garden city. He added, however, that 'you still have to convince the country', no doubt an acknowledgment of the hostility of many country dwellers to planned new communities in the heartlands of rural England.[119]

Welwyn Store's opening crowd, 1939. *(Courtesy John Lewis Partnership)*

One young woman who moved to Welwyn Garden City from south London ten years later, in 1936, was originally in need of such convincing, partly because of her emotional attachment to Lambeth, and partly because it now meant commuting from the new railway station back to London. She and her family already had relatives in WGC, but when her father moved them all to a house near Sherrardspark Woods, she remembered: 'I wasn't very happy about coming.' She had left school and had (unspecified) work in London, while her older brother, an accountant, commuted with her to Holborn. She recalled how they took 'the workman's' train for 1 shilling and 3 pence return (about 6 pence today). A Londoner, she became a commuter from WGC to her old city. She only stopped commuting after three years when she became an accountant at Welwyn Stores, on the eve of the Second World War.[120] Another example of a skilled worker who commuted to London was the father of Beth Day, who moved to WGC in 1925, but following the opening of the station in 1926 could more easily take the train to London.[121]

Her testimony also revealed that her family moved into a house in Applecroft Road, next door to an uncle. The remaking of the extended family network in internal migration is a key theme in the social history of moving from old cities to new communities. (At the time of her interview by the WGCHT, she was still living in the same road, Applecroft, although her uncle and his family had moved away.[122])

Clothes manufacturing came to WGC during the 1930s, the best-known factory being Cresta Silks. Based in a unit in the sectional factory, Cresta made ladies' dresses, famous for their high-quality design and fabric. They also made the curtains for the Shakespeare theatre in Stratford-upon-Avon. Cresta moved to a bigger factory in 1938 in Howardsgate and were eventually taken over by Debenhams during the post-war years.[123] Another company associated with clothing was Catomance. Established in WGC in 1936, it made waterproofing for textiles.[124]

In addition to construction, retail, finance, food and clothing, other key sectors were all established in WGC between the wars, namely engineering, pharmaceuticals, chemicals, electronics, fashion, radio, cinema production facilities, plastics and a variety of small-scale workplaces. In sharp relief, and in the relatively unique context of an interwar new city, WGC was representative of the new industries that established themselves in Britain during the 1920s and '30s, as opposed to the older staple industries of the Industrial

Film Studios film set. *(Courtesy Hertfordshire Archives & Local Studies)*

Revolution, namely textiles, coal and iron and steel production, which were in decline. The only exception to this was British Lead Mills, which set up on the corner of Peartree Lane in 1932 and has remained in the town ever since. WGC also reflected the burgeoning service sector, the growth of office and administrative employment in the new industries.

The radio and the cinema played an important role in WGC, both economically and socially. In 1928, British Instructional Films Ltd set up in WGC, making mostly documentaries but later also fiction feature films. Among their best known films was *I Was a Spy* (1933) about a Belgian nurse spying for the Allies in German-occupied Belgium during the First World War. Local children used to love going to watch the films being made:

> One of the things my friend and I liked to do was to go over the other side of the railway line where the Welwyn Film Studios operated … quite a large arched building, which was the studios, and hiding ourselves in the grass and seeing them filming. I can remember the title of the film *I Was a Spy* and it was about the First World War and there were explosions and all sorts of things going on … And another film was filmed in the woods – there used to be a part of the woods that was called 'the dell', which was an indentation, and I think they had play readings there but the film company used it as a film set and when we went there after the filming we found a lot of the woods had been made up as jungle and there was still jungle pieces of vegetation all over the place …[125]

British Instructional Films was later renamed Welwyn Studios, making movies such as *A Cottage in Dartmoor* (1929), the celebrated *The 39 Steps* (1935), *The Avenging Hand* (1937) and *Dark Eyes of London* (1939). The company made films during the war, while among its best-known post-war films was *Brighton Rock* (1947). Yet just a few years later it succumbed to competition from nearby Pinewood Studios. Still, Welwyn Studios put WGC on the global map as a modern centre for film production.[126]

Welwyn Garden City Film Society was also a child of the interwar period, enabling its members to watch films made both at home and increasingly from overseas. As Fred A. and Stephanie M. recalled, 'The WGC Film Society watched a lot of foreign films' and they also recalled many of the movies were 'very gruesome'.[127] This was allowed because of the lack of censorship and licensing of smaller film societies, suggesting they were watched during the 1920s and '30s. Although the British Board of Film Classification had begun in 1912, its recommendations for films were often interpreted differently between local authorities, and frequently ignored in film clubs. It was not until 1948 that a nationwide system of censorship was introduced to exclude children under 16 years of age from watching horror films.[128] The 'Welwyn Studio Weekends' were popular, and also showed children's films and Christmas films during the festive period.[129]

A significant chapter in WGC's industrial evolution came with the arrival of Murphy Radio in 1929, reflecting the growing popularity of the wireless for news and leisure. In line with the multiplier theory of the economist John Maynard Keynes, it spawned other smaller local firms making radio parts. As Angela Eserin notes, it was originally located in the sectional factory, but it became so successful that the company moved to a purpose-built factory in 1932:

> … as the workforce had grown from 8 to over 500. By 1939 Murphys was one of the 6 biggest radio manufacturers in the world. [Remember that hardly anyone had a television at this time, so radios were what everyone listened to.] They made all sorts of radios, including special ones packed in suitcases which were parachuted in to occupied France for the French resistance. After the war they also made communication and navigation equipment for aircraft and medical diagnostic equipment.
>
> The company made a unique contribution to the Allied war effort, and was later taken over by the Rank organisation in 1962.[130]

The expansion of inward investment was particularly impressive during the 1930s. Although the slump of 1929 and the Great Depression that followed it sharply cut economic growth rates across the world, WGC performed better than many other longer-established towns and cities. A sample of the companies that came to WGC evidences the successful strategy for inward investment pursued by WGCL during this difficult period in the history of modern capitalism. These companies helped WGC become famous not only for its fine housing stock, spacious environment and social amenities, but also for its enterprising businesslike spirit. An emergent sector comprised a number of new companies associated with motor car and car

Birkin's 'Le Mans' Blower competing in the 2019 Mille Miglia.

engine production. These included Bentley, which moved to a new factory unit in WGC in 1929. At WGC, Henry Birkin developed the 'Bentley Blower' which won at Le Mans in 1929. Birkin had been well-known as a racing driver at Brooklands during the 1920s.[131] John A. Weir Ltd, who made car bodies and other car parts, Lacre Lorries and WGC Coachworks Limited were all established in WGC between the wars, reflecting the fact that motorisation was changing the face of British towns between the wars, as well as the economy. As Betty W. recalled, her father was an unemployed engineer in London, but following a word-of-mouth interchange he gained employment at Jenner Parsons Garage on Hunters Bridge during the mid-1920s. He also got a house for himself and his family in Verulam Close.

While most people in WGC could not afford a car, a fortunate few could. The redoubtable and seemingly unpopular Miss Coe, who became the Head of Parkway School in 1934, had an Austin 7 that she conspicuously drove around the garden city.[132] One man recalled the family pride in their possession of what was not only a means of mobility, but state-of-the-art modern automobile engineering, and a status symbol, too. This has been called the 'technological sublime' by social historians:[133]

… Father bought the car – Morris 10 – they changed them once a year, can you imagine for something like £50 – we used to buy them from a showroom in Hatfield – and then my father went a bit mad and bought this enormous Rover and it had a bonnet about 5ft long and it had a 'Viking' thing on top of the radiator – it was a magnificent machine. My sister had just then reached 17 so I was 13 and she and my father drove us all the way up to Filey in Yorkshire, where we spent a holiday there.[134]

Other key sectors included toy manufacturing, heating and ventilation, electricity, gas, clothing, engineering, photography, plastics production, and, notably, food production. The teething biscuits manufacturer Bickipegs was based in WGC from 1929. Each of these sectors was indicative of the types of employment that would become increasingly important in the wider national economy.[135]

The growing significance of photography in wartime Britain was strongly evident at WGC. The rise of photojournalism meant that daily and weekly newspapers and magazines were increasingly including photos to embellish their articles and reports. The opening of Studio Lisa in 1934 in a house in Parkway was significant, as it would play an important part in democratising photography, particularly of the Royal Family. The studio was named after Lisa Sheridan. As Marion H. recalled, many people in WGC had their photographs taken at Studio Lisa, especially the children of proud parents. She could also recall the famous actress Dinah Sheridan, the daughter of Lisa and James Sheridan.[136] Another woman recalled how:

When Lisa Sheridan was looking she used to go round looking for children that were suitable for films – for photographing – photogenic children. When I was at the Day Nursery she came and had a look at them and picked out several children who were photogenic and spoke to their parents of course – they were often on the cover of magazines and advertising baby foods and things like that, and knitting patterns, and we could often see children we had had in the nursery – we picked out their pictures in the magazines.[137]

New technology reflected inward investment not only from elsewhere in Britain and from North America, but from European countries. The founding of the German chemicals company Beiersdorf in 1931 was a key example.[138] Four years later, Neosid Ltd was established at WGC. One of the two founders of Neosid moved to England in 1935 to escape from Nazi Germany. This story reveals the modernity and the global reach of the economy of WGC, and is brought to life by the Welwyn Garden City Heritage Trust:

> In 1932 IG-Farben (now BASF) launched a new material called Carbonyl Iron Powder. For high-frequency applications this caused an entire change in the field of electronics. Coils could be reduced by up to 10 per cent in size with better performance and quality.
>
> Hans Georg Pemetzrieder saw the potential of carbon-iron and became a pioneer in the technique of miniaturisation. In 1933 in Berlin he and Eduard Michaelis Neosid founded Pemetzrieder with just six staff. The company name Neosid derives from the Green NEOs SIDeros, meaning 'new iron'.
>
> Eduard Michaelis emigrated to England in 1935 in order to escape the Nazi movement. The two founders had already agreed that he could use the company's name, knowledge and patents in the UK.
>
> A suitable site for a factory was needed. Eduard was attracted to Welwyn Garden City's tree-lined streets and convenient proximity to London. Neosid Limited was located in Hydeway for over fifty years until 1977.[139]

Michaelis was Jewish, and his escape to WGC unwittingly antedated a later Jewish migration to the town.[140] Hence both the location of WGC near London, and its fine environment, attracted investment from overseas. Other pharmaceuticals and chemicals companies locating to WGC included the American firm Carnegie Chemicals in 1936, Roche Ltd in 1937 and the British Imperial Chemical Industries (ICI) Ltd in the same year. Maurice F. moved to WGC from Northampton as a young man to work in ICI during its earliest years. He recalled the relative isolation of the ICI factory in the fields, and how he and so many others cycled to work. He was also given part-time day release to study at a London college.[141]

As the great industrial cities of northern England, central Scotland and South Wales suffered from a narrow and ageing industrial base, WGC was in a sense showing the way for post-war prosperity in the increasingly affluent south-east of England. As the economic situation eased both nationally and

globally during the 1930s, WGC continued to build on these modern sectors, and by the time war broke out it was in a much more secure economic
position than it had been just ten or twenty years earlier.

The workplaces of WGC were important in other contexts: that of industrial architecture, and the rise of the Modern Movement in the design of
corporate buildings. Here, WGC made a distinctive contribution. The new
workplaces in WGC were grouped together in the industrial zone, and in
his summary of the most important new places of employment, Pevsner was
quite complementary. He wrote during the 1950s:

> The factories at Welwyn Garden City, begun later than those at Letchworth,
> show how from the 1920s the best industrial architecture, inspired by
> continental examples, was developing a new confidence and original-
> ity. This still continues. Architecturally best among the factories are the
> Shredded Wheat Co., 1925 by L. de Soissons, and Roche Products, by Otto
> Salvisberg of Zurich, 1938–40. The latter is of two and four storeys, white
> and unadorned, and still refreshingly modern.[142]

Yet while the co-ordinating role of Welwyn Garden City Ltd had delivered
real growth, and helped to foster some notable architectural achievements,
any notion that the Company was a unified and conflict-free operation must
be dispelled. As the new garden city weathered its problems, and overcame
many of them, divisions became apparent on the Board. These were most
clearly exposed in 1928 and in 1936.

## 'A Certain Disharmony': the Purdom Crisis of 1928 and the Resignation of Osborn in 1936

The collective and communal project of Welwyn Garden City Ltd was always
at the heart of the actions and rhetoric of the development company, but
human nature being what it is, there were often tensions between different
members of WGCL bubbling under the surface of day-to-day operations,
which sometimes burst out into the open. Such was the Purdom Crisis of
1928. According to a number of writers, Purdom was by no means an easy
person to get along with, and his relations with Frederic Osborn in particular

were not always cordial. This became brutally apparent in 1928 when Purdom was ousted from his executive responsibilities, notably as finance manager of Welwyn Stores, a subsidiary of WGCL. Osborn played a leading role, authoring the main case against Purdom as a poor communicator and, worse, as less than scrupulous with the accounting:

> These details were given to an enquiry by Sir Harry Peat, a chartered accountant, on behalf of Osborn and other leading signatories to a petition to relieve Purdom of his duties. The enquiry into Purdom [focused] on nothing less than 'character and personality as well as organisation and business methods'. [143]

Alongside FJO, others who ranged against Purdom included Louis de Soissons; W.E. James, the Company engineer; A.E. Malbon, manager of Welwyn Builders Ltd; E.G. Parsons, farm manager for the New Town Trust; and A.R. Pelly, the Company's financial secretary and staff manager of Welwyn Garden City Stores Ltd. That Purdom was at the helm of Welwyn Stores suggested a significant measure of internal conflict in the retail wing of WGCL. Most tellingly of all, perhaps, even Ebenezer Howard, in what was to be the final year of his life, attacked Purdom in a letter to WGCL, claiming he was 'entirely unfitted' for the tasks he performed, and 'a source of very great danger to the interests of the company, of the Town, and of the whole garden city and allied movements'. His opponents finally called upon Sir Theodore Chambers to sack Purdom, claiming that 'defects in the working of the business are due primarily to Mr. Purdom's policy, methods and personality'. [144]

This was damning stuff, but Purdom did possess allies, notably Chambers himself, who accused FJO of essentially leading a campaign to 'force the company to dispense with Mr Purdom's services', requesting that Osborn himself might also quit his positions. [145] Relations between Chambers and Osborn remained somewhat strained until 1936, and may well have influenced the termination of Osborn's role as secretary to WGCL in 1936, about which more below.

Yet the crisis of 1928 also perhaps revealed a frustration that the development of WGC should have been more rapid, basically more successful, after almost ten years of early growth and expansion. That the garden city began to establish its economy more successfully during the difficult years from

1929 begs the question of whether the co-ordination required to attract British and overseas companies had been to some degree undermined by the Osborn side, or by those who supported Purdom.

Whither Purdom? After all, he had been a long-standing ally of the Garden City Movement since his days in Letchworth. He was one of Howard's 'New Townsmen' during the First World War, and along with his official roles had also written the introduction to de Soissons *Site Planning in Practice*. As he tendered his resignation he must have felt hurt and rejected by many of his of former colleagues, not least his mentor Ebenezer Howard. He certainly seems to have apportioned no blame on himself for his dénouement. In his autobiography *Life over Again* (1951) he contextualised the problem as one of slow growth during the 1920s, and the consequent 'financial insecurity' of WGCL that exacerbated 'personal rancour' against himself and Chambers and a number of other Board members. Purdom argued that there was a definite tension between the more business-minded leaders such as Chambers and himself, and those who were more socially minded, notably Osborn, who was of course also a socialist.[146]

Purdom became a local councillor, and was elected to the UDC in 1930 as an independent member. But soon after the publication of his autobiography he faced another rebuff from Osborn, who along with Reiss wrote to the *Welwyn Times* in 1951, firmly rejecting Purdom's version of events in *Life over Again*.[147] More recently, however, the website www.ourwelwyngardencity.org.uk sought to rehabilitate Purdom, arguing that he was 'ruthlessly' treated by old friends and colleagues.[148]

Frederic Osborn suffered a similar fate to Purdom some eight years after he had led the coup against his colleague. As the entry on Osborn in the *Oxford Dictionary of National Biography* claims, despite his hard work and superior organisational and propagandist skills:

> It was, therefore, something of a bombshell when he was abruptly dismissed from his job in 1936, when the Welwyn Company was restructured. Within the year, however, he was appointed financial director to the local Murphy Radio Limited and became honorary secretary to the Garden Cities and Town Planning Association (subsequently the Town and Country Planning Association).[149]

As Maurice de Soissons argues, it is difficult to find any detailed information on why, after sixteen years of service to the Garden City Movement, one of Howard's brightest and best should have resigned. A 'bald statement' in the *Welwyn Times* announced the departure, and Osborn wrote to Chambers asking for his compensation to be raised in view of his service to the Company and to the wider cause of the garden cities movement. De Soissons suggests that a new emphasis upon the professionalisation of executive roles may have disadvantaged Osborn, but his self-removal may also have been about the lingering resentment felt by Chambers to Osborn over the dismissal of Purdom some eight years previously.[150]

Liberated from his administrative role, Osborn now took on leading roles in the Garden Cities and Town Planning Association, and he was able to become a much more active freelance advocate for the garden city influence on the professional town-planning culture that was expanding during the 1930s, and which would become increasingly influential in Government during the Second World War. Osborn's home in Guessens Road was literally at the epicentre of the escalation of town planning during the 1940s.

## Image Problems, or External Perceptions of WGC Between the Wars

As a mark of recognition that Welwyn Garden City had 'arrived' by the 1930s the Garden Cities and Town Planning Association, in association with the Town Planning Institute (TPI) held its first ever Town and Country Planning Summer School at WGC in 1933. As one of Britain's foremost planning historians, Gordon Cherry, argued, its aim was to 'broaden the planning outlook' and to publicise the aims of the Garden City Movement by publishing the proceedings of the summer schools. The driving force behind the initiative was Thomas Adams, the long-standing head of the GCTPA, who also financed much of the event.[151]

Town planning had established itself as a profession by the 1930s, and was exerting a growing influence over the Labour Party, particularly the London Labour Party, which committed to introduce a planning apparatus for the entire LCC area if it was elected to power in 1934, which it duly was, under the leadership of Herbert Morrison.[152] However, beyond the Labour Party, town planners and their garden cities were much less influential with the wider public. In some quarters, they were decidedly unpopular.

The wider national reputation of the Garden City Movement had not always been a positive one. Since its role in hosting conscientious objectors during the First World War, and given the strength of nonconformist religious groups there, Letchworth had long been castigated as the home of pacifists, puritans, teetotallers and vegetarians, causes that were much less accepted during the twentieth century than they are today. A similar set of critical judgements was applied to Welwyn Garden City between the wars. One of the main reasons for this was the 'healthy living' ethos with which the Garden City Movement was strongly associated. This gave critics of WGC the opportunity to attack it as an antiseptic and soulless environment, lacking in the urban welter and spontaneity of the older city centres. As Maurice de Soissons argued, 'the trouble was that garden cities were associated with the social conscience complex rather than the business-interest complex'.[153] This is an interesting and revealing observation but it does not completely stand up to scrutiny. First, although it helps us to understand the conflicts between the more business-minded Chambers–Purdom axis and the social conscience reformers of which Osborn was a key representative, the simple fact remains that one of both Letchworth's and WGC's most eloquent and famous detractors was George Orwell, a socialist who cannot be accused of favouring the business over the social interest. So what was the problem?

In a nutshell, the problem was that the social reform impulses in Welwyn Garden City appeared to Orwell and others to be puritanical. They were part of a 'cranky' culture of anti-drinking and anti-smoking, middle-class elitist hobby horses, and intellectual confections of an educated minority that had little in common with the working-class mainstream in interwar Britain. We must remember that the working-class population between the wars was almost 70 per cent of society, and was widely viewed by left-wing writers such as Orwell himself as possibly open to socialism, but only if that socialism more keenly embraced popular culture and commonplace working-class values. Writing in his travel-based social observation *The Road to Wigan Pier* in the mid-1930s, a book commissioned by the left-wing publisher Victor Gollancz, Orwell was uncompromisingly rude about Letchworth and the cadre of socialists who flocked to live there, 'every fruit-juice drinker, nudist, sandal wearer, sex maniac, escaped Quaker, "Nature Cure" quack, pacifist and feminist in England'. But he also laid into the second garden city for continuing to give socialism a cranky image: 'If only the sandals and the pistachio-coloured shirts could be put in a pile and burnt, and every vegetarian, teetotaller, and creeping Jesus sent home to Welwyn Garden City to do his yoga exercise quietly.'[154]

This is a fascinating passage, because while we can understand why a socialist like Orwell would be enamoured of a less middle-class 'lifestyle' kind of socialism, today drinking fruit juice, being a feminist, a vegetarian, and taking yoga exercises are much more commonplace. In these contexts, Letchworth and WGC were trendsetters, their emphasis upon healthy living encouraging emergent consumerist and lifestyle trends that became more popular throughout the rest of the twentieth century and into the present one. It remains to argue, though, that Orwell was not implicitly anti-feminist, or anti-progressive, but frustrated at the chasm between the values of the patriotic beer-drinking majority and the 'faddists' inhabiting the garden cities. As we will see, however, Orwell was both right and wrong in his assessment of the social and cultural character of WGC and its impact upon political life.

Nonetheless, it appears that Orwell's critical observations did catch the attention of some citizens in Welwyn Garden City. As a local councillor argued in 1939, the name itself 'conjured up in most people's minds': 'a town of peculiar people with peculiar clothes and ideas, sandals and homespuns, whose religions, homes, lovers and recreations were tainted with politics of many hues, generally pink to blood-red'.[155]

And as one man interviewed by the WGCHT recalled of the 1930s:

W R Hughes and his wife were early Garden City citizens – the sandal brigade they used to call them … A delightful couple – they were vegetarians and it was very unusual in those days to be a vegetarian and I used to sample some of them and my mother was quite horrified – I think she thought I was going to die![156]

In other words, people in WGC were well aware that their town was sometimes regarded as full of 'cranks'. Yet its social and cultural life was by no means dominated by religious nonconformity and 'lentil munchers'.

## Sport and Social Life in Interwar Welwyn Garden City

The master plan for WGC made ample provision for healthy sports and leisure pursuits. Within the first decade of the new garden city, WGCL in alliance with the Urban District Council (UDC) and the Hertfordshire County Council in some instances, had provided outdoor pitches for football and cricket, an eighteen-hole golf course, tennis courts, croquet and putting lawns, other recreation grounds for more informal play, an outdoor swimming pool, indoor meeting halls including church and school halls, boys' clubs, Parkway Café, the Cherry Tree Restaurant, various smaller clubrooms and clubhouses, and Welwyn Theatre. Among many other activities, the Cherry Tree hosted amateur dramatics from the early 1920s, and from 1932 the Barn Theatre would follow, becoming a hub of drama in WGC. And schools also enjoyed indoor and outdoor recreational spaces. Some of the larger companies in WGC also provided indoor leisure facilities and sports pitches.[157] Here was the infrastructure within which the social and cultural life of the fledging garden city would flourish.

The Welwyn Garden City Heritage Trust's *Where Do You Think We Played?* is a pretty comprehensive compendium of the leisure-based groups that came into being from 1920, supplying the social fabric alongside the developing infrastructure of facilities supplied by WGCL. The WGCHT website also contains many testimonies of living and playing in interwar WGC.

In an article entitled 'Social Life' in *Welwyn Garden City News* in 1921, a company-sponsored newspaper, 'the value of social life' was emphasised:

… it helps people to understand one another. Clubs and societies, like towns, need to be of the right size; if too large, the community spirit becomes atrophied; if too small, they degenerate into mere coteries. In WGC there exists already a many-sided social life, which encourages what we may term the social life of its citizens. The social contact is real. The social instinct is not forced to confine itself, within the boundaries of sect or creed. The bulk of the clubs and societies in the large towns are associated with particular sets of people who share, perhaps, one idea in common, with the result that most of the members never gain social contact with those who differ from them in religious, political or social ideas.

At WGC the citizens are brought together in many ways. Citizens who differ on philosophy or religion, say, at the citizens meetings, may find a common interest at the informal dances on Fridays, or join in harmony at the choral practices. The Anglican and Freechurchmen, the Rationalist and Agnostic, may meet as members of the Book Club or the Theatre Society, at whist or bridge, at chess, tennis, football or hockey. These various social activities help to foster a real community spirit, a social life having its roots in understanding and tolerance.[158]

Organised sports were at the heart of local participation in interwar WGC, as they were in most towns and cities. By the end of the 1930s, there was a variety of football teams, competing in a number of local and regional leagues, and the sport was also played informally by boys and young men on the parks. Cricket, golf, hockey, tennis and rugby were also played by a number of amateur clubs and teams. Athletics clubs and a swimming club also graced the sporting scene. More informal sports such as bowls and darts were played in church halls, youth clubs and pubs.[159]

In common with those earlier paternalistic industrialists and philanthropists who had funded model communities and worker's villages, the Garden City Movement evidenced a top-down involvement in the social life of the town. Leading members of the WGCL were active in sports, and often took on organisational roles. Richard Reiss, for example, was the president of Welwyn Garden City Football Club and also the Welwyn Garden City Cricket Club, both formed during the early 1920s, while vice presidents included Chambers, de Soissons and Purdom.[160]

WGC Cricket Club at tea with a Harpenden team, 1947.

Football is a great example of the vitality of sporting life in the garden city. The early role of the Company in promoting WGCFC laid the foundations for other clubs to follow suit. There were at least twelve local football teams by 1939. Richard Reiss was a keen sportsman and actively promoted football. Other leading members of WGCL served in WGCFC, as well as other sports. A little local history of football in WGC emphasised why football was the most popular sport:

Football was a cheap and healthy leisure activity for the labourers and craftsmen on whom the construction of the new town depended. Also, clubs and societies would bring people together and provide the social events that would give the town life. The Football Club held a Carnival Night in July 1922 to raise funds and it received extensive coverage in the *Welwyn Garden City News* as the social highlight of that week.

To encourage younger players and to increase participation in sport, Capt. Reiss presented a shield to be played for by teams made up of Welwyn Garden City residents and workers. Eleven teams competed for the WGC Football Cup during August and September with the winners being J 20 – the jobbing staff from the Company's Welwyn Builders workforce. Beaten finalists were Valley Road A and other teams in the tournament were Brocket Close; Council Houses United; Estate Office (referred to as "the pen-wielders" in reports); Hall & Bartholomew; Nondescripts; Valley Green; Valley Road B; Welwyn Stores; and Welwyn Transport.

In 1927 a new Welwyn Garden City Junior Association Football Club was also set up with the aim of getting local residents to play football amongst themselves. Four teams, Applecroft (based on the hostel there), Gaieties (soon to change its name to the equally incongruous Inertia FC), Pear Tree (sic) and Old Stagers (veteran players encouraged to coach and mentor their younger colleagues and opponents), played each other weekly. Soon they were also arranging games with other sides from around the town such as Hatfield Hyde, Welwyn Stores and Welwyn Thistle, a team mainly made up of workers from Welwyn Foundry on Bridge Road East.

As the town grew so did the ambitions of WGCFC. In the summer of 1926 the club moved into senior football by joining the Bedfordshire & District League (later the South Midlands League). Season tickets were made available at 4/6-, or 2/6- for the half a season (about 23 and 13 pence).[161]

Economic growth in WGC also increased the number of football clubs. Shredded Wheat and Murphy Radio were among a number of employers supporting works-based football teams between the wars, and providing pitches for play.[162]

Cricket was a favoured sport of Richard Reiss, who became secretary and treasurer of the newly formed Welwyn Garden City Cricket Club (WGCCC) in 1921. It competed against other local cricket teams, integrating the garden city with nearby towns and villages. One man who had been an active cricketer between the wars recalled that:

> There were two XIs who played on Saturdays and Sundays, and there was a flourishing Wednesday XI because there was early [shop] closing on Wednesday to give poor shopkeepers a rest. [I] think they tried a Wednesday League at the KGV playing fields. Our milkman was the captain of the Wednesday XI … One summer when I was home for the holidays he suggested that I played. I was the youngest at 15, most of the chaps were in their forties.[163]

For some historians, cricket was the national sport of interwar Britain, participated in and watched by all social classes, and across all regions of the country.[164] WGCCC probably reflected this. The club continued to thrive after the war and the sport is still going strong today, as are rugby, tennis, hockey, athletics and swimming, among many others.

The Mid Herts Rugby Club was the first rugby team to be formed during the mid-1920s, followed by Welwyn Rugby Football Club (RFC) from 1931. The growing numbers of Welsh men, and some Scots, moving to WGC to find work during the Great Depression boosted the popularity of the sport. Irish workers at ICI also formed a rugby team, some playing for Welwyn RFC. Most of the team's captains between the wars and into the post-war years were not from England but Wales, Ireland or Scotland.[165] Many in the Irish, Scots and Welsh communities also enjoyed their traditional dancing clubs, and the Welsh also developed a male voice choir during the 1930s, practising in church halls.[166]

Tennis was a very popular sport in interwar WGC, and mostly played by the wealthy and comfortably off amateurs.[167] The large middle-class population of WGC participated in a considerable number of tennis clubs, some with excellent facilities, the first being Welwyn Garden City Tennis Club, formed as early as 1921. Other clubs followed, including works-based tennis teams at Shredded Wheat, Murphy Radio, Norton Grinding Wheel and Unity Heating.[168] Most tennis clubs continued into the post-war years, reflecting within sporting circles the wider segregation in WGC, although this was a nationwide phenomenon. Golf also reflected class divisions in WGC. The eighteen-hole golf course to the north of the town required a subscription of three guineas a year, and while this was relatively low, it maintained the exclusivity of golf between the wars.[169]

Hockey was commonly played at schools in interwar Britain, and although not the most popular sport it had an active following. Many towns and cities had hockey clubs. In WGC, the WGCHT found evidence that the sport was being played on a small pitch just off Parkway as early as 1921, and by 1929 a new, larger hockey pitch was added to the garden city. The WGC Hockey Club was formed soon afterwards, although like most clubs it was disbanded during the conflict of 1939–1945.[170]

Swimming was also an informal leisure activity promoted by Doctors John Fry and Gladys Miall-Smith for its health-giving properties. They set up a swimming club in 1922, to make use of the outdoor pool in WGC. The WGC Swimming Club was also known for the success, both locally, nationally and internationally, of its water polo team.[171] Badminton, squash and weightlifting were also established during the first two decades of the garden city.[172] Another healthy outdoor activity, and sport for the more competitively minded, was cycling. The Welwyn Garden City Wheelers were in existence by 1932. Athletics facilities were introduced from the early 1920s, on land where sand and gravel had been dug out for the construction of the town. That site would eventually become the Gosling Stadium by 1960. The Welwyn Harriers Athletics Club was formed in 1927, and following its temporary disbanding during the Second World War, would go on to make an impression on the national and international stages, one of many sporting and cultural contributions that engaged WGC with the wider world.[173] A lively sporting life had irrupted in WGC in less than twenty years, as a consequence of a grassroots desire for participation, and the facilities and active encouragement provided by Welwyn Garden City Ltd.

## Arts and the Cultural Life of Interwar WGC

The arts and drama were among the earliest organised cultural activities at WGC. As Purdom noted, 'drama was one of the new town's first social activities' and he played a leading role in developing it, just as he had done at Letchworth.[174] The Welwyn Garden City Theatre Society gave its earliest performances at the Cherry Tree, including plays by George Bernard Shaw, William Shakespeare and other esteemed playwrights, as well as performances scripted by Osborn, Purdom and others with thespian tendencies who lived locally. Purdom was delighted when in 1928, the year of his denouement at WGCL, the Welwyn Theatre was opened, offering not only drama but also films. As Purdom recalled with some sarcasm, Welwyn Theatre 'was only a highly decorated barn' and for some years it was dubbed 'Purdom's folly' before being sold in 1939: 'the Garden City Company did well out of it, as it has done out of all my follies'.[175] Purdom continued to live in WGC, however, and to play his part in its amateur dramatics and other areas of social life, and serving as a UDC councillor.

Welwyn Theatre, 1940s.

One of the most famous people to come out of WGC was Dame Flora Robson, an actress who moved to the garden city originally to take work at Shredded Wheat. With Frederic Osborn she launched the Welwyn Drama Festival from 1929, and was actively associated with the Barn Theatre for most of her life. She transitioned between both stage and screen and was internationally renowned by the 1930s, starring in famous films such as *Wuthering Heights* (1939). As Richard M., then a young boy, recalled, the African American actor and singer Paul Robeson came to stay, as he was acting in a film being produced at Welwyn Studios:

> I've just remembered that Flora Robson's parents lived in Elmwood at no. 7 and he worked in the Garden City at the Shredded Wheat Factory and it was there that they invited Paul Robeson to come and stay and I had my first sight of him. I'm trying to think back to little boys of that age and their gang in the back garden and suddenly being confronted over the fence with a very large black man – we naturally got very excited and jumped up and down and I began to chant 'Hey Mr Black man' and was duly brought into the house and told off by my parents and sent round there with a message of apology – so I have had the honour of sitting on Paul Robeson's knee being fed biscuits – a really lovely man …[176]

The *Welwyn Garden City News* first mentioned an arts club in 1921. Its members included Osborn and Chambers, suggesting further Company patronage in the promotion of the leisure culture in WGC. Other members included local artists and budding painters, and as the club grew its success depended upon subscriptions of members as well as the popularity of its exhibitions.[177] These were held in empty houses and local church halls, and one included a 1928 event that included paintings by Laura Knight, Stanley Spencer and Camille Pissarro, temporarily loaned by WGC residents.[178]

The pervasive popularity of the radio and the gramophone between the wars led many in WGC to listen to music or to make it. The WGC Music Society came into being as early as 1921, playing concerts at the Cherry Tree and other venues.[179] Moreover, the Thalians have remained one of the leading cultural groups in WGC. Formed in 1929 from the WGC Barnstormers and the WGC Operatic Society, the Thalians staged light operas and musical shows. Between the wars they were well-known not only in the garden city but in London, from where special trains were laid on to some of the events.[180] The increasing presence of Welsh people in WGC, looking for work away from the dormant coal fields and industries of South Wales, led to the formation of the male voice choir in 1935. And during the Second World War the WGC Music Club was formed, with the assistance of the famous pianist Myra Hesse. A gramophone club was formed soon after the war, and throughout the post-war decades most genres of music were enthusiastically played and listened to in the town, as many recordings in the WGCHT *Where Do You Think We Played?* collection demonstrate.[181]

Another of the most enduring clubs, also formed in the late 1920s, was the Ladies Luncheon Club. Its membership included some notable local women:

> The Welwyn Garden City Women's Luncheon Club prides itself on being one of the oldest consistently active clubs in town. Not many women went to work then and so it was decided to form a group where they could meet, socialise and have an interesting talk. It met fortnightly through the school term to suit the original members who had children – they could get away during the middle of the day whilst the children were at school and get to know people and have some cultural interest. Its inaugural meeting took place in the Parkway Cafe on Wednesday, 29 November 1929, with thirty people present. Meetings were to be held fortnightly in the Cherry Tree Restaurant with subscriptions initially of one-and-a half guineas to include a luncheon of 'a very simple meal cost no more than 1/- to provide'. Its objectives included 'fostering friendship, increasing the efficiency of its members by the exchange of ideas and working together for civic, social and industrial development.' WGC ladies, who worked in a professional or business capacity or were involved in public duties, had to be proposed, seconded and voted in as members. Founder members include Dr Gladys Miall-Smith, the first female doctor in the garden city in 1922, and Mrs M. Crowley JP (one of the first women magistrates in Hertfordshire), Mrs Celia Reiss (Health Association Chair 1922–48), Mrs FJ Osborn (wife of FJ Osborn the first secretary of the GCCo.), Miss AM Coe, headmistress of Handside Junior School and Mrs de Soissons (wife of Louis De Soissons). Talks in the early days were very erudite, dealing with the position of women, e.g. women's position in the Argentine, local needs such as sex education in Welwyn

Garden City and international and national issues, e.g. the abolition of the death penalty; prisons and prison reform.[182]

This also reminds us of the didactic ethos in the garden city's social life, as well as the fact that social life was organised around gender as well as class.

## Providing for Young People in Interwar WGC

The provision by local places of worship for young people reflected an age-old concern to ensure that youth matured into responsible God-fearing citizens who would not succumb to temptation. A secular version of such concern was also evident among local educational advisers and the UDC, in the provision of youth clubs, and activities and facilities to keep children and teenagers on the right path. The Welwyn Garden City Heritage Trust's *Where Do You Think We Played?* notes that:

The first boys' club was started by the WGC Educational Association in September 1922. Initially open to boys aged 12 to 16, it met on Friday evenings at Lawrence Hall. A girls' club that met on Wednesdays began a few weeks later. As the population of the Peartree area of the town grew in the late 1920s, it became clear that a social centre for this side of the town would be a real boon. In January 1927 the Peartree Clubhouse opened. It was used as a school and clinic by day and for social events in the evenings and weekends. A branch of the boys' club was quickly established here. The opening social, at the end of January, featured a physical drill display by the members featuring boxing, gymnastics and an exhibition of rapier practice.

In the summer of 1927 the first annual sports day was held on the Handside School playing fields between the Handside Boy's Club and Peartree Boy's Club. Over 750 people attended. The sack race alone attracted over sixty competitors. Girls were allowed to take part in a few races, including skipping backwards! The club flag of scarlet and gold was won by the Handside Club. Both clubs still existed in 1929 – Handside opening two evenings a week, Peartree three evenings a week.[183]

This quote alludes to the fact that keeping the boys and young men occupied was more important than involving girls and young women, possibly because most petty crimes and minor misdemeanours in interwar Britain involving young people were perpetrated by the male of the species. As the collection of the WGCHT's *Where Do You Think We Played?* demonstrates, the boys' club at Peartree, the gymnasium and recreational facilities in schools, and church halls, all hosted sports such as boxing and athletics. Many also joined the Cubs and Scouts, or the Boys' Brigade, meeting at church halls and engaging in philanthropic behaviour as well as bonding with each other. Many young women and girls joined up with the Brownies and the Girl Guides. More informal leisure was common in the public spaces of WGC. Children made use of the culs-de-sac for playing outdoors because they were free of through traffic. And playing in Sherrardswood as a young boy or girl was a shared memory of many interviewed by the WGCHT.[184] Teenagers would meet for coffee at Welwyn Stores. In summary, children's and young people's recreation in interwar WGC was both informal and spontaneous, and also organised by adults.

## Segregation in Interwar Welwyn Garden City

Although George Orwell tended to ignore the complexity and vibrancy of social life in Welwyn Garden City, and preferred to present a picture of a town of cranks, in one sense his critical observation on the normative differences between middle-class garden city activists and the working classes did have an unfortunate expression in both the built environment and social scene in WGC. Unfortunately, the ability to access the increasingly impressive social amenities in interwar WGC was compromised by the class-based, socio-spatial segregation unfolding in the garden city. And in this context, a railway line ran right through it!

In his detailed studies of class in late-Victorian London, Charles Booth had observed that the effect of railway construction and railways lines was to encourage greater spatial mobility but also, ironically, to increase social segregation. Railways lines sometimes acted as barriers to walking and other forms of street-based mobility, reinforcing spatial disadvantages through access issues by adding time and sometimes costs in journeys to work, to shops or to places of leisure.[185] We saw above that during the site planning for Welwyn Garden City, the railway line bisected WGC. Those living to its west were spatially at an advantage compared with residents on the other side of the tracks.

During the late 1920s the American housing reformer Louis H. Pink, undertaking a tour of new housing developments in Europe, was mostly impressed by WGC and its town plan. However, he made an early unfavourable judgement on the segregation he observed at WGC, a consequence of both the location of the railway line, and the plan itself:

> The railroad cuts the town into an eastern and western half. In the westerly portion, where the commercial and civic centres are located, the expensive dwellings lie close to the centre and taper off almost imperceptibly to low-cost cottages around the edges. The entire easterly section has been given over to a factory area along the railroad, and beyond this, to the workers' houses. The town plan is remarkably well done, but it is unfortunate that the low-cost cottages should have been entirely segregated, and set apart from the rest of the town. Such segregation is hardly democratic and smacks of the old order rather than of the ultra-modern ideas which this, the most advanced of garden cities, is supposed to spread.[186]

This led to greater inconvenience for many poorer people in the garden city. In January 1931, a letter from a Dr S.J. Clegg to the *Welwyn Times*, entitled 'A Socialist's Accusation', berated the Company for installing all of the 'special amenities' of the garden city, notably the public gardens, shops, business premises, post office, theatre and restaurant, on one side of the railway line, while 'the necessary evils' such as factories and small workers' homes on the other:

> The result is that Welwyn is a most pleasant and convenient place for middle-class folk, but the factory workers – i.e. the very people for whose more especial benefit Garden Cities were originally intended – are largely isolated and cut off from the town.[187]

The workers were unimpressed with the class structure, and less keen on participation than the earlier pioneers, and some better-off social groups. In 1937 the Company, to its credit, established the Welwyn Garden City

Research Committee.[188] The first major piece of research it produced was the aforementioned *Life and Work in Welwyn Garden City*. This resulted from a conference held early in 1939 involving a number of local groups and societies, notably the Chamber of Commerce, the Trades Council, WGCL itself, the Rotary Club, schools, the Council of Christian Congregations and other voluntary organisations.[189] The report focused on labour conditions in WGC, the standard of living when compared to existing towns such as Bristol, and 'general amenities'. The methodology included not only employer surveys but household visits and questionnaires. The research team included leading statisticians from the Universities of Oxford and Manchester, and Margaret Osborn, a teacher by profession and the wife of FJO. The social scientist Jaqueline Tyrwhitt, a researcher at the GCTPA, was commissioned as the lead investigator on the project.[190]

Tyrwhitt has been belatedly recognised by historians of town planning. She personifies the often-neglected role of women in planning research and its relationship to urban policy. As Ellen Shoskes has argued, Tyrwhitt was a global figure in town planning both between the wars and in the post-war years, and was qualified in both architecture and town planning. During the 1930s Tyrwhitt spent some time in Nazi Germany, observing the application of garden city principles to National Socialist schemes for new communities. Tyrwhitt was employed as a part-time research assistant for the TCPA, of which Osborn was Honorary Secretary. In securing the post as researcher, Tyrwhitt was obliged to live in the garden city, where she rented a small semi-detached cottage.[191]

Research was undertaken in the spring and early summer of 1939 and put into hard covers by 1940. *Life and Work in Welwyn Garden City* argued that considerable social change had impacted WGC since its pioneering phase:

> The character of the resident population in the town has changed considerably since its earliest days. It had a predominantly dormitory aspect until after 1926 when manufacturing industries began to be established. Their relative importance has since grown and the dormitory population has now numerically become of minor importance.[192]

These generally positive findings were augmented by the discovery that most people who had moved to Welwyn Garden City by choice were pleased with their house and garden, and enjoyed the parklands, access to the rural belt, and the general lack of overcrowding and pollution encountered in the older cities.[193] But it was clear that some, particularly those who had moved to WGC to take up industrial and manual work during the 1930s, were segregated from aspects of the new town. The report echoed the observations of Louis H. Pink some twelve years earlier:

> [Many] complained, either directly or by implication, about the great social cleavage caused by the railway line, which could be crossed only by two bridges situated at the two extremities of the town. The result of this state of affairs was that the East side of the railway was highly inaccessible from the shopping and entertainment district that had been placed centrally upon the West side. In consequence, 'better-class' houses built upon the East side could only be let or sold with great difficulty, and that district became, in fact, almost wholly a working-class area, well separated from the concentration of middle-class houses upon the 'other side'.[194]

As the report noted, 'Direct complaints about this state of affairs were rare but were implied by frequent statements that "they were putting everything on the West"'.[195] The report also recorded grievances about the high price of food, a consequence of the retail policy of Welwyn Garden City Co., and the near-monopoly in the Welwyn Stores building and its offshoots. And this was despite the fact that the Co-operative had opened a store in WGC during the mid-1930s, and other small shops had come into being. Furthermore, residents from older and larger cities also complained about the lack of leisure facilities, for example the one cinema, and the absence of a music hall, or an indoor heated swimming pool. Some garden citizens also felt that the place was 'terribly unsociable'. They were not only from the 'distressed areas' but also from London and other parts of the south-east. They were, however, 'almost entirely large-town folk'.[196]

The reference to the distressed areas, an interwar term for the declining industrial areas, was significant. The Conservative Government of Stanley Baldwin had introduced the Industrial Transference Scheme in 1928, to assist workers from areas with high unemployment and low levels of opportunity to find work in the more prosperous regions. Partly due to the contribution of the scheme, Tyrwhitt found that during the 1930s about one-third of the working-class households in WGC had moved there from the north of England, Wales and Scotland, compared with 30 per cent from Greater London, and about 20 per cent from Hertfordshire. Two examples from the depressed north-east provide a powerful impression of how the Industrial Transference Scheme worked. As one man, originally from Sunderland, recalled:

> Well, I was born in Sunderland, in 1922. When I was about 10 my father was out of work and I don't know how he came to know that it was worth coming to Welwyn Garden City but I have a feeling that we knew somebody that was down here and that's why he came. He was down here about eighteen months or so, by which time he'd settled, got a job, and he was happy that the rest of the family should come down. Now, because I am the youngest of three boys, things that were decided and talked about tended to be between the elder two and there could be lots of things that I don't know.
>
> … my father was unemployed so he came to the garden city and in those days the labour exchange, as it was known as, they did all sorts of funny things that I didn't really understand because, as I say, I was the youngest of the three. But apparently my father was given either a rail ticket or the money to buy a ticket, and he came down to Welwyn Garden City. And he was down here about eighteen months getting things sorted out and eventually just before Christmas my mother was given either a rail ticket or money, I don't know, to bring us to Welwyn Garden City, and they also provided a furniture van to bring the furniture down. This was paid for somehow by the labour exchange because they were getting somebody out of a depressed area, Sunderland, where there was high unemployment at that time.[197]

Gordon A., from the north-east of England, was one such migrant to WGC. Like others before and after him, other extended family members had already moved to WGC, thus easing the transition:

> I was actually born on Tyneside. There was a famous shipyard there called Palmers which closed down in 1934 due to the banks being a little reluctant to hold over the 'tiding loan', and the shipyard got into the hands of the assets figures and that was it. The shipyard closed and that put about 8,000 people

in a small town out of work – unemployed – a great deal of it. There was a general exodus over a number of years – people leaving the area – it was actually called a 'distressed' area and they spread around the country.

I already had an aunt and uncle down here – they obviously got here before we did – two of my brothers – I am one of four – the youngest. The two middle brothers in their early teens … they came south and found work in the garden city and carried on from then.

We then moved here in 1936 – that was [with my] widowed mother – my father died in 1935. My mother and eldest brother came down and my other brothers had found a house – there were empty houses then – and we moved into St Audrey's Green at the time.[198]

WGC residents also hosted the unemployed from the north-east on the Jarrow March of 1936, which also brought the garden city to the attention of people from the declining staple industries. As Joan S. recalled, moving to WGC for work also meant a rise in living standards for those from Jarrow:

When they heard about the garden city, many of them came here to live. They got jobs straight away, Shredded Wheat, Dawneys, Norton Grinding Wheel, and of course Murphy Radio. Then they got houses. One of the girls who sat next to me in my class, her name was also Joan and another lad in my brother's class, his name was Matthew. Of course, they had never seen houses with hot water. Some moved to Ludwick Way, Mill Green Road, and of course bathrooms were not outside like they were used to, and toilets were in with the bath.[199]

Unemployed people also came from poor areas in Scotland and Wales, making little communities that in time produced Scottish and Welsh clubs and societies, such as Gaelic dancing and the male voice choir.[200] (And although he was not unemployed, the novelist Leslie Mitchell, better known by his pen name of Lewis Grassic Gibbon, moved from Scotland, via London, to WGC in 1931. He was not well-off or well-known by then, but would become so.)[201]

As Ward argues, migration from the poorer regions of the UK increased the working-class population of WGC and also assisted the local economy.[202] This was in tune with the aim of a socially mixed demographic as Howard had wished for, but actual social 'mixing' between the classes remained rare.

Another plus factor was the growing level of self-containment within the local economy. As more skilled, semi-skilled and unskilled workers moved to WGC to take employment in local industries, the relative proportion of those commuting to London or elsewhere declined. By 1926, more than half of the resident working population worked elsewhere. By as early as the census of 1931 this percentage was in decline, and by 1940 about four-fifths worked in WGC itself.[203]

A significant minority of poorer working-class residents, however, continued to feel at a disadvantage within the garden city to which they had moved, and were alienated by its small-town atmosphere. According to one historian of the garden cities, some of the responsibility for segregation lay with its master planner:

> de Soissons's scheme had destined the area east of the main line the wrong side of the tracks and essentially working class. The privately owned homes of the middle class were almost invariably built in the northwest and southwest parcels. In a sense of creating a community that transcended social distinctions, Welwyn Garden City proved no more successful than Letchworth.[204]

Welwyn Garden City Ltd was displeased with many findings in the report. A lengthy article in the *Welwyn Times* in October 1940, just a month after the Blitz on London had begun, criticised the 'general amenities' and 'standards of living' sections, which had been rendered 'in a sketchy and incomplete way':

> The report has an academic rather than a human interest, and, as the war has changed conditions so extensively, it has a slight historical interest as a transient indication of probable tendencies in the spring of 1939.[205]

It also pointed out that evacuees and war workers had swollen WGC to at least 18,500, above the figures given by Tyrwhitt.[206] This was essentially a rebuttal tactic by WGCL via the pages of the *Welwyn Times*.

## Health Services in Welwyn Garden City Between the Wars

A further issue in the social development of WGC concerned the lack of a general practitioner surgery or a hospital suited to the needs of an expanding population. The issue was first raised in 1921 when the town was little more than a year old and had 700 residents. A number of local people invited the King's physician, Lord Dawson of Penn, to advise on initial health facilities. A provisional committee then worked on a scheme and a Health Council was established in WGC in 1922. The town's first GPs were Dr Gladys Miall Smith and her husband Dr Hubert John Fry. Most of the work undertaken by the Health Council was funded by the Ministry of Health and Hertfordshire County Council. Apart from Miall Smith and Fry, most people working at the Health Council were volunteers.[207] The Council was later replaced by the Health Association.

The work of the Health Association was aided by the simple fact that WGC had created a salubrious environment in which to live, work and play. In 1930, the *British Medical Journal* reported that, ten years into its existence, the health of WGC citizens was better than that of Londoners. Lower mortality and infant mortality rates in WGC were seen as positive consequences of the Garden City Movement.[208] Yet as the population grew, healthcare facilities struggled to keep pace.

As the local historian Angela Eserin shows in her history of the town's QEII hospital, there were a number of abortive attempts during the interwar period to finance a new larger hospital in WGC, as an alternative to patients being sent to Hertford and other hospitals for treatment. In 1926 a start was made when the Health Association took over two beds at a private nursing home, The Hollies. This laid the basis for turning it into the Welwyn Garden City Cottage Hospital in 1929, with six local GPs and eight hospital beds, three of which were for private patients. The consulting staff at the Hollies numbered a surgeon, an ear, nose and throat specialist, a gynaecologist and an eye specialist.[209] As the *Welwyn Times* reported in May 1929, the 'outstanding feature of the year's work' of the Health Association had been the establishment of the cottage hospital. The newspaper also reported that Dr Hubert Fry had been elected as Vice Chairman of WGCUDC, indicating a growing pressure for more health facilities.[210] In 1929 the Garden City Health Association, with Fry now on the UDC, put forward a tentative proposal for a new hospital with a minimum of thirty beds.[211]

Clifford B. recalled that his mother, 'a restless soul', found meaning in her life in WGC partly as a Quaker but also by working at the cottage hospital and engaging in wider healthcare activities:

> My mother was the AD nurse at the little cottage hospital in Elm Gardens – that was the only hospital the town had in those days – and she would disappear for several days on end – she was inundated with work of course – I think she must have come home to sleep but she just disappeared. She was in the St John's Ambulance and I have photographs of her in a tent at the sports days on the fields – which is now Handside playing fields – it was then the Murphy Radio football ground. Murphy Radio was a big employer in the town in those days and they used to have sports days and a great big fair there – she used to act as the first aid tent [*sic*].[212]

During the 1930s the health services in the garden city were administered by the Hospital Committee and the Health Association, under the jurisdiction of the Medical Officer for Health and the Sanitary Inspector of Welwyn Garden City Urban District Council. The National Health Service was still some years away, and many people who could not afford private medicine were members of the Industrial Scheme of the Central Civic Fund. By 1937 the Hospital Committee reported 'increased difficulty in meeting the needs of the town due to the small hospital containing only eight beds for a population over 11,000'.[213] Many patients had to be sent out to other hospitals for more serious or complicated operations. By the end of the 1930s the Industrial Scheme was digging deep into its finances to meet demand within WGC but also to send patients elsewhere. The Medical Officer of Health expressed cautious optimism that the UDC would gain the sanction of the Ministry of Health to raise a loan for the purposes of a new larger hospital.[214] WGCL gave over some land for the anticipated healthcare facility, and in 1938 the plans were unveiled for the new hospital, containing forty-four beds, an operating theatre, outpatients department, an X-ray unit and an adjacent nursing home.[215] Unfortunately, 'war clouds were gathering, and all such plans had to be put on hold'.[216] WGC would have to wait until the heady days of the 1960s before it gained a modern hospital sufficient for a growing new town. During the war, however, WGC gained expanded hospital facilities as a consequence of extra Government funding for anticipated bomb casualties. In 1940, as wartime demands intensified on the health services, the cottage hospital was moved to Fretherne House in Church Road (now the Doctor's Tonic public house), and both Peartree Boys' Hostel and Brocket Hall, a nearby stately home, provided healthcare facilities.[217]

## Politics in Interwar Welwyn Garden City

Following the formation of the Urban District Council (UDC) in 1927, the dominance of independent members, and the growing influence of the Labour Party, were undeniable. Many independent councillors may have possessed Conservative sympathies, but the local political culture of interwar WGC tended towards a marginalisation of the Tory presence as named 'Conservative' councillors. This was evident in the political parties active in WGC since its earliest years. Osborn had been instrumental in establishing the WGC Labour Party in 1921, which was a kindred spirit of the Co-operative Men's Guild, and the Co-operative Women's Guild, formed in 1932. The WGC Labour Party was affiliated, via the umbilical link between the trades unions and the Labour Party, to the WGC and District Trades Council, formed in 1933. Three years earlier, the WGC Communist Party was established, 'by a group of socialists to find ways and means to build up strong Trade Unions and Labour organizations in Welwyn Garden City'.[218] As the industrial base of WGC grew, so the influence of Labour and the trades unions became stronger. Adding to the left-leaning mix, during the 1930s a Left Book Club was offering radical literature to the local trades unionists, Labour and communist supporters, and others interested in questioning capitalism.[219]

The Conservative interest in WGC was initially represented in the 'Constitutional' group formed by garden city residents in 1921, and the following year a separate Conservative and Unionist Association was founded.[220] This was the nucleus from which the Conservative organisation and vote would establish itself during the post-war period. The president of the Conservative and Unionist Association was Lord Brocket, living nearby in his eponymous Hall. Nonetheless, the presence of the Conservative Party and Tory voters in interwar WGC has been marginalised by the existing historiography.

The president of the Welwyn Garden City Conservative Party between the wars was the aforementioned Lieutenant Colonel Francis Fremantle. Fremantle was the candidate for the St Albans Division, which included a large district of Welwyn Garden City. A smaller area of WGC at Digswell came under the Hitchin Division, where Lord Lytton Cobbold was an influential force in Hertfordshire county politics. The Liberal vote, weakening rapidly nationwide, was so fragile in Hertfordshire that in the General Election in October 1931, for example, held at a time of national crisis during the slump, the Liberals did not even field a candidate. The result of that election was a thumping majority for a Conservative-dominated National Government, and Fremantle, standing as the 'National Conservative' candidate, soundly defeated the Labour hopeful Miss Monica Whately, gaining 36,690 votes to her 10,289.[221] His victory in the General Election of June 1929, which had brought about the ill-fated minority Labour Government of 1929–31 had been smaller, but still decisive, despite the election of a second minority Labour Government.[222] The headline in the *Welwyn Times* for 6 June 1929 was simply 'Conservative Hertfordshire'. And in the last General Election before the Second World War, held in 1935, Fremantle was also elected as MP for the St Albans Division. There thus appears to have been a superficial disconnect between the influence of the Labour Party in local elections for the UDC and the preference for choosing Conservative candidates at national General Elections. However, we need to consider the important point that WGC fell under two wider electoral constituencies, so its vote in national elections was subsumed into the wider pattern of Hertfordshire's Conservatism.

The history of the Liberal Party in interwar WGC is something of an enigma, particularly given the active presence of the Free Churches and religious nonconformity there.[223] Although the *Welwyn Garden City Directory* for 1938–40 lists the communists, Conservatives, Labour, the Independent Labour Party, trades unions and the Left Book Club under 'Clubs and Societies' there is nothing for the Liberal Party. Nor was there any listing for the Liberal Party under the 'Politics' page of the Jubilee *Welwyn Garden Citizen's Handbook*. This may partly be explained by the rapid rise of Labour during the 1920s, and the eclipse of the Liberals into a poor third place in the party political system. During the Victorian years and the early twentieth century nonconformity had a closer relationship to Liberalism, but the nonconformist conscience increasingly, if unevenly, transitioned towards the Labour Party between 1918 and 1939.[224] Another problem for the Liberals could simply have been a function of the related fact that a declining national party had difficulty sowing seeds in relatively new soil, and finding the resources to do so. The local Conservatives had the patronage of Lord Brocket, a number of members of the Board of WGCL, and the support of many business interests and landowners. By contrast, Labour was funded by subscriptions of trades unionists, was also represented locally in the leadership of WGCL, and enjoyed the support of a number of benefactors. The Liberal Party was now at a funding disadvantage both nationally and locally when raising income to fight elections.

All new cities and towns encounter initial problems and develop issues that have to be addressed both by officials and others in the general population. Yet it was with some justification that Osborn could argue in 1945 that WGC 'carried further than Letchworth the technique of civic design and architectural harmony':

> … and in the organisation of its shopping centre and factory area it conducted interesting experiments which merit careful study by all who are concerned with the economics of large-scale development. Being nearer London than Letchworth it has a more appreciable proportion of residents who travel daily into the metropolis, but at least 85 per cent of its working population find their employment in the town, which has a wide variety of industries and some large commercial office businesses – a class of enterprise now found to be more susceptible of dispersal than has been hitherto proposed.

Despite some periods of slow growth and controversy, and an undeserved and unflattering reputation, the interwar years witnessed the successful establishment of Welwyn Garden City. Osborn was writing in the autumn of 1945, furthermore, following a war that had proven to be a major catalyst for a new nationwide apparatus in town planning. His endorsement of the merits of WGC and the principle of decentralisation of industry was also partly tactical, as he saw WGC and the Garden City Movement more widely as the templates for a generation of post-war new towns. Osborn himself played a major role in agitating for such development, and WGC would develop a unique relationship with the post-war settlement in town planning, as the next chapter demonstrates.

# 4

# FROM GARDEN CITY TO NEW TOWN: WELWYN GARDEN CITY 1939-48

As the Great Depression wreaked havoc in the traditional industrial areas of Britain, and as the storm clouds gathered over Europe during the second half of the 1930s, a new garden city was unwittingly inspiring hope for a new, better and different future. Yet ironically, WGC had been a child of the First World War, and the Second World War would lead to a new phase of life and influence for the garden city. As this chapter demonstrates, planners, politicians and the people of wartime WGC were conjoined in fighting a conflict in which the communitarian values of the Garden City Movement were strongly in evidence. And as war ended, WGC would play an important role in the rebuilding and urban renewal of Britain's blitzed and blighted city centres.

The historic victory of the Labour Party in the General Election of 1945 brought about the first majority Labour Government of the last century. Alongside a legislative programme that introduced the Welfare State and a mixed economy, the government introduced two seminal pieces of town planning legislation, namely the New Towns Act of 1946 and the Town and Country Planning Act of 1947. The link between the two is personified in Frederic J. Osborn. And the connection between WGC and the new towns was encapsulated in the designation of Welwyn Garden City as a new town in January 1948. As we will see, there was both support and opposition to the decision to make WGC a new town under the terms of the 1946 Act.

Yet that designation was itself hugely symbolic, demonstrating the close relationship between the principles of the Garden City Movement and the fact that the new towns of post-war Britain were designed according to those principles.

## A Garden City at War

In a number of important ways, WGC was no different to other towns and cities across Britain as war was declared in September 1939. It had been preparing for air raids and possible invasion since the Air Raid Precautions Act of 1937. As part of the air raid precautions (ARP), children from London had been evacuated to WGC in early September 1939, swelling its population by 2,600 souls. The Welwyn Garden City Heritage Trust DVD *A Brave Vision* (1996) contains some contemporary footage of evacuees turning up in WGC. Those living in WGC were obliged to take in evacuees. As Pat L. recalled:

> The first three we had were children, they came from a Convent in north London – I don't know the name of it – and then we had somebody else and I don't know whether she didn't like us – I can imagine my mother not being very welcoming, having somebody foisted on her – and we ended up with this lady called Pamela Davidson and she was a real feisty sort of girl. We never knew what happened to her after she left us but they all started drifting back to London because there was nothing very much going on.[225]

Elizabeth D. remembers seeing the evacuees coming off the train 'in a crocodile' to be allocated accommodation. Her own family took in two evacuees from London. One was a young man called Ronnie, who became a paratrooper and was killed in the war. Another young evacuee was homesick and took himself back to London after an unspecified time.[226] The wilful decision by children to return home was a common phenomenon during the nonevent of the so-called 'Phoney War' from November 1939 to spring 1940, before the Battle of Britain.[227]

The very late 1930s saw a different enforced migration to WGC as growing numbers of Jewish refugees from Nazi Germany escaped the fate of those left behind. The Quaker tradition in Welwyn Garden City deserves

Evacuees outside Cresta Silks, 1940.

praise here. Its emphasis upon non-violence had invited opprobrium during and in the aftermath of the First World War, but its sentiment towards the oppressed facilitated the movement of many Jewish people to WGC. Of particular note was the role of Richard and Celia Reiss in helping to smuggle out young Jews from Nazi Germany in 1938, who were given board and lodging in Applecroft Hostel.[228] The Reisses, with the help of the Dutch engineer-businessman Wim Van Leer, who had set up General Stampers Ltd in WGC in 1936, and aided by a young German student Edgar Reissner, brought the fourteen young men from concentration camps.[229]

Just prior to the Second World War, moreover, Jaqueline Tyrwhitt, still living in WGC, invited a German Jewish refugee family, the Hammerschlags, to live with her, as long as they could assist with the rent.[230] WGC was a friend to the oppressed during a dark period in European history.

A number of German Jewish refugees were interviewed by the Welwyn Garden City Heritage Trust. As Freddie G. recalled, when Adolf Hitler was elected to power, and the Nazi Party seized control of the German state, 'Things obviously changed dramatically in 1933':

My father was always an optimist. He never thought anything like that could happen to a so-called civilised country. So he left it rather late to leave Germany, although all my brothers and sisters had left already. Fortunately, we left just in time in July 1939, six weeks before the War started.

And now, why Welwyn Garden City? We came straight to Welwyn Garden City. I don't know if you know that there was a hostel in Welwyn Garden City, next to Applecroft School, which has now been converted to flats. It was a hostel for German refugees. There was a committee formed after the notorious Kristallnacht in 1938, which I am sure you've heard about, and the committee was formed under the chairmanship of Captain Reiss – I don't know if you know the name but he was one of the founders of Welwyn Garden City – and a Dutch industrialist with a factory in Welwyn Garden City, Wieman Leer, went over to Germany and collected sixteen young men straight from concentration camps and brought them to Welwyn Garden City, and they all lived in the Applecroft hostel. I wasn't one of them. The hostel at that time had a warden, Mrs Anida Zander, who was a friend of my mother, and that's how we came to Welwyn Garden City.[231]

And Sam O. remembered that Quakers from Welwyn came to his German home city of Leipzig in January 1939, offering a visa-free escape to WGC to stay in the hostel on Applecroft Road, the Quakers 'looking after us perfectly.' He was about 21 years of age. He left Germany with 10 German marks, or 17*s* 6*d*. It was 'heaven' in the hostel and they were found unpaid jobs. Sam, for example, got a job in Digswell Nurseries, as an apprentice gardener. A friend of his called Charlie also worked at Digswell.[232]

This was another of many examples of where WGC was internationally engaged, and its humanitarian culture has since been celebrated. At an event held at Friend's House in London in 2010, which also acknowledged the ninetieth anniversary of Welwyn Garden City, elderly Jewish people movingly recalled how they escaped fascism to establish a new life there:

Peter Zander was 11 when he came to the Garden City with his parents in 1933 from Berlin. His mother, Anita, joined the committee to help Jewish refugees and was appointed Warden of the hostel in Applecroft Road. Peter was able to read her account of how the hostel was furnished with donations and of how several professionals offered free services to the refugees as well as to recall episodes of his own life as a teenager and young man in Welwyn Garden City.

Sam Ostro, who was 21 when he joined Wim van Leer's party of fourteen Jewish young men, spoke of his desperate situation in Leipzig, his journey to England and his arrival at the hostel on 15 January 1939. He felt that if the 'hostel wasn't heaven, it must be next door to it'. Freddy Godshaw and Peter Zander were childhood friends in Germany. The Godshaw family came to Welwyn Garden City from Hanover because the Zanders were here. Anita Zander and another Jewish friend sponsored the family, who were then granted entry visas. Freddy was just 16 when he arrived with his parents in July 1939. He and his brother stayed very briefly at Applecroft Hostel until his parents found a house to rent.

Ena Wyatt was a young woman and member of 'The Ring' Quaker Youth Group. She told the gathering how the members of the youth group befriended the Jewish refugees and included them in their activities. Ena told how she was a member of a party of twenty-five young Quakers who went to Germany on a peacemaking quest to befriend young Germans during a Youth Hostel holiday. Three of the refugees in the Applecroft hostel had asked her to visit their parents, which she did, taking entry visas for two members of one of the families. This couple reached England the day before war was declared. Ena arrived back two days before.[233]

The ethos of volunteering that had been encouraged by Welwyn Garden City Ltd and local civic societies fused with the need to get involved on the Home Front, and that included Jewish refugees. By 1944, a Zionist Youth Club had been established in WGC, run by Esther I. Samuel and meeting weekly at Handside Farm House. Its membership was not restricted to Jewish people. Activities included discussions, socials and rambles, all with a view to promoting interest in anything that might concern Jewish youth, particularly in the building of the Jewish National Home in Palestine.[234] While helping to defeat fascism, Jewish people in WGC were also looking to the future.

The garden city was suffused with social capital during the war, possibly more so than at any other point in its history. Although the Government deployed a constant stream of propaganda in the form of posters, cinema films, radio programmes and newspaper and magazine articles to whip up involvement in the war effort, this to a degree echoed the volunteering and patronage encouraged by WGCL during the 1920s and '30s. Often, a top down approach encourages bottom up participation, a lesson the Garden City Movement was well-placed to deliver. Working with the Company, the Urban District Council had established the Civil Defence apparatus before the conflict broke out. The Home Guard, the Women's Voluntary Service (WVS), Air Training Corps, Army Cadets and Sea Cadets were all active as soon as war was declared. Of the ATC, one who joined when he was young recalled 'a great time':

> We were taken up in aircraft. My first flight was in an Airspeed Oxford … We used to go up in Tiger Moths from Panshanger. I remember flying in an Avro Anson … And we used to spend Sunday afternoons on Panshanger Airfield doing gliding. I only got as far as what we called 'high hops' where you were towed up by a winch up to heights of 50 or 60ft, then they released the cable and you came down within the airfield. Some of the bright ones got as far as circuits. It was all part of our aircrew training.[235]

A British Restaurant, as part of the Government scheme to supply cheap nutritious food at a time of rationing, was also opened. Two day nurseries were provided to enable mothers who would have otherwise have been at home to raise their children to undertake industrial employment and other work given the shortage of labour caused by men serving in the Armed Forces.[236]

The Local Defence Volunteers (LDV) was the initial name of the Home Guard, the 'Dad's Army' of the Home Front. Gordon A. and his family did their bit for the war, and Gordon attempted to join the LDV. But there was a minor problem:

> Two of my brothers went into the Services: Stan, who by the way is 92, he is the only one left out of the lot of us, he went into the Army at the start of the war. Bill, who was the next one up from me, went into the RAF, so being keen to do something I offered myself as a runner for the LDV, Local Defence Volunteers, later to become the Home Guard, but at 12 years old I was deemed to be too young. So I thought, fair enough I'll try the Fire Service – it was probably the Auxiliary Fire Service by then because I think most of the professional retained firemen were already in the services, and

they decided that I was a bit too young to be a runner as well. I didn't think I was too young but they did! But they had a suggestion, which tickles me: why don't I go and make collections to buy stirrup pumps and whatever in case of an air raid as they would come in handy for putting out house fires. I used to do a weekly collection and I would hand over this to a young Salvation Army couple who lived in Barnfield Road over the other side and, having collected as much as I did over whatever period of time, they suddenly moved and the funds went with them, which was rather disappointing but somewhere my little collection notebook still exists.[237]

The *Welwyn Times*, in line with official diktat from the Ministry of Home Security, referred to WGC as a 'town in South-East England' when the garden city was bombed in October 1940.[238] Two people were killed, the only mortalities in the town as a consequence of enemy action during the war. Mary H., who was a young girl during the war, remembered the aftermath of one night of bombing of WGC just a few weeks into the Blitz:

Yes – there was one on September 26; he [Hitler] dropped one in Handside Lane, one Guessens Road and one actually by Parkway School. I slept through the lot and when I woke up next morning all I could see was these two houses completely gone in Guessens Road, which was almost opposite to me, and all I could worry about was the little Scots girl that lived there – they were all right, no one was killed there. But there were quite a lot of bombs in the garden city – he was after Hatfield de Havilland. In fact, a big land mine was dropped in Mandeville Rise and when my dad went back to work the next morning, he worked for Welwyn Builders – that was where Woodside House is now in Bridge Road – which was one of the main firms in WGC, he found this great big piece of bomb – curved – and that stood behind our toilet for years and years.

Why I don't know but the actual wartime is quite vivid to me. I didn't realise then the horror of war; to me it was fun because we had the RAF and a lot of Army chaps. I've got a sister who is ten years older than me, so she was out with the boys and I was tagging along.[239]

And one woman, a little girl at the time, vividly recalled how her home was one of the few to be hit by a bomb:

Bomb damage, Second World War.

The week before a family up off Pentley Park – Woodland Rise area – perhaps it was Mandeville Rise – yes they had a bomb there and a little girl was killed and she had been evacuated … she had been an evacuee from London – the Skinners' school who were evacuated here.

AE: So you were lucky – were any of you hurt?

SL: No my father was out because all the men had other jobs – he was an ARP warden – and he had certain hours after work and he didn't come in until 3 o'clock in the morning. Well this had happened at ten minutes past one. We were bombed out and I had a brick wall on me [and] my mother started to drag me in and I think other people had helped, and when he came home the front of the house was perfect and he had put his key in the lock, opened the door and NOTHING.

AE: You were so lucky.

SL: My mother had managed to rescue me, and my sister, who was in another room, was all right because it hadn't brought the wall down on her side and we nearly lost mother because she reacted very badly and was taken into a neighbour's house and fortunately the woman had been a nurse and she nursed my mother but it was touch and go for a week and my sister and I were taken in further down Blakemere Road. They lived at the bottom, they were school teachers at what was then Handside School – is now Applecroft – and Miss Ward and Miss Smith, their names were, and we stayed with them for about five days … [240]

Facilities in the garden city were repurposed for the war effort. The Barn Theatre was requisitioned for war purposes, and other halls had to be used by the amateur dramatic societies in WGC. All through the war the various drama, music and theatre groups staged plays and shows in between the working day and Civil Defence duties.[241] Such activities were essential for wartime morale. As one woman, who had been in her twenties during the conflict, said, the air-raid sirens and the blackouts made for 'a very dreary sort of time' but she also recalled the dance evenings in the canteen in Lawrence Hall, where she and her friends 'used to have a bit of a hop' with the soldiers.[242]

Another woman, a young girl during the blackout, recalled that 'everything was in darkness, of course':

> There were no lights in the evenings and if you didn't draw your curtains and had a chink of light you were fined, or warned. There were air-raid wardens who walked around. In fact, we had to be air-raid wardens, and you had to walk around when it got dark, to spy on people to see whether they had any lights showing, and then knock on their door to tell them to draw their curtains properly.[243]

She and her friends became informal assistants to ARP, rather than signed-up wardens.

Domestic food production was essential during a conflict where imports were disrupted or destroyed by enemy action. 'Dig for Victory' was a famous wartime slogan, and the generous provision of back and front gardens at WGC came into its own to maximise vegetable and fruit growing. Additionally, allotments were dug in public parks and on the golf course. Many of those tending the allotments were women. The Home Food Guild had a particularly impressive rabbit club, too, and a number of pig clubs produced bacon and pork for wartime consumption.[244] The town was adept at growing food during the war. A good example is the testimony of Les B., who had grown up during the 1930s in Longlands Road. The garden was important to his family's life, and it came into its own during the war:

> When I was born my father was at home but within about six months he was called up and went off into the army and at that time there was my mother and … my elder sister, who was about eighteen months [older] than me and that carried on until about 1946 when my father returned from the army.

Interviewer: So what are your earliest memories of that house, did you have
a back garden?
We had a massive back garden and my father started off growing vegetables
and my mother carried on with the garden when he was in the army so
we always had fresh potatoes, greens. One thing I remember: my father
had a thing about blackcurrant bushes and I got sick and tired of blackcurrant pie, blackcurrant jam, anything you could do with a blackcurrant my
mother did, and to this day I cannot stand the taste of blackcurrant. Oh,
and we had chickens.
Interviewer: In the back garden? Yeah, you had to get permission to have
a chicken run and I maybe wrong but I had a feeling you had to donate
some of the eggs.[245]

And Brian D. recalled how he improvised to get fertiliser for the garden
during the war:

All the milk and coal and everything was delivered in horse and carts when
I was a real youngster so you got sent out with a bucket and cleared up after
the horse and that went on the tomatoes. Well yeah, like everybody in the
war you had your own, you had a garden, which was basically fruit and veg,
and then a small bit of it would be lawn or something like that or flowers.[246]

For children and those with a sweet tooth, the appearance of favourite con-
fectionary broke the monotony of the ration diet. One woman recalled how
excited she was when Handside Stores put up a notice saying 'Cadbury's in'.[247]
      An event of note was the rousing speech by the novelist Dorothy L. Sayers,
who spoke to a packed meeting at the Parkway Restaurant during the war about
work as a vocation.[248] As with the First World War, the total war of 1939–45
mobilised almost everyone in one way or another, and women came to the fore
to take up employment and public roles reserved in peacetime for men. The
women of WGC, and female workers transferred to the garden city, were essential to the war effort. And the Brownies and the Girl Guides were also prominent
in doing little jobs for people, as were the Cubs and the Boy Scouts.[249]
      The Home Food Guild also began a co-operative potato growing scheme,
too. The Women's Voluntary Service (WVS) 'busied itself with comforts for
the services and running troop canteens' for soldiers and service personnel

billeted in WGC.[250] Many and varied events and parades were held in WGC throughout the war, including Spitfire Week, War Weapons Week, Warship Week, Tanks for Africa Week, Wings for Victory Week and Salute the Soldier Week. The War Weapons Week Parade in 1941, for example, between the Campus and the council offices and other areas of the town centre raised more than £150,000 to equip two military battalions.[251]

Historians have critically debated the impact of war on technology and the research and development of weapons, generally and unsurprisingly concluding that the demands of war tended to escalate the process. The obvious reasons were the need to keep abreast of the enemy's capability in order to defeat him. During the Second World War an important if often overlooked contribution to weapons development was made locally in the form of the so-called Welgun and the Welrod. The Welgun was a prototype submachine gun, developed by the Birmingham Small Arms Company, and trialled for the Special Operations Executive (SOE), which assisted resistance movements and covert operations in Axis-occupied countries. The SOE had secret research departments hidden across Britain, one of which was known as 'Station IX', tucked away inside the Frythe, a secret site just outside Welwyn Garden City. This explains the use of the prefix 'Wel' used by Station IX. The Welgun went through various iterations as a short-range, rapid-fire weapon, of particular use to soldiers and resistance fighters at close quarters with the enemy. Yet it was ultimately rejected for the Sten Gun Mark IV.[252] Nonetheless, its importance in the evolution of the British gun is acknowledged by the Imperial War Museum, where it is an item in its collection.

Another significant weapon to which WGC lent the first syllable of its name was the Welrod, or the 'Assassin's Pistol'. Also made by Birmingham Small Arms, and developed at Station IX, it was a bolt-action, magazine-fed pistol, whose use was intended for irregular fighters with the SOE, and by resistance fighters. The Welrod saw more action that the Welgun in the war as it was dropped into Denmark and a number of other European countries from 1943 to assist retaliation against the Nazis. It is likely it was used in 'Ratweek' in France during 1944, for example, when Gestapo officers were assassinated by the French Resistance.

The Frythe was also the site of other important wartime weapon innovations. A large hangar was erected in the grounds for the testing of limpet mines and small one- or two-man submarines. Corgi scooters and folding bicycles for paratroopers, and small arrowheads for use in jungle warfare, were also tested at the Frythe.[253]

During the Cold War, the Frythe was also to be used by NATO in the event of an invasion of Western Europe. This was as part of the so-called Operation Gladio, which ran from 1956, following the Soviet invasion of Hungary, to 1990, when Gladio was stood down during perestroika.

The Welrod was deployed during the Falklands War in 1982, and in Northern Ireland during the Troubles of 1968–98. It was also used in the Gulf War in 1991–92.[254]

Murphy Radio made a significant contribution to the war effort. As noted, during the war the Ministry of Information and the Ministry of Home Security had mostly prevented newspapers and other media from individually naming towns affected by bombing, or those towns and cities involved in essential war work. In March 1944, the *Welwyn Times* carried an article entitled 'Praise for Radio Workers. A-A Chief Visits Home Counties Factory'. The Commander-in-Chief of Anti-Aircraft Command, General Sir Frederick Pile, praised the contribution made by local workers in developing specialist radio parts for the Ministry of Supply. This followed an 'urgent telegram from Mr Winston Churchill' in 1940 calling for trials and testing of such parts. The general congratulated the factory on reaching full production within a year of the telegram, adding that the parts were now used in thousands of operations, though he added that he would like to see more German aircraft 'killed'.[255]

Yet a number of employees of Murphy Radio were made to feel unwelcome during the war, not necessarily by the company but by wartime regulations. As Freddie G., the German Jewish refugee from Hanover, recalled:

I had already begun an apprenticeship in Germany as a watchmaker, and I got a job at Murphy Radio working as an instrument maker in the test instrument department, which I loved: it was a lovely job. But when we arrived in this country we obviously had to register as 'aliens', so unfortunately, when the war broke out, we suddenly became 'enemy aliens'. And I was called in, together with I think two or three other German refugees, into the office of E.J. Powell, who was managing director at Murphy Radio, and shown a letter from the Air Ministry stating that they were no longer allowed to employ non-British subjects. Then I immediately got a job as a watchmaker at Mr Faulty – I am sure that name doesn't mean anything to you! He had a workshop over the cinema …[256]

Other companies based in WGC during the war, British, American, Swiss, and even German, made essential contributions to the war effort. Beiersdorf employed German nationals who were arrested and interned in 1939, and it soon changed its name to Herts Pharmaceuticals, for reasons both patriotic and practical. The company made chemicals and drugs for civilian and military use during the war.[257] Neosid, another German company in WGC, also played a key role in defeating the Third Reich. At its factory:

> components essential for the war effort were manufactured for use in communications equipment (transmitters and receivers) for Army backpacks, and Air Force Spitfires. Day and night, ammunition tin after ammunition tin of components were delivered to Marconi for assembly.[258]

Norton Grinding Wheel, a US-based company, also did its bit for the war effort. Its factory became a control centre for industrial civil defence in WGC. In common with Shredded Wheat, it operated its own Home Guard platoon, and also a bomb disposal unit. Many women replaced men on the production line during the conflict.[259]

The Swiss company Roche played a very important role in wartime WGC. The roof of one of its buildings was the site of an air-raid warning siren. As with 'the Wheat', many of its workers volunteered for ARP, Fire Guard and Civil Defence duties.[260] Women employees became members of the Home Guard Auxiliaries, making meals and providing refreshments for the men in the platoon. Others joined the Civil Nursing Reserve.[261] An independent Roche Fire Brigade was formed in 1940, made up of twelve workmen (women were not allowed to fight fires, only to watch out for them). In 1943 the Roche Fire Brigade was affiliated to the National Fire Service, hence its activities were extended to the entire garden city, not only the defence of Roche sites. A first-aid room was also based at Roche. As a history of Roche during wartime also noted:

> The Roche building was one of the chosen official 'Keeps' to be held to the last man, the Battle Headquarter of the 4th Herts Home Guard, and on any

night you could see one of the commercial rooms transformed for martial purposes; while about our grounds, where, a few hours before, wagons and lorries had been discharging raw materials or picking up packages of 'Roche' preparations for despatch to every battle front and the countries of the Empire, soldiers moved intent upon their military business.[262]

Further anecdotes and details on Roche at war can be found in its own history of the company, *Roche in Wartime*.

Meanwhile, what of WGC as a business concern during the exigencies of war? As Maurice de Soissons notes, the Company enjoyed its twenty-first birthday in 1941, a good year for profit margins that remained sound throughout the war.[263] The Company saw a number of staff movements during the conflict. W.E. James, the engineer, retired after twenty-five years of service; John Eccles was elevated to a seat on the Board, and H.T. Tigwell became Chief Executive Officer, while Fred Page was elevated to Secretary and Estates Manager.[264] Eccles, who will resurface in a later chapter, was remembered as a '*very* charming man' by a female accountant at Welwyn Stores.[265] The first generation of the Company's leadership had been characterised more by continuity than by conflict and change, despite the earlier fates of Osborn and Purdom.

Yet despite the general mood of keeping calm and carrying on, there was some discord in the garden city. Concern was expressed that the bomb shelters were not bomb-proof but bomb-resistant, a common complaint about Anderson shelters, as a direct hit meant death or very serious injury. Some residents were angered at the employment of conscientious objectors by the UDC, while various complaints were sent to the *Welwyn Times* about inadequate air raid precautions, poor food distribution and the uneven collection of salvage. This reflected 'no corporate spirit, no sign of communal enterprise, no leadership …'[266] In his seminal revisionist histories of wartime Britain, *The Myth of the Blitz* (1991) and *The People's War* (1969), Angus Calder emphasised that conflicts and divisions between individuals and different sections of society tarnished the notion of wartime unity. Yet he over-egged his pudding of discontent, as a number of historians have argued. Despite wartime grumbles and resentments, most people in WGC, as in Britain, 'went to it', in the words of one wartime poster, and saw the war out to the best of their abilities. As Maurice de Soissons stated:

Certainly it seems that the ARP was seriously hampered by lack of equipment and of properly protected posts, and a number of wardens complained until matters were put right. But there is little evidence of a lack of spirit and leadership in the garden city.[267]

One woman recalled how her house near Handside Lane was full of visitors during the war, because her mother was a salvage steward, and her father volunteered both for bomb disposal with the Home Guard, and as an ARP warden. The home kitchen doubled up as an ARP post, and the air-raid shelter built in the back garden was still there at the time she was interviewed, though with changed use, of course.[268] Another woman had a photograph of her father in uniform. He was a member of 'The Home Guard of the Shredded Wheat' and she dated the photo to about 1943.[269] As the Welwyn Garden City Heritage Trust argues, Shredded Wheat made a further unique contribution to the war effort as 'the only breakfast cereal house in the country able to maintain a fleet of vans under war conditions'.[270]

The father of Shirley H. was a key figure in air-raid precautions, another example of the culture of wartime voluntarism in WGC:

> While I was young my father was appointed chief air raid warden for WGC and one of my memories is of the house smelling of rubber, which was in fact rubber boots issued to the air raid wardens, and we had tin hats hanging up, jackets and trousers hanging up, in fact the whole house became like an office or factory and I have a very clear memory of my father having received a message to press a button and warn the air raid wardens in WGC when they scuttled down either into the Morrison shelters or Anderson shelters or under their dining tables, and he also used to receive the information when it was time to give the 'all clear'. He took his job very seriously. One day when I was at home we were having the red warning, so it was a little bit dodgy, and my mother decided to cut my toenails. My father said: 'You can't do that, you can't do that. There's a red warning,' and my mother said: 'Red warning, war, I don't care – I am going to cut Shirley's toe nails,' and to this day I can remember the look my father gave her at the time.

As the war began to take decisive turns in favour of the Allies in 1943, that year also became a profound one in the history of British town planning.

In no small part thanks to the efforts of Frederic Osborn, the Ministry of Town and Country Planning was established in 1943, leading to a grow-ing public interest in and debate about the matter. WGC was, of course, pivotal to so much of this new interest. In 1942, Osborn had redrafted and republished his *New Towns After the War*, originally a call for a programme of new towns post-1918 but now made strongly relevant to the imminent period of reconstruction that would follow the Second World War. Osborn now, however, argued that WGC should enjoy more licensed pubs and bars, cafeterias, restaurants, and a more generous provision of informal leisure facilities. This was an optimistic, morale-raising vision, and the Company took it on board, as well as proposing further shops and homes in its post-war plans.[271]

Coterminous with the gathering momentum in Britain for post-war town planning, the Welwyn Garden City Post-War Committee was also set up in 1943. As the war drew towards its conclusion, and victory appeared increas-ingly likely, reconstruction matters were increasingly discussed in the *Welwyn Times* and in public meetings. The war had to be won first, of course, and by the time VE Day came along in May 1945, WGC 'had escaped relatively lightly'. Only two people had been killed. The sundry bombs and incen-diaries that had fallen on the town had destroyed only two homes, badly damaged nine more, and caused minor damage to 216 houses. Only one factory, in Tewin Road, had been seriously damaged.[272] The rest of WGC's industries had played their part in wartime production, and in the case of the cinema production company, in raising morale through documentary films.

A brains trust was formed during the war, partly to discuss key issues from the form and wording of the war memorials once the conflict was over, to the implications of post-war planning for Welwyn Garden City. The term 'brains trust' is interesting, as President Roosevelt had established an outfit of the same name during the Great Depression to pursue collective thinking and imaginative solutions to the crises facing America.

In common with the rest of Britain, the wartime moratorium on housing construction led to a shortage of homes. In January 1944, R.L. Reiss addressed the Welwyn Garden City branch of the Common Wealth Party. Formed in July 1942, it was made up of left-leaning politicians and planners, and celebrities such as J.B. Priestley, who wanted a socialist and egalitarian vision for post-war reconstruction.[273] Reiss was adamant that the majority of new houses required after the war would need to be built by the Urban District Council, thus supporting a prevailing call among Labour and Common Wealth activists for a new post-war programme of public sector housing locally and nationally. True to his garden city form, he also insisted the new housing estates should be 'of strict limitation of density' and that the people deserved houses with gardens both front and back. In the short term, however, he noted there was a need for emergency housing in the form of prefabricated houses. In the USA millions of prefabricated housing units had been built around large-scale munitions factories and key industrial sites for war production, hence Reiss felt that 'America had a lot to teach us'.[274]

In spring 1944, the *Welwyn Times* commented upon the 'grave housing shortage' as the main 'problem of reconstruction' in the town, but it gave an upbeat summary of the financial position in WGC, claiming its council was one of the most financially solvent of councils across the country.[275] Prefabricated housing was now viewed by the UDC as a temporary solution to the housing problem. Yet the use of prefabricated homes was akin to placing a sticking plaster over a gaping hole, as the number of prefabs provided in WGC during 1944–45 was inadequate. Following correspondence between the Housing and Town Planning Committee of the UDC and the Ministry of Health, in November 1944 the Minister of Heath agreed to a mere fifty homes to alleviate the problem in WGC.[276] This was not really the fault of the UDC or WGCL. As the eminent historian David Kynaston argues, in 1944 Prime Minister Winston Churchill had promised half a million new prefabs, but in the event fewer than 160,000 were built.[277]

Against a backdrop of serious material shortages and a dearth of construction labour, however, the UDC managed to complete its first post-war council houses in 1946. Once the war had ended, the UDC and WGCL had also begun to formulate plans for the provision of a fresh programme of housing across the town, and to increase the population significantly, perhaps up to 50,000. Yet such planning was distracted, to say the least, by the priorities of the first majority Labour Government, elected in the summer of 1945. And to understand those priorities, we must return to the figure of Frederick James Osborn.

# The New Town Cometh

Since the 'restructuring' of WGCL in 1936, Osborn may have no longer been a leading player in the governance of WGC, but he was still very much a prominent public figure, living in Guessens Road and remaining a frequent contributor to the correspondence columns of the *Welwyn Times*. While he was aware of the findings of *Life and Work in Welwyn Garden City*, he did not let them interfere with his drive for wartime planning, or his goal to put WGC at the heart of debates about the decentralisation of Greater London.[278] Liberated from his administrative role in WGCL, Osborn now, in effect, used his hands-on experience at WGC to promote garden city town planning:

> [As] honorary secretary, chairman of the executive committee, editor of *Town and Country Planning*, chairman of the association, [Osborn] worked with astonishing energy, single-mindedness and political acumen to further the association's policies for limiting the size of cities, industrial reloca-tion, low-density housing, green belts, and planned decentralisation to new towns. The report of the Royal Commission on the Distribution of the Industrial Population (1940), for which he had prepared and argued evi-dence and whose findings were something of a triumph for him, marked the beginning of seven intense years that proved also to be his most active and effective. He sat on the government's Panel of Physical Reconstruction, was on the Labour Party Post-War Reconstruction Committee (while advising the Conservative and Liberal equivalents), and advised Patrick Abercrombie over the County of London and Greater London Plans.[279]

In December 1940 his article 'Replanning Britain' was published in *Town and Country Planning*, the journal of the GCTPA. The article was heavily reported in the *Welwyn Times*, because it emphasised 'the popularity of planning', the opportunity opened up by the appointment of Sir John Reith as Minister of Works and Planning in 1940, and 'the importance of the garden city idea in national planning'. Despite his differences with WGCL there was common ground here, as Osborn was keen to extol the virtues of both Hertfordshire garden cities as models for future new towns.[280]

Peter Hall and Colin Ward have emphasised the tireless contribution of FJO to the growing influence of the Garden City Movement within the emerging town planning apparatus in wartime Britain. He was long a man of both words and deeds and now he saw his opportunity to put Howard's ideas into operation on a much grander scale than before. His catalogue of wartime achievements is impressive. In 1941, as Secretary of the GCTPA, he successfully lobbied with his allies to change the name from the Garden Cities and Town Planning Association to the Town and Country Planning Association (TCPA), the name it still enjoys today. Osborn's *New Towns After the War* (1942) argued strongly that the Blitz had opened up 'new vistas' both for people living near the ruins but also for town planning.[281] After all, the consequences of the official call for 'Homes Fit for Heroes' and the campaign of the New Townsmen during the First World War had been largely disappointing. Now a second terrible total war provided the catalyst for a new culture of planning, not least because the destruction of the built environment by air raids and fires was extensive when compared with the earlier conflict. Osborn and other leading garden city planners were instrumental in the formation of the Ministry of Town and Country Planning (MTCP) in 1943, and in promoting new towns through lobbying for the New Towns Act of 1946.[282] His leading role in the TCPA enabled FJO to exert his influence over architects, civil servants, leading politicians and media figures who might be sympathetic to decentralisation and a large-scale programme of new towns. He was also at the heart of a network of influential non-governmental organisations, such as the conservationist Campaign for the Preservation of Rural England (CPRE).[283] Osborn was more than a little pleased when the Report of the Commission into the Distribution of the Industrial Population, chaired by Sir Montague Barlow, published in 1940, endorsed the principle of decentralisation of the older cities. Its recommendations were endorsed by Osborn but also by Labour politicians such as Herbert Morrison, the leader of the London Labour Party, who became Home Secretary from 1940.[284]

In *Garden Cities of Tomorrow*, Howard had discoursed upon 'the future of London' and called for a programme of planned decentralisation of 'social cities' in 'new town clusters' to ease the burdens of the capital city. These burdens were inextricably worsened by the air raids on the Home Front. Due to its size, London had suffered more destruction than any other British city from bombing and the consequent housing shortage, and here the figure of the architect Patrick Abercrombie becomes important. Osborn was in contact and correspondence with Abercrombie, the Head of Architecture and

Town Planning Department of the London County Council. Abercrombie was also a member of the Town and Country Planning Association, and the CPRE. In 1943, Abercrombie's *County of London Plan* was published, to some criticism from the TCPA and Osborn for its failure to embrace a more extensive vision of decentralisation. Hence in his *Greater London Plan* of 1944, Abercrombie and his associate J.H. Forshaw fully accepted the case for dispersal, and used the example of WGC to justify a programme of carefully planned dispersal of population to new towns beyond the green belt.[285] Osborn successfully persuaded the London Labour politician Lewis Silkin 'to co-operate in a joint TCPA–LCC study' of the potential for new towns. Silkin became Minister for Town and Country Planning in Clement Attlee's Cabinet, following the General Election victory of the Labour Party in 1945.[286] As David Kynaston puts it, the 'Howardian agenda' was ultimately realised in the *Greater London Plan*.[287]

As the town planning historian Stephen V. Ward has argued, London was presented as four rings: the inner-urban ring; the lower-density suburban ring; the green belt; and the outer-county ring where the new towns, and also some large-scale council estates (social housing projects), would be built.[288] Here, the figure of Lewis Silkin, a qualified barrister, became increasingly significant. Before the war, he was Chair of the Housing Committee of the LCC, but became Chair of its Town Planning Committee on the outbreak of the conflict. Silkin was in favour of high-density housing as a solution to the problems of inner-urban areas, rather than dispersal, but he became the target of what one historian has termed a 'courtship' by Osborn:

> The setting for this courtship seems to have been the Labour Party's wartime Reconstruction Sub-Committee. Silkin had not hitherto been deemed an enthusiast for decentralisation, and his conversion marked an important turning-point. Elevated after the war to Parliament, he was to be given immediate charge of the young Ministry of Town and Country Planning and to embark upon the New Towns Policy with remarkable fervour.[289]

In common with pre-war Silkin's ideas, many leading housing reformers in London, whether on the LCC or as independent advisers, preferred not dispersal but, in the words of Elizabeth Denby, 'to go to work on the mess we have made' in the existing cities suffering from blitz and blight.²⁹⁰ Denby was an out-and-out critic of decentralisation. In other words, she wanted to keep the population where it already was and 'renovate' the industrial city. So there was a strong urbanist tendency, as it would now be called, within the architectural and planning elite of the capital city. Despite his conversion of Silkin, this rang alarm bells with Osborn and others in the TCPA fearful that their proposals might be significantly watered down, and that the recommendations of the Barlow Report might be ignored. In 1944, Osborn wrote to Viscount Astor, a leading exponent of bold town planning during the upcoming era of post-war reconstruction, lamenting Denby's attack on 'overspill' new towns and population dispersal. He rather patronisingly argued that she knew more about maternity and child welfare and had less than an elementary knowledge of housing and town planning.²⁹¹

Denby was an important figure in housing and architecture, however, and Osborn knew it. During the 1930s she had won Leverhulme funding for her project, which led to her book *Europe Rehoused* in the 1930s, where she claimed the most successful cities in Europe were higher density: 'How lazy to advocate decentralisation and the creation of satellite towns.' Instead, each city should be researched and rebuilt according to its housing needs and its own social, economic and cultural profile.²⁹² She had also published on housing 'from the slum dwellers' point of view'. She was one of the first women to become an honourable member of the Royal Institute of British Architects. As a housing expert and an activist for affordable housing, she made many public speeches in favour of 'living in cities'. A modernist, she also worked with the architect Maxwell Fry who, from 1948, perhaps with a touch of unintended irony, would play a leading role in Hatfield New Town, bringing his mark to bear upon it.²⁹³

Ultimately, FJO need not have worried. His efforts were not in vain. The programme of decentralisation to new towns went ahead, but not always according to the preferences of leading lights in the Garden City Movement.²⁹⁴ Yet Osborn's long-standing involvement with Labour politics and his connections at both Letchworth and WGC greatly aided him in his calls for a new towns programme. The capture of the London County Council by the London Labour Party in 1934 had advanced the cause of town planning in London. The LCC pioneered the adoption of a green belt, an inviolable ring of countryside, around the capital city.²⁹⁵

Osborn continued to lobby hard for a programme of new towns, keeping up his efforts in WGC, too. In 1945 as the war moved towards its conclusion, he addressed the WGC Labour Party, reminding them of their 'pleasant community-minded town' and reiterating his position that WGC was 'an example' for future planned environments and an alternative to 'evil' overcrowding in unplanned cities.[296]

As the *Greater London Plan* was finalised towards the end of 1944, and as the place of WGC within it became starkly evident, there was much debate in the garden city about the future of the town. Just before Christmas 1944 the *Welwyn Times* reported on Abercrombie's *Outline Plan for Greater London*. The architect-planner viewed WGC as an 'obvious' centre for industrial relocation from London due to its 'thriving and expanding industries' and the simple fact that it possessed 'the necessary spaciousness to make it the nucleus for a much bigger population'. Abercrombie also pointed out that Hatfield would be conjoined with WGC in his plan. It would expand the de Havilland operation by building more accommodation to house those workers living some distance away. It would also be a centre for relocated employment from London. Abercrombie estimated that the combined future population of WGC and Hatfield would amount to 60,000 people, two-thirds of them living in WGC, 20,000 in Hatfield.[297] The justification for expanding WGC and Hatfield in tandem was straightforward: they were accessible from London, within the 'outer-county ring' some 22 and 20 miles from central London respectively, so industry could be dispersed from the capital city relatively easily, as advocated by the Barlow Report.

Partly thanks to Osborn's efforts, and also to those of the Luftwaffe, town planning became a more prominent subject of public debate as the war went on. The need to clear up and clear out the blitzed and blighted industrial city was transmitted to the wartime public in a variety of media, notably instructional films at the cinema, radio broadcasts and public exhibitions. In 1943, for example, a sixteen-minute documentary film entitled *The Development of the English Town* was released by GB Instructional Productions. Every screening at a British cinema was approved by the Ministry of Information. The film began with the ancient village, moved through Roman and Anglo-Saxon and feudal towns, and the legacy of overcrowding and the environmental degradation of the industrial city. This included the commuting problem caused by suburbanisation and the long-range separation of housing from employment. Its solution was the planned garden city as proposed by Howard. Letchworth and WGC were presented as the brave new world. The last five minutes of the film depicted images of WGC as the narrator called for the new post-war towns to be planned so that work and homes were close to each other but separate, and where families could enjoy gardens and parklands, and other conveniently placed leisure amenities.[298] This was wartime propaganda for the Garden City Movement.

Yet many living in WGC were concerned about the post-war expansion and its impact on the social and environmental character of the town. The spirit of wartime unity, tangible but sometimes on the verge of fracturing during the conflict, soon collapsed once the war ended. This was evidenced locally within the long-standing rural-versus-urbanisation divide. As Maurice de Soissons argues:

> The Second World War was hardly over when the village of Welwyn began a battle for its independence from the thrusting and uncouth neighbour to the South. There were Hertfordshire County Council plans to place Welwyn [village] previously in the North Herts planning area, in the East Herts area with Welwyn Garden City. The village felt it would be in danger of joining the garden city in more ways than this – that it would be the beginning of the end of its separate identity, especially if Welwyn Garden City spread north of the Mimram. It fought successfully to remain in its planning area.[299]

The importance of maintaining the identity, and peace and quiet, of Welwyn village from planned urbanisation revealed both the continuation of rural localism and status consciousness, but it also reflected a deeper cultural nostalgia for the Welwyn area before it became a garden city, and was now under further threat. The opposition of 'Old Welwyn' to the new planning dispensation also demonstrated a kind of dress rehearsal for the opposition to new towns that would be manifest in almost all designations following the legislation of 1946. The anger of the residents of the old Hertfordshire town of Stevenage is a famous episode. Stevenage saw itself as 'an idyllic small town in North Herts until 1946 when it was designated as a new town'.[300] Soon after that decision by Lewis Silkin, opponents of the new town carried out a clever attention-grabbing campaign, daubing the signs and notices for Stevenage with 'Silkingrad'.[301] This strongly suggested not only fear of urbanisation but of socialist interference from the state.

The year 1946 looked promising for Welwyn Garden City Ltd, but it would also initiate the ending of the Company's life. The following quote from Maurice de Soisson's history of Welwyn Garden City is important for both of these reasons:

> Accompanied by Lewis Silkin and Lord Reith, Chairman of the New Towns Committee, the Crown Prince of Sweden visited Welwyn Garden City. At the time the figure of 50,000 for the eventual population was again raised. Welwyn Garden City Limited had already purchased the Danesbury Estate of 202 acres (82 hectares) to the west of its Lockley Estate, and north of Welwyn village. Much closer to its needs in having adequate land to complete the town and provide it with a greenbelt, the Company had bought 565 acres (228 hectares) from Lord Salisbury. This would fix the final southward extension and the greenbelt between the Garden City and Hatfield. While some of it would be for housing, the majority would be for agricultural and recreational purposes – relieving the pressure for more playing fields. At the time both parties to the sale agreed a new boundary on which there would be no building for a certain distance on either side. This became known as the 'Salisbury Line'.[302]

Silkin would go on to abolish WGCL, but in the meantime the UDC and WGCL submitted a proposal to the Minister for Town and Country Planning in 1946 for an expansion of the population of WGC to 50,000 people. This was opposed by both the village of Welwyn and also the Welwyn Rural District Council, long resentful of the loss of countryside but also of its declining powers in the face of both the Company and the Urban District Council.[303]

Yet Welwyn Garden City itself was divided over plans for its future, and had been so for some time. Many members of the Urban District Council had not always agreed with Welwyn Garden City Ltd on some key issues. Among the citizens of WGC, many wanted their town to remain much as it was before the war, while others understood the need for growth, and welcomed it.

At a meeting of the local 'brains trust' in November 1944, a Mr Langdon-Davies had asked 'will our town be better when bigger?' He was accused of being a 'narrow-minded bigot with long hair' as Osborn sought to reassure the locals that a larger population certainly posed problems but mostly advantages in the form of greater social amenities. He also pointed out that the estimated population was closer to Ebenezer Howard's call for 30,000 people to make a viable community than the 14,000 or so living in WGC by 1939.[304]

Subsequent concerns expressed by both WGCL and local citizens suggest a significant level of cynicism in WGC about planned growth. In March 1945 the *Welwyn Times* announced the forthcoming arrival of Sir Patrick Abercrombie, who was to speak to the local Chamber of Commerce on his *Greater London Plan*, 'which is, of course, the proposal to decant population and industry from London's congested areas into a ring of satellite towns, of which we are one'.[305] Abercrombie shared Osborn's view that Welwyn Garden City had been making an important contribution to the decentralisation of London, and repeated his view that WGC was 'an obvious centre for planned industrial expansion' and one of the places where Hertfordshire would make a significant contribution to solving the problems of overcrowded London.[306]

It is more than likely that Abercrombie was not greeted with universal enthusiasm, both within WGCL and among the politically aware citizens of WGC. Many had shared or enjoyed the patronage of the Company, so they resented the imposition of a Development Corporation. While Osborn embraced the wartime opportunities to develop a centralised Ministry infused with the ideals of Ebenezer Howard, his long-standing opponent Theodore Chambers remained unconvinced. Chambers had strongly opposed the change of name from GCTPA to the Town and Country Planning Association in 1941, and he lamented that the idealism of Howard was now 'entangled in the mazes' of the wartime town planning and reconstruction report. Chambers was fearful of the growing bureaucratisation of town planning, and of the manner in which the Garden City Movement had become so influential within a centralised planning machinery: 'I think it is a rather sad departure from the true faith. I wish it had remained the "Garden City Association".'[307]

So this leads to an intriguing proposition: was Osborn's drive to get WGC recognised as a major model for the post-war new towns, and to call for such an extensive state-supported programme, partly a kind of dish of revenge, which he began to prepare in 1936 following his resignation from WGCL, and served up cold as the New Towns Act of 1946? Osborn, Reiss, Chambers and others associated with WGCL remained in contact and correspondence with each other, but Osborn had fought hard for a state-sponsored programme, while Chambers remained sceptical about the role and fate of WGC within it.

Osborn was, perhaps understandably, a little immodest about his contribution to the promotion of town and country planning in general and of the new towns in particular:

> I personally have been a decisive factor in the evolution of new towns policy and [this] evolution is extremely important historically. I mean no less than without my fanatical conviction and persistent work in writing, lecturing and especially lobbying, the New Towns Act of 1946 would not have come about, at any rate in that period.[308]

The New Towns Act was preceded by the establishment by Silkin of the New Towns Committee, which met in 1945–46. Headed by John Reith, the founder of the BBC, and Minister of Works and Planning in 1940–42, the committee provided the opportunity for supporters and also critics of new towns to make their case. Although Chambers, Osborn and Reiss contributed to the New Towns Committee, and made the case for WGC as an exemplar of new towns, they did not bargain for the decision by the Labour Minister for Town and Country Planning, Lewis Silkin, to transfer governance of the new town from the hegemony of WGCL to a Development Corporation, which was also to be responsible for Hatfield, a small town brought into the designated area. The New Towns Committee debated at length the most effective mechanism for delivering the new towns, and ultimately settled upon the new town Development Corporation model. The Development Corporations were to be funded by significant Treasury loans, and each corporation was to be terminated once the new town was built, and the new town's assets handed over to the local authority. Yet unlike the other new towns that came into existence after 1946, WGC already possessed a delivery authority, Welwyn Garden City Ltd. This would cause significant local tensions, as we will see.[309]

Silkin, however, had local allies beyond the Company. The Urban District Council requested of the Ministry of Town and Country Planning that Welwyn Garden City become a new town. Osborn and Whittick viewed this as a key factor in Silkin's decision.[310]

Following the recommendations of the New Towns Committee, the New Towns Act was passed in 1946. Steered through the House of Commons by Silkin, it was redolent with the ideas and practices once promoted by Howard, and operationalised in Letchworth and Welwyn Garden Cities. The idea of social mixing, for example, was emphasised by Silkin, within the social planning concept of the 'neighbourhood unit'. This was an American innovation in town planning between the wars, owing a great deal to the 'ward' in Howard's writings. The social planning of the new towns was clearly an extension of the Hertfordshire exemplars, particularly WGC, and influences from the USA and Europe. Silkin envisaged genuinely mixed and interactive communities, as he stated to the House of Commons during the second reading of the New Towns Bill:

> The towns will be divided into neighbourhood units, each unit with its shops, schools, open spaces, community halls and other amenities. [I] am most anxious that the planning should be such that the different income groups living in the new towns will not be segregated. No doubt they may enjoy common recreational facilities, and take part in amateur theatricals, or each play their part in a health centre or a community centre. But when they go home I do not want the better off people to go to the right, and the less-well-off to go to the left. I want them to ask each other 'are you going my way?'[311]

Silkin was consciously drawing upon the wartime spirit of co-operation and the need to pull together beyond class and sectional differences in order to defeat a common enemy and build a brighter future. That was certainly the view proposed by the Labour Manifesto for the General Election of 1945, which emphasised how the Blitz spirit could be drawn upon once more to build a modern, egalitarian 'New Jerusalem'. Yet Silkin may also have been subliminally thinking about WGC's social and spatial division as he spoke about his desire to avoid class divisions in everyday life. He was at best a critical friend of WGC, and his emphasis upon social mixing in the new towns as an extension of wartime unity jars with his evaluation that the garden city was a 'dormitory town that was started for the middle classes'.[312]

Silkin was by no means alone in his critical views of Welwyn Garden City Ltd. The announcement of the imminent new town, and the inevitable opposition of WGCL towards it, led to a number of stated impressions, not always favourable, of the legacy of the Company. Councillor Donald Daines of Welwyn Urban District Council argued that the Company as a commercial concern, run partly in the interest of the shareholders, had not fulfilled the true communitarian and co-operative spirit that Howard had wished for, and while he acknowledged some success in the establishment of the garden city, he felt that 'the financial interest of the shareholders' was always too much of a concern for WGCL: 'perhaps the Development Corporation will bring us back to the ideals of Howard?'[313]

In his nuanced assessment of the legacy of WGCL, Maurice de Soissons acknowledged the 'vibrant cultural and social life' and the impressive levels of civic participation among the citizens of WGC, but he shared some of those earlier concerns of Daines that Howard's ideals had been 'strayed' from by WGCL policies:

> Under tremendous financial pressure it had certainly done away with the 7 per cent limited dividend, with profits over and above to be spent for the town's benefit. In fact, dividends had been limited to below that percentage, and there had been little left over for development work to be expended as Howard had envisaged. But the principle had gone, thus giving the company's critics a stick to beat it with, although Welwyn Garden City Limited's financial history to date gave little reason for supposing that it would in future become a greedy landlord. Certainly, the idea that everyone would be within a quarter hour of open country and town centre had been abandoned. The reduction in the size of families coupled with density limitations meant that more dwellings were required to house what to the company had been an eventual population of 50,000, necessitating more land.[314]

De Soissons also reiterated the significance of housing and spatial inequalities between the poorer east and the west of the garden city, claiming that a mixture of human nature and the failure of the Company 'to build the full range of housing on both sides of the railway line' meant Howard's idyllic view of an harmonious mixed social city was not properly realised.[315]

Others living in WGC picked up on the anger that some leaders of the WGCL felt at the imposition of the new town. As Elizabeth F., whose parents knew Frederick and Margaret Osborn and Theodore Chambers, recalled:

I know there have been some nasty rumours, maybe true or not, about the people running the company and then the Government … well it was the Labour Government decided that Welwyn and Hatfield ought to become new towns and they were to be taken over and I can remember the old stagers who my parents knew … I got the feeling that they weren't at all happy about what was going to happen and that the ethos under which the garden city had evolved, things which we now call building regulations I suppose, were all going to be changed and they were going to develop the area round the edge and it wasn't going to be like Ebenezer Howard … that was when I became aware of his original plan, the one that is reproduced so often now with how everybody was going to be able to live in their own house and have a garden and cycle or walk to work, and well he was long dead, of course …[316]

The designation of WGC as a new town must be viewed within the wider context of reconstruction and the planned decentralisation of blitzed British cities. The New Towns Act created more than twenty new towns in Britain, all of them adhering to a considerable degree to the garden city principles proposed by Howard almost fifty years earlier. London gained eight new towns beyond the green belt, four of them in Hertfordshire, the 'home' of the Garden City Movement. The first new town to be designated was Stevenage in 1946, 10 miles (16km) further north than WGC along the Great Eastern Railway line, but sharing convenient access to the road and rail networks.[317] The next Hertfordshire new town to be designated was Hemel Hempstead in 1947 and Welwyn Garden City and Hatfield followed in 1948. They were the eighth and ninth new towns to be designated. (The other London new towns were Basildon and Harlow in Essex, Crawley in Sussex, and Bracknell in Berkshire.)[318] Each new town was to be guided into place by the aforementioned Development Corporation. Each Development Corporation was given a lifespan, which varied between corporations, to ensure the new town under its auspice was established as successfully as possible.

The designation of all post-war new towns was accompanied by a local inquiry, during which support, objections and a variety of practical and ethical issues could be expressed. Silkin's actions in transforming WGC into a new town were by no means popular with the leaders of WGCL and many of its citizens. Some of those fears about expansion, expressed during 1944–45, were reiterated in the inquiry. And the Company was forthright in its opposition to the planned transition from its control to a new Development Corporation. Its statement to the shareholders, issued in August 1948, drew attention to the 'serious complication of the Company's affairs arising out of the formation of the Development Corporation', and the 'little likelihood of any further dividend being paid in respect of the year ended 31 March 1948'. In other words, the 6 per cent dividend less tax enjoyed by the shareholders was coming to an end. Yet it would be erroneous to view this purely in terms of individual and corporate self-interest, for the proposed winding up of WGCL was entwined with wider concerns for the viability of the principles of the garden city and its interwar achievements.

Speaking at the public local inquiry into the Draft Welwyn New Town (Designation) Order, 1948, held on 22 and 23 March 1948 at the Cherry Tree Restaurant, Chambers pointed to a meeting of the shareholders of WGCL, held on 6 February, in which the shareholders had strongly supported the actions of the directors of the Company in opposing the formation of a Development Corporation. Unsurprisingly, he stated the need for shareholders to be 'equitably treated', meaning that negotiations between WGCL and the Ministry should ensure that 'equitable compensation is obtained for the acquisition of the Company's land and buildings within the designated area for Welwyn Garden City', and a host of reassurances about the continuing viability of the Company's enterprises and the disposal of assets in the event of the liquidation of WGCL. These statements were transmitted back to the shareholders in the form of extracts from the enquiry.[319]

Under questioning from Arthur Capewell, Reiss, the Vice Chairman of WGCL, and Chair of Hampstead Garden Suburb Trust, recalled his original bemusement at the original proposal by Howard of WGC and his pride in creating 'London's first satellite town' in spite of difficulties in raising capital. He praised the social balance in the town, and expressed his concerns, shared by Chambers and Osborn, that the expertise and acquired working knowledge of the Company would be dispersed in the new dispensation.[320]

Charles Purdom was bitterly critical of Silkin too, arguing that he bore 'animosity' to the idea of garden cities, and was appropriating the aspects that he liked and rejecting those he disliked for his new towns programme. He was particularly scathing of Silkin's claim, made in a booklet on behalf of Stevenage New Town Development Corporation, that 'the policy of aiming at a self-contained community is new, and the methods for attaining it are still untried'. In common with Chambers, and to a degree with Osborn, Purdom viewed the Ministry of Town and Country Planning as steamrollering over the legacy of the Company.[321]

The *Welwyn Times* in the winter and spring months of 1948 contained many articles both opposing the new town and putting the case for retaining WGCL. Chambers was particularly offended at the notion that a public corporation would be more even-handed than a private organisation.[322] And as Chairman of Welwyn Garden City Ltd, he had worked hard to assure shareholders that their financial interests would be best served in maintaining the status quo, while insisting to the Ministry of Town and Country Planning that shareholders were being treated unjustly.[323] Silkin played a clever game, praising WGCL for blazing a trail for the new towns, before announcing that it was ill-suited to the task of co-ordinating the planned growth of the garden city within the wider decentralisation from London. He also claimed that WGC required a more democratic and representative body, insisting that both existing and future citizens needed a governing and developmental authority that was answerable not to shareholders but to the people of the garden city.[324] Silkin may also have had in mind the earlier financial difficulties of WGC Ltd.[325] Ultimately the Ministry bought out the properties held by WGC Ltd, leading to its imminent demise.[326]

During the local inquiry into the Draft New Town Designation Order, Chambers and Reiss continued to voice their objection to the transfer of the town from WGCL to a Development Corporation. Deliberately ignoring earlier conflicts, Chambers was adamant that the Company had worked for almost thirty years 'with a real team spirit and a strong sense of public responsibility for their work and its results'. He praised the enterprising spirit of the Company and justified its practical successes by pointing to quality of the built environment and the international reputation of WGC, invoking once more the 'the personal devotion of the early pioneers'.[327] As might be expected, the *Welwyn Times* remained a staunch ally of the Company, restating Chambers' view that 'the knowledge and experience gained in the course of twenty-eight years work at Welwyn' had informed many recommendations in the New Towns Committee's reports.[328] Chambers, Reiss and others accused Silkin of a 'complete travesty' and of naivety in his prognosis for WGC.[329]

The Company was not alone in its opposition to the instigation of a Development Corporation. It had worked closely, both for the purposes of economic growth and community building, with the Chamber of Commerce, the Ratepayers Association, the Rotary Club, the Welwyn Association, and leading industrialists in the garden city. Each of these organisations raised objections to the transfer of power from the Company to the development corporation, and called for 'reasonable continuity' between the policies of WGCL and the new dispensation.[330] The Labour manifesto had promised more public ownership of industry, leading to worries about the nationalisation of local industries in WGC. And within the context of housing, concerns were expressed that the new corporation would change the leases on the houses, thus converting private owner-occupiers into mere tenants.[331] This was partly the fear of socialism, but also, arguably, an expression of the defensive snobberies that came with home ownership, rather than the idealism of the mixed community cherished by Howard.

Osborn was in a uniquely privileged position. He had been an advocate of the apparatus and principles of large-scale, state-sponsored decentralisation, and of the contribution WGC could make. Chambers, by contrast was fearful for the future of his beloved garden city, not least because of the achievements of both businesses and private interests at WGC. Once the public enquiry was over Osborn stated to the citizens of WGC and also to WGCL that he was 'all in favour of public control' of the garden city in particular and the new towns in general.[332] This would have rankled with Chambers. Osborn appeared to be less concerned about the fact of the Development Corporation, however, than with the lack of continuity between the planners and experts who had created the inspirational garden city, and the 'untrained people' of the future. He made clear that he was with the majority of the New Towns Committee, who believed that when new towns were complete they should become public property, a long-standing goal of the Garden City Movement. Yet he was not convinced that elected urban district councils were the best tools for this task, and attacked Welwyn Urban District Council for 'contemptuous treatment' in their apparent 'secret' support for the Development Corporation model. In so doing he exposed a certain controlling tendency. Quoting the American writer and poet Walt Whitman, he referred to the 'never-ending audacity of elected persons' and argued that citizens 'should never leave their affairs solely in the hands of their elected representatives'. He called for a politically non-partisan collection of voluntary groups to help take the new town forward.[333]

It is also possible that Osborn was concerned that the team that the Ministry of Town and Country Planning had selected to advise Silkin on the Welwyn and Hatfield New Town Advisory Committee, which included D.H. Daines and other leading Hertfordshire politicians and professionals, included few of any significance from WGCL.[334] Ultimately, however, some continuity was assured when Silkin invited Richard Reiss to become Vice Chairman of Welwyn and Hatfield New Town Development Corporation, a role he duly accepted, with the support of Chambers, in May 1948.[335] Reiss was obliged to dispose of all his financial interests in WGCL in order to clear the way for his new role.[336] Although Reiss had many concerns about the transition from WGCL to the Development Corporation model, he replied to Silkin's 'flattering' invitation thus:

> I think it is well that I should explain to you the reasons which have led me to this decision despite the fact that I expressed my disagreement with the proposed change both at the Shareholders' meeting and at the Inquiry.
>
> At the Shareholders' meeting I expressed the view that despite the objections to the proposal, I thought that if the Designation Order was confirmed the position should be accepted in the interests of the town, provided steps are taken to ensure equitable treatment for all concerned. In arriving at my decision, therefore, I had, in loyalty to the Company, of which I have been a director since its first inception, to decide as to whether, in my view, there was sufficient ground for thinking that equitable treatment would be accorded within, of course, what the law allowed.
>
> The fact that I am personally sufficiently satisfied that this will be the case to justify my accepting the Vice-Chairmanship, if offered, must not be taken of course as in any way compromising the position of the Company, of which I am no longer a director.
>
> If, as you kindly suggest, you consider that my experience and knowledge will be of value to the Corporation in the important task which they are undertaking then I feel it my duty to do all I can to assist in the work.[337]

A number of other personnel transferred from WGCL to the Development Corporation, ensuring there was no clean break between the garden city's past and the future new town of WGC. As noted, de Soissons was appointed as the architect-planner for the new town in July 1948, and began to prepare his outline plan, which was published in 1949. The Company's former landscape architect Malcolm Sefton took up much the same role in the new dispensation. A former member of the Company's finance department, H.T. Tigwell, took over as comptroller for the new corporation, along with J. Skinner, a company engineer.[338]

There was, of course, much new blood. The first Chairman of Welwyn Garden City Development Corporation was Reg Gosling, while the General Manager was James McComb. The two men could hardly have come from more divergent backgrounds. Gosling was born into a working-class family, and was a dedicated Labour Party supporter and member of the Co-operative Movement. McComb by contrast had been educated at the elite Stowe School in Buckinghamshire, was a solicitor in his professional life, and had served as a squadron leader in the Royal Air Force.[339] Other elite appointments included the architect and polymath Lionel Brett (4th Viscount Esher), who became the new master planner for Hatfield.[340] (This was the same Esher who was very critical of the de Soissons composition for WGC.)

The new Welwyn Garden City Development Corporation was given responsibility for developing 4,231 acres (1,712 hectares) and 'to provide satisfactory living and working conditions for a total population of 36,500'.[341] This was a doubling of the 16,000 population who then lived in WGC. The First Annual Report of WGCDC also emphasised the new 'green belt of not less than 1,000 yards' or 914m.[342] Many enthusiasts for Welwyn Garden City would have been more than a little pleased at the *cordon sanitaire*, which had initially been purchased by the Company. Its aim was straightforward: to 'divide the one from the other and thus keep the characteristics of the towns separate'.[343] Hatfield was to remain the smaller of the two, with a population rising from 8,000 to 25,000.[344]

Although a Development Corporation was appointed for both Welwyn and Hatfield, many of the same personnel worked on the Board of each corporation, and administration was carried out by the same staff. The administrative tie-in between Welwyn and Hatfield gave rise to more than a little snobbery among some citizens of the garden city. Advocates for WGC were bitterly critical of the decision by Silkin to include Hatfield into the post-war new town plan for 'Welwyn New Town and Hatfield New Town'.

Although this story is mostly beyond the scope of this book, certain aspects of it are very revealing. The achievement at WGC was contrasted with 'deplorable Hatfield', the unplanned and untidy creation of a nearby aerodrome and some new private industries:

> The former is a world-famous modern new town developed as an experiment in community planning by public-spirited private enterprise. The latter is a modern new town presenting most of the deplorable features of an unplanned settlement, created by the sporadic building of industry and houses in the open country, near to an ancient and ordered village with a house and park which are national treasures.[345]

Welwyn Garden City, once associated with cranky socialists and lentil-munching freaks, was now presented as an enclave of socially responsible capitalism. At a stretch, it also appropriated the 'national treasure' of Hatfield House for the cause of the garden city rather than the suburban town of Hatfield itself. WGC was now heir to a well-ordered and long-established village and the referred nobility of Hatfield House, home of the local aristocracy.

Such elitism found short shrift with some of the more left-leaning key officials in the Ministry of Town and Country Planning. Chairing the public inquiry was Baroness Evelyn Sharp, Deputy Secretary to Silkin, and well-known in political circles as 'never one to mince her words'.[346] This was, moreover, the first time a new town public enquiry had been chaired by a woman, and she did a good job. In her 'Foreword' to Osborn's *The Genesis of Welwyn Garden City* (1970), Sharp noted how the enlargement of WGC following the New Towns Act of 1946 generated 'a great deal of opposition' from residents. She argued WGC was by 1970 'more of a true city now, and no doubt some regret this'.[347] In her mind, Sharp viewed WGC, as did Silkin, as a small town infused with local patriotism and reverence for garden city principles promoted by the interwar elite of WGLC and adopted by its more defensive residents.

Antipathy towards Welwyn Garden City Ltd lingered after it was wound up in 1949. This sentiment was expressed in the early 1950s, in an audit of the historic buildings and landscape of the Digswell area by the Welwyn and District Regional Survey Association. The former Welwyn Garden City Co. was damned by faint praise:

The late Welwyn Garden City Company sought in the tithe maps for old names to give to the new streets and 'closes'. In this way they tried to preserve some slight continuity with the character of the place. In most cases the names do not fit in their old position; it is difficult to change the name of a small field to fit into a long street. Where it has been possible the old name has stood: Handside, Stanborough, Ludwick, Brockswood, Coneydale and many others. Mandeville Rise, Walden Road and Walden Place must remind residents of past history which those names suggest.[348]

The author went on to argue 'lest it be forgotten and buried forever under the rapid development and urgent life into the new phase of planned post-war urban development'. There was a certain nostalgic dissonance in this lament, however. While WGC retained 'Garden City' in its title, it was by the early 1950s also a new town. Moreover, why 'must' previous field names remind incoming migrants or recently established residents of the medieval, feudal or rural heritage? Both WGCL and WGDC maintained as many palimpsests of the past as they could, while driving the new town forward. Yet this was only one local complaint among many others.

Alongside the inclusion of Hatfield and the problems that this unplanned suburban small town raised for original garden city principles, opposition to the new town and the Development Corporation emanated from other quarters: from the business interests of WGCL; from the mostly middle-class composition of the active citizenry of WGC; and from the many separate interest-based cliques that made up the social life of the town. During the 1930s, the expanding demographic of unskilled workers and their households, and the geographical segregation of large sections of the skilled and semi-skilled working classes, did some damage to the principle of social mixing at the heart of the garden city ethos. It is difficult to avoid the conclusion that many of the more active citizens in WGC were fearful of sacrificing their garden city to a more utilitarian future. This was also completely understandable. Those middle-class pioneers who moved to WGC had become enamoured of its social and recreational amenities, and felt safe within the exclusivity of the interest groups to which they belonged. The Second World War had seen a rude interruption into the social evolution of WGC, and a desire for a return to normality was an overriding aspiration among the local and national population by 1945. Yet the new normal in WGC was to be a Development Corporation.

The problem of segregation by class would continue into the post-war years.[349] The goal of complete self-containment was not achieved either in WGC or any other of the post-war London new towns. Most have not even achieved 60 per cent of a population both living and working in the new town.[350] The experience at WGC between the wars was indicative of the only partial realisation of some of the initial ambitions initially claimed by Ebenezer Howard, and operationalised by WGCL between the wars. Yet despite these difficulties, WGC was only partly what Lewis Silkin polemically accused it of being: a 'dormitory town that was started for the middle classes'.[351] It was no dormitory, nor was it completely dominated by the middle classes, despite their undoubted social, cultural and economic influence. And as we will see in the next chapter, the working classes were set to become an increasing presence in WGC, as in all of the post-war new towns.

# 5

# GROWING UP AND SETTLING DOWN: WELWYN GARDEN CITY 1948-2020

The second half of the twentieth century saw Welwyn Garden City mature into a mostly successful and attractive place to live. The early post-war years were certainly difficult ones, as we will soon see, but the many challenges and problems, major and minor, were met and mostly solved by the different organisations governing post-war WGC, and by the people of the town. David Kynaston draws attention to the achievement of the new towns in general during a period of austerity that stretched from wartime until the mid-1950s, and WGC had a unique role within that achievement.[352] As the British economy began to return to growth and relatively full employment after 1953, the simple fact was that, thanks to the mixed economy that Welwyn Garden City Ltd had produced by the end of the 1930s, the town now began to prosper once more following the interruptions and depredations of war. There were still developmental issues to be addressed as the garden city expanded, and there would be further significant changes to the governance of Welwyn Garden City during the 1960s and '70s. But the social, cultural and economic life of post-war WGC would become a very English success story.

De Soissons' master plan, 1949.

## Reconstruction and Readjustment in Early Post-War WGC

The new towns were an ambitious nationwide programme, a key element in the post-war reconstruction of Britain. For most urban and planning historians, the reconstruction era began with the end of the Second World War and lasted until the mid-1950s, or at the very latest 1960. Every new town had to plan for the dispersal of population from existing cities; the construction of enough housing; the provision of social and cultural amenity; the laying down of infrastructure; and of course the promotion of as high a level of internal employment, or self-containment, as possible. And all of these goals had to be pursued within a context of rationing, shortages of primary (raw) and secondary materials, and labour supply issues. Whilst WGC had something of a head start on the new towns built from scratch, its existence since 1919 also meant that it had unique transitional factors to get to grips with.

First and foremost, perhaps, WGCL was wound up, and its assets transferred either to WGCDC or to new companies. As de Soissons notes, all its land assets beyond the designated area were taken over by a new company, Danesbury properties. The Company's successful businesses – Welwyn Stores and Welwyn Builders – now came under the auspices of the Howardsgate Trust Ltd.[353]

## Growing the Post-War Economy

Following the war, existing industries in WGC returned to their original purpose and to full-scale production. Despite the greyness of post-war austerity, 1947 was a good year for fashion both internationally and at WGC. In the same year that Christian Dior launched his New Look, Cresta Silks became a listed exhibitor at the British Industries Fair. It was still a leading manufacturer of hand-printed silks, linens, woollens and rayons for dresses and scarves, and its goods continued to be sold in upscale fashion shops at home and abroad.[354] There was also an important new start-up in 1947, with the launch of Eylure Ltd. In a sense Eylure was a spin-off from Welwyn Studios, as the founders David and Eric Aylott had worked on make-up for the actors there. As the magazine *Herts Countryside* reported in 1970, Eylure was originally run part-time from the family sitting room, but in 1947 they moved to a 'shack' on the current site of Gosling Stadium:

> Until the late-1950s the brothers worked on film sets by day and ran Eylure part-time; some of the films they worked on are now appearing on our television screens. They include *Look Back in Anger*, *Road to Hong Kong*, *The Millionairess* and *The Journey*. The real breakthrough for the company came with the introduction of ready-shaped and trimmed lashes which were mounted on curved platforms shaped to the natural contour of the eye. With the addition of self-adhesive fixative, Eylure lashes could be fixed straight from the pack, making them the most instant make-up ever and bringing the film-star look within the reach of the average woman.

So successful was the business that the brothers concentrated on lashes only, receiving the Queen's Awards for Industry in 1966. Other branches of the company were established in Britain and in Europe.[355]

The fact that Eylure pre-dated Welwyn Garden City Development Corporation was significant. WGCDC possessed the advantage of an already successful, mixed local economy, and it built upon the achievements of Welwyn Garden City Ltd during the post-war years. During the 1950s, among the important companies locating in WGC were Smith and Nephew, the manufacturers of Nivea hand cream, which took over Herts Pharmaceuticals in 1951; Anglo-Swiss Food Products (Knorr) from 1958, and the pharmaceuticals company Smith, Kline and French from 1959. A 1969 *Guardian* survey of the new towns stated that the Corporation had been responsible for adding twenty-one new companies to WGC since 1948.[356] The inclusion of Hatfield, with its aerospace and manufacturing assets, was also advantageous to the Development Corporation. As soon as the London new towns were designated, the Government and the LCC encouraged companies to relocate from the capital to the most accessible new town for their needs. This included larger firms and what are now called small and medium-sized enterprises (SMEs). Greater London was divided into five administrative sections for the purposes of planned dispersal of industry, each linked to the selected new towns, called, somewhat akin to the towns nominated for evacuees during the war, 'reception areas'.[357] When relocating, employers needed to be satisfied there was a good labour supply, access to transport and communications, and WGC was still very much at an advantage here, with its proximity to London, its railway sidings, and the main arterial road running north from the metropolis, the A1. Hemel Hempstead and Stevenage also shared some of these locational advantages, but lacked the robust economy of an already established garden city. The incentives on relocation costs and reduced business rates were also a clincher for many firms deciding to relocate from the capital. And the availability of new housing for their workers was another key deciding factor.[358]

Many of the established industries in WGC continued to thrive until the latter decades of the twentieth century. ICI was at its peak during the late 1960s, with more than 4,000 employees.[359] Shredded Wheat expanded its operations in early post-war WGC, introducing 'Welgar Shreddies' named after Welwyn Garden City, later shortened to 'Shreddies'. During the 1950s, Imperial Preference tariffs were jettisoned, bringing an end to cheaper wheat imported from the Dominions, notably Canada, and encouraging greater use of home-grown crops. During the 1960s, the garden city was increasingly viewed by Nabisco as a base from which to grow sales into Europe, and the expansion of the British and European motorway networks led to more exports using lorries rather than the railway.[360]

Food, pharmaceuticals, electrical goods, radio parts, publishing and print, and machine parts manufacturing all characterised the post-war economy of WGC.[361] In addition to Danish Bacon and Shredded Wheat, Bickiepegs, the makers of teething biscuits for babies, and Suchard, the Swiss chocolate manufacturer, helped to make WGC a household name. In 1968, Rank Xerox took over Murphy Radio, which had been in the garden city since the late 1920s. Dawneys continued to manufacture steel for construction purposes in WGC, until the steel industry mostly collapsed in Britain during the 1970s.[362]

A keyword in understanding the changing economy of post-war WGC, however, is deindustrialisation. As Maurice de Soissons argues, 1982 was a transitional year in WGC. ICI closed down most of its operations. Norton Abrasives laid off more than 100 people, as did Rank Xerox.[363] Smith and Nephew quit WGC. As noted, Dawneys, the first company to relocate to WGC, closed operations during the 1970s. In contrast, Roche invested £4 million in a new laboratory. Yet while manufacturing was declining in WGC, in common with sectoral trends across the UK, retail and services were expanding. Tesco, the supermarket chain, occupied the former Smith and Nephew building in 1982, and by 2010 the former Suchard factory. Sainsbury's supermarket opened in WGC in April of the same year. The previous cottage hospital became a restaurant and pub. Unemployment was lower in WGC in 1982 than the national average, and lower than in some other south-east towns.[364] Most of the smaller food manufacturing companies had left WGC by the beginning of the present century. The Danish Bacon Co. continued at WGC.

The new hi-tech employment zone called Shire Park was announced during the mid-1980s. Just 200m from the town centre, it also symbolised the growing significance of retail and services to the local economy. At the time of writing, Tesco PLC headquarters was based at Shire Park, as was HSBC's Global Data Centre. Roche Products, which still has a significant presence in WGC, run a number of operations out of Shire Park, and there are many SMEs in design, media, consultancy, deliveries and other expanding areas of the mostly post-industrial economy of the South-east. Ease of access to the national road system, the railway and London continue to play a significant role in the economic fortunes of the WGC.[365] The opening of the Howard Centre in 1990 also signified the importance of retail to WGC.

## A New Era in Housing?

In 1949 the Development Corporation acquired property worth £28 million from the Company. A programme of housing, building upon the existing stock, but also in areas earmarked for new build, was soon under way. The Second World War had exacerbated an already existing housing short-age, both through a moratorium on construction, as well as a consequence of bomb damage, and WGC was to play its part in alleviating that shortage. The development company divided the garden city into four areas: north-east, north-west, south-east and south-west, and different targets were given to each area. In the south-east for example, the Beehive area would be given some of the best housing. In the north-east, Panshanger was also expanded according to an ambitious scheme for new housing announced in 1953. Both the Beehive area and Panshanger drew many incomers from London, and from elsewhere in the UK.[366]

The early provision of housing in post-war WGC lagged behind industrial relocations and new business start-ups. There was also concern about the quality of some early post-war housing and its relationship to the Neo-Georgian aesthetic established by Louis de Soissons. As a contributor to the Planning Exchange's *New Towns Record* (2002) argued, the 'underlying princi-ples' of the original master plan were not so much threatened by the takeover of Welwyn Garden City Ltd by the Development Corporation, but by the material conditions of post-war austerity into which the new town was born. A shortage of labour and also of building materials exacerbated the problems of housing supply as the local population grew: 'Through necessity houses were designed for economic viability and speed of erection and the underly-ing principles of the garden city were often compromised.'[367] The writer was also critical of the 'cautious' provision of flats for smaller households during

Early post-war housing, Beehive Lane, 1953. *(Photographer Ken Wright)*

Panshanger, Broomhills, 1973. *(Photographer Ken Wright)*

the 1950s, but noted that many larger households living in flats preferred a house.[368] Yet as a local resident has countered, the de Soisson partnership's basic post-war house was 'excellent'. She lived in one for years, and also noted the continuation of the cul-de-sac principle established between the wars, 'albeit with higher densities'. Most of the Beehive area, south-east of the town, is now a conservation area.[369]

Housing construction in WGC during the second half of the twentieth century partly reiterated the social divisions in the form of the east–west divide established between the wars. The east saw higher levels of housing construction, and a continuation of industrial workers moving there rather than to the centre and the western residential districts. Yet more than 6,400 new homes were added between 1948 and 1968.[370] More shops and offices were added to WGC.[371] The physical expansion of WGC was mostly complete by the end of the 1960s.

## Social Development in Post-War WGC

Social development consisted of three main activities in new town Development Corporations. One was arrivals work: the welcoming to the new town of immigrants with little or no knowledge of the town. Another was the use of a social planning device known as the neighbourhood unit, discussed below. And the third strategy was to work with local clubs, groups and associations, and providers such as commerce, organised religions and the Urban District Council, to enhance and maintain social life in the new town.

Among the first practical expressions of social development were the two clubs built by the Development Corporation, one at Ludwick and one at Hatfield Hyde, where new housing was being built. In its report on the Ludwick Family Club in 1952, the *Welwyn Times* pointed out how this local experiment was of national and international significance, and it indicated the continuing role of religion in community building. Yet it implicitly also reflected the growing understanding within social planning that interest-led groups were as important as locality when people joined together:

**Whole Family Can Join New Club**

A novel experiment in developing the social life of a new community is to be tried in WGC. Presiding over it will be Mr Joseph Trenaman of 138 Parkway, who has had a unique experience in the study of certain aspects of social development. He has just completed for the BBC an enquiry that has taken him three years. It has been to go among people all over the country to find out how far the various educational broadcasts were being assimilated and how far they are completely missing the mark. During the war he evolved a method of teaching adult illiterates which was a considerable advance on anything previously known in any country.

**Shopping Area**

The experiment with which he will now be associated will centre on the shopping area, still to be built, and to be known as Ludwick Green. To some extent it will follow the lines of the very successful community associations which have grown up in the Nottingham area, sometimes in rather tough districts. An ordinary local citizen, perhaps a bus driver, has been asked to invite a few of his neighbours to a little meeting in the front room. Subject for discussion: 'is there anything you would like to start?'

As a result of these tactics, there have developed old people's clubs, whist groups, language studies, and many other activities. The essence of the scheme is that the social life of the new community shall grow naturally out of the interests of the residents and shall not be imposed upon them. This is one aim of the Council of Christian Congregations in sponsoring the experiment. [Their] other chief aim is to ensure that the family group shall be specially catered for. There have been talks for many months between the Council of Christian Congregations and the Development Corporation about the scheme.

A first step has now been taken by the acquisition of Ludwick House, a four-bedroom private dwelling just beyond Ludwick Hall, to serve as a club.[372]

The Hyde Family Club was begun soon afterwards in 1953 in Hatfield Hyde. In common with the Ludwick Centre, a warden was appointed to oversee social interactions. In the words of the *Herts Advertiser*, it was 'getting ready to receive new population'. The club was based in The Hyde, Hatfield Hyde, once a large private house repurposed by WGCDL to accommodate the free-time aspirations and needs of a mostly working-class population largely coming from London. Youths and 'housewives' figured prominently in its preparations, signalling a growing official awareness of the problems faced by women and young people when adapting to a strange new town.[373]

Both the Hyde and Ludwick clubs hosted an impressive variety of local clubs, groups and societies. For youths, Cubs, Scouts, Brownies and Girl Guides, and young Christian groups were based in them. The family clubs themselves were at the hub of activities, but a housewives club catered to the needs of younger women. Beyond these interest groups, wider functions included Christmas parties, fetes and harvest festivals, all of which were designed to encourage local participation and local patriotism.

In its 1956 report to Duncan Sandys, the Minister of Housing and Local Government, WGCDC was generally upbeat about its social development strategies, and the new facilities coming on stream to boost the community life of the town. Arrivals work also remained a key activity, one inherited from practices pioneered in WGC during the 1920s. Acknowledging its general success in maintaining social development, it drew attention to the greeting of new arrivals with parties and information, assisting new societies to establish themselves and withdrawing as much as possible when the new organisation was up and running. The Development Corporation co-operated closely with the Urban District Council and the Council of Christian Congregations in its arrivals work, and emphasized some success in providing new neighbourhood centres in Ludwick and the Hyde: 'Both these clubs are physically limited in their activities, but they continue to flourish and are indeed a source of social comfort to many newcomers.'[374]

Overall, the Development Corporation felt its social development programme was successful:

> Work of this nature does not show obvious results and one must consider many matters in attempting to gauge success, such as: Is there in the town much misery, loneliness, juvenile or adult crime, drunkenness, indebtedness or mental ill-health? Looking around it would seem there is considerable success.[375]

Assessing the legacy of the social development is a difficult exercise, and such considerations must be borne in mind when reading contemporary official publications. Yet those in charge of the garden city had faced significant challenges in keeping pace with social change.

Social development had another role to play: to ward off, as far as possible, the criticism of the new towns from certain quarters that newcomers were left isolated and confused on moving away from their old place of residence to a strange and ostensibly bleak new housing estate. During the 1950s, for example, studies of Crawley New Town in Surrey, and of Harlow in Essex, found that some young women of child-bearing or child-rearing age were particularly prone to a sense of disassociation from their new environment, as they were cooped up at home all day, and cut off from old friends and neighbours while their husband was out at work or socialising in the evenings. Something akin to 'the Crawley neurosis', or what was more generally and critically referred to as 'the new town blues', was a problem that all new towns, including WGC, wanted to avoid.[376]

The memories of Francesca H. throw some light on to how some women felt about moving to Welwyn Garden City. Her mother and father and she as an only child moved to WGC from Islington in north London in 1958. They would have moved earlier but the council flat they were moving to was occupied by local people from Hatfield, rehoused when the roofs blew off some modern houses designed by Maxwell Fry during the mid-1950s. Francesca recalls that her father worked as a television cabinet maker for Murphy Radio, while her mother was almost completely home-centred, taking a short spell of work at Danish Bacon, but as a woman of 40, she felt separate to the other mothers with more and younger children. Francesca mentions that as her mother got older, she felt both ill as well as lonely, and was given a placebo by the doctor, which made her feel better. So was it all in the mind? Possibly, but as Francesca recalls, back in London her mother was the youngest of a large family, and was 'spoiled rotten' because everything she needed was given to her. She therefore found it hard to make friends, unlike most of the younger mothers who forged relationships with others. Despite that, she viewed WGC as 'heaven', and became very house proud. As for Francesca herself, she recalls being bored every day because there was little provision for young people, as she saw it: 'Welwyn has always been an old people's city.'[377]

Another woman who moved to WGC in 1956, Gillian L., remembered that as she was a shy person and 'not clubbable' she did not make many friends at first: 'I was quite lonely to start with because people who had been there for some years already had their friends, they didn't need me as a friend.'[378]

This was a temporary feeling, however. During the later 1950s and the '60s she was busy raising her children, meeting fellow mothers, even dog walkers, and once her children went to school she did have a little more time to have coffee with people. Later she joined the Women's Voluntary Service. She also met people through a shared interest in gardening. Her husband, a research chemist at ICI, also played cricket for Welwyn Garden City Cricket Club.[379]

Ultimately, as research by this writer has demonstrated, the new town blues were largely a myth got up by critics of the garden cities and new towns who preferred the busier, mixed-use streets and higher densities of the older towns and cities. Partly thanks to social development strategies and arrivals work, and also due to the existing social and cultural facilities at WGC, the problem appears to have been kept to a minimum, and levels of active participation in WGC and other new towns remained higher than in longer-established urban areas. Indeed, the very doctors who had first identified the psychological problems of newcomers reversed their diagnosis during the mid-1960s following a study of 'mental health in new towns', arguing there was little evidence to substantiate the case, and that most people who moved house might exhibit some temporary insecurities at some point.[380] The study was carried out in Harlow, but the psychiatric department at the newly opened QEII hospital also dealt with patients suffering from anxiety about the move to a new town.[381]

Yet there was another, positive outcome from the national debate about the new town blues and suburban neurosis. The Housewives Register was formed in 1960 to bring 'housebound housewives' together, and there was soon a branch in Welwyn Garden City. This was a good example of the collective tradition of self-help in the garden city:

Interviewer: The National Housewife's Register, how did that start?
Well that was a national thing, it started quite specifically in 1960 when a housewife called Maureen Nickle with small children whose husband's job meant she kept moving round the country went to *The Guardian* … You know housewife then was a valid term. If you had small children you didn't go back to work, you stayed at home with the children and there were no evening classes and not many women would have had a second car and been able to drive, and really women with small children were stuck at home all day and had no conversation.

Maureen Nickle wrote and said wouldn't it be a good idea if there were a register of housewives at home with small children who wanted to meet for intelligent conversation, and Betty German, the journalist on *The Guardian*, picked this up and wrote an article on the women's page about all this, women in suburbia, and lots of letters came in. She mentioned Maureen had written and gave Maureen's address again, and Maureen, having said wouldn't it be a good idea if there was a register, found she was running it.

Letters poured in from all over the country and all she could think of to do was put them in touch with each other, so she kept all the letters for each county in a separate paper bag and then wrote to them all and it grew and grew. [It was] originally called 'Housebound Housewives', but because of the connotations of disability they changed that … and then I think it was 'Likeminded Women', but finally it settled on 'National Housewives Register' … Olive Cast, who lived in Welwyn Garden City up in The Templewood area, read about it in the national press and with her friend Mary Ooton, who lived very near her there, they started it, I'm not sure exactly what date … [in] 1967. I wanted to join and by then Olive had moved to The Ryde in Hatfield, that new estate, and she remembers me knocking at her door and saying: 'Please, I want to join the National Housewives Register'. She and Mary had started when they were in Welwyn Garden but they had members in Hatfield, Welwyn Garden and Old Welwyn and I chiefly remember going over to Old Welwyn. I was the first one from Hatfield and I remember being driven in the car with Olive and others. We had a lot of members in Old Welwyn and finally Hatfield split off. We had enough members in Hatfield to make our own group by 1969, but it did all start in Welwyn Garden thanks to Olive Cast.[382]

## Arrivals Work

Arrivals work was important for all new communities in Britain. The original garden cities in their earliest years, and the new communities built after 1946, were relatively raw housing environments compared to the older-established neighbourhoods of traditional towns and cities. In common with most large-scale developers of new residential areas, both the pioneers of garden cities and the later leaders of the new towns understood that people who moved from a familiar urban neighbourhood to a new housing estate might feel disorientated, possibly homesick for their older town, and required reassurance and guidance.

The Corporation was concerned with the problem of possible loneliness of families coming into the town from London and elsewhere. As Philip Gosling, the son of Reg Gosling, remembered, his father was an avid participant in arrivals work:

> My father loved the work that he did for these two towns. He came from east London, like many of the other new residents. Dad particularly enjoyed attending the fortnightly Saturday welcoming parties – organised for the new residents when many of the local organisations introduced themselves and helped them settle in.[383]

The Development Corporation and its leaders were thus keen to make arrivals work a success, and some were personally invested in it. Looking back at 'the social aspect' of WGC since the war, Osborn and Whittick argued in 1969 that although there had been setting-in problems for some incomers during the early post-war years, particularly those who missed the urban lifestyles of established cities, community development work had generally created a satisfied population who were pointed towards the social and recreational facilities provided by WGCDC. For its part, the corporation argued that throughout its life it had been there to welcome newcomers from the earliest rental housing until the last days of its existence.[384]

Yet one woman who arrived with her husband on her wedding day in November 1956 remembered that no one came to welcome them, not even their neighbours. This may have been because they moved to a 1920s house in The Links, and not a Development Corporation or council-built house.[385]

While the garden cities of Letchworth and WGC both took steps to welcome newcomers, providing written and visual materials on the benefits of living in the new town, the new town Development Corporations took arrivals work to a higher level, building on a variety of established practices. The idea and practice of welcoming new households to residential districts was not new. Since the Victorian years, the followers had pioneered social work within a system of rent collecting, facilitating new arrivals into their council homes and paying regular visits to families deemed to be in difficult circumstances, or 'problem families' as they would later be termed. Between the wars, as the mass programme of council housing expanded Britain's towns and cities, many councils adopted the strategy of collecting rents, checking on new arrivals and monitoring their morale via the Society of Women Housing Estate Managers.[386] This was the practice pioneered by the housing reformer Octavia Hill during the late-Victorian and Edwardian years. She felt that tenants should be responsible, clean and tidy, but that they also required guidance in difficult times.

## The Neighbourhood Unit as a Social Planning Tool

The original 1920s master plan for WGC had delineated a number of neighbourhoods, each with a measure of facilities and social amenities, based upon the system of local wards redolent with active and socially engaged citizens envisaged by Ebenezer Howard. With the onset of the new town, the neighbourhood idea now became more explicit in the social planning of Welwyn Garden City. This took the conceptual and applied form of the so-called 'neighbourhood units', about which Lewis Silkin had been so optimistic in his reading of his New Towns Bill to the House of Commons in 1946.

The neighbourhood unit was of American provenance. Through the work of the National Council of Social Service (NCSS) and leading advocates of garden cities and garden suburbs, the neighbourhood unit became increasingly popular between the wars as a planning mechanism to encourage local identity in new housing areas. Each unit was to be supplied with essential shops, schools, health facilities, places of worship and social and recreational facilities. At Wythenshawe in Manchester, for example, a huge working-class housing development of the 1920s, no less a planner-architect than Barry Parker had designed the residential areas according to neighbourhood unit principles and by 1933 about 25,000 people lived in the three neighbourhood units there.[387]

The first post-war new towns were designed to neighbourhood unit principles, but of course WGC had a head start. The existing neighbourhoods of WGC were already well provisioned with social amenities, and a pretty vibrant social life in most areas of town. As the new town grew, both the established and the new neighbourhoods were fitted with new facilities. Yet it is one of the finer nuances or paradoxes of town planning history, and of the history of WGC, that as the Development Corporation was building new neighbourhoods according to neighbourhood unit principles, the chief protagonist of WGC wrote to Lewis Mumford expressing his scepticism. In an argument worth quoting at length, FJO revealed himself to be a thinker more in tune with the emergent Californian notions of patterns of social interaction, stressing interest-based connections and wider spatial interactions, than those envisaged within cosy conceptions of overweening localised communities. He also anticipated some of the findings of social scientists during the 1950s about the restrictions of the neighbourhood unit:

I have not written much about the neighbourhood, but you will have noticed from my occasional notes on the subject that I do not really believe in the Village within the Town; I mean that I do not believe it can be created by the physical structure of a neighbourhood and its centre.

[As] a resident for thirty years in WGC, which has grown from 400 to about 20,000 in that time, I am conscious of various groupings: my family in its one house; the over-the-garden-fence community of the immediate neighbours (perhaps six to ten families); and then WGC as a whole; then Greater London; and then Great Britain. Inside WGC I have no consciousness of a larger neighbourhood than the six to ten houses; but of course I am conscious of lots of such communities at the factory in which I work, the political party to which I belong, the Chamber of Commerce etc. I draw my friends more from WGC than from outside – that is, I see my WGC friends more often – but from any part of WGC and from other parts of GB and the world; not particularly from a neighbourhood within WGC. I do not believe much in attempts by organising community centres to make people especially ward-conscious; they will naturally be so to a slight extent; but unless there is an obstacle or an interval of distance they will not be neighbourhood-conscious to any important extent ...[388]

Osborn was writing at a time when the ownership and use of motor vehicles was expanding rapidly, further enabling people to traverse distances more easily to forge or maintain social connections beyond the immediate locality. The neighbourhood had its uses, providing schools, and a limited range of shops, services and leisure facilities, but was mostly out of sync with rapidly expanding patterns of spatial mobility. While undermining much of the validity of the neighbourhood unit, moreover, motorisation generated other consequences, causing increased traffic flow and some serious practical problems that the planners of WGC soon had to get to grips with.

Osborn also anticipated the radical thinking that led to the new city of Milton Keynes being planned as 'the little Los Angeles of North Bucks'. The planning of the new city of Milton Keynes in Buckinghamshire was strongly influenced by such phrases as 'the non-place urban realm' and 'community without propinquity', terms used by the Californian academic Melvin Webber.[389] Sadly, Osborn died when Milton Keynes was in its first decade.

He had been prescient. By the time the WGCDC was wound up in 1966, the neighbourhood unit was indeed out of fashion with town planners and social scientists. Instead of an insistence upon a delimiting localism in the provision of urban resources, a new emphasis upon spatial mobility through motorisation, and as a consequence of affluence and more freedom of choice, was at the heart of intellectual ideas for new town planning. Sociological studies made of neighbourhood units in both new towns and post-war council estates during the 1950s and '60s found that many households made little use of neighbourhood retail and leisure facilities, preferring to head 'down town' or further afield for a night out or to enjoy sports and other pastimes. The growth in ownership of motor cars among working-class households was the key to increased choice and spatial mobility.[390] Hence a 'friendship map' made by the renowned sociologist Peter Willmott in his study of Stevenage, published in 1962, found that neighbourhood had little influence on informal friendships.[391] The fashionable approach in the planning of new communities and new towns was not focused on 'belongingness' to the locality, but on 'interest groups', the clubs, groups and organisations that brought people together over space and time through shared enthusiasms.

Yet such thinking was always in danger of throwing the metaphorical baby out with the bathwater. For those on limited incomes, adjacent schools, shops and places of worship were a great help. The neighbourhood units built following the 1946 New Towns Act may have done little to encourage local pride and patriotism, but they were still useful in a practical sense. WGC was mostly fortunate in terms of its provision of facilities but also its social scene. Despite some teething problems in the early post-war neighbourhoods, the provision of local amenities improved during the Development Corporation era. And since its earliest days, WGC's citizens had demonstrated that not only localism but interest groups were at the heart of social connection, across the town and beyond it.

## Sports and Social Life in Post-War Welwyn Garden City: Continuity and Change

Frederic Osborn was not alone in understanding a basic fact about human sociability in an urban society: localism and neighbourliness are important, but people mostly come together on the basis of interests and enthusiasms that are not necessarily based on propinquity. Moreover, class, gender and age all influence the social and cultural life of a town. During the second half of the twentieth century, WGC continued to experience growth and inward migration, alongside the so-called 'baby boom' of the 1940s and '50s. But its original population was ageing as the decades rolled on. These key demographic phenomena all shaped the pattern of post-war sociability in WGC.

As the garden city also became a new town, there were considerable continuities as well as changes in social life. Leisure groups, sports clubs, places of worship, schools and other outdoor and indoor facilities remained as bastions of community and participation. Most of the clubs, groups and societies formed before the war had continued throughout it, or were renewed as the town, and the nation, returned to peacetime normality.

In addition to the facilities and groups supported by Welwyn Garden City Ltd, individual companies had also sponsored and supported sports teams, and other leisure activities, and this continued from the second half of the 1940s. One man recalled the Christmas dances at the Cherry Tree organised by ICI during the late 1940s and '50s. As there were at least 3,000 employees each department had its own party:

> Later on … they did something for all the employees' children, it depended on what age they were as to what they did. They got a present or took them to a pantomime, or they had a party in the restaurant on site and there could be up to 1,000 kids there.[392]

Gosling Stadium ceremony.

While such events were intended to promote loyalty to the Company, they also reflected a kind of employer paternalism of which Ebenezer Howard would have approved.

The death of Reg Gosling led to a significant elevation in sporting facilities. The eponymous Gosling Stadium was opened in 1960. It was a fitting tribute to a working-class man who had 'made good', rolled up his sleeves, mixed with people of all social classes, and promoted the best interests of WGC and Hatfield during his time as head of the Development Corporation. In a sense, Gosling personified the ideal town leader and citizen that Howard had in mind. He also inspired the spirit of collective self-help that characterised the spirit of social life in garden cities. As Philip Gosling recalled:

A Sports Park had always been on the plans for the garden city. However – as happens too often – a recession came along … and the development of leisure facilities was halted. With my dad as chairman of the Development Corporation of Welwyn Garden City and Hatfield and a strong local determination not to lose this part of the two town's development … a 'devious plan' was hatched. There was a great deal of other building work going on in the immediate area, houses, factories, shops and roads – and builders, working in the vicinity, were given the opportunity to dump their soil, sub-soil, rubble and such around the oval outline of the present amphitheatre. For this convenience the builders were asked to donate money. It was much cheaper for them – and more convenient – than taking hundreds of lorry loads to distant landfill sites.

Therefore, by the time my father died, enough money had already accumulated in the fund to drain and lay the football pitch and create the banked, tarmac cycle track and the cinder first running track was also under construction. In brief, that was the start of a great social venture for the emerging communities. More money was forthcoming from Industry in the new towns and from many individuals who could see the need for this achievement.[393]

Sometimes within but mostly beyond the social development programme, sports and leisure continued to thrive in post-war Welwyn. As the WGCHT's *Where Do You Think We Played?* collection of oral testimonies and other materials demonstrates, many if not most of the clubs, teams and societies formed between the wars were re-formed after the interruptions of 1939–45, or continued throughout the conflict. New ones came into being, some even during the war, others during the post-war years.

Of those clubs formed during wartime that went on to become staples of WGC's sporting culture, the bowling club was established in 1942, when many other sports clubs were in abeyance due to wartime conditions. Many emergency workers and visitors to the garden city were keen to participate in this relatively accessible sport. Based at the Cherry Tree, and with investment in an improved bowling green after the war by WGCL, bowls became a popular local sport in early post-war WGC. The WGC Bowling Club became active and successful in local and regional leagues from the 1950s to the '70s, extending the sporting influence and reputation of the garden city across the country.

Key sports established in WGC between the wars were actively participated in during the second half of the twentieth century, and many brought the garden city to the attention of millions abroad. The Ludwick Badminton

Norton's football team, 1940.

Club played in Denmark in 1965. Football teams from WGC have played in European competitions since the early post-war years.

The Hockey Club Easter festivals were international events. WGC Rugby Club saw some of its players included in the England squad. And on the global stage of the Olympics, WGC made its mark. In the 1952 Olympics in Finland, Denys Carnill captained the British hockey team. In 1960, WGC Athletics Club, formed in 1953, provided two Great Britain team members for the Rome Olympics. Leading WGC cyclists competed in road races abroad during the 1950s and '60s, and in the Olympic Games of 1964 and 1968, members of the Welwyn Wheelers Cycling Club represented their country, town and club.[394]

Cricket remained essential to the sporting calendar. Richard Reiss had played both as cricketer and organiser since the earliest days of the garden city, and following his death in 1959 it was decided that WGCCC should have a new pavilion named after him. There had long been complaints that the social facilities of the cricket club could have been improved, and 1965:

saw, at long last, the completion of the R.L. Reiss Pavilion and we were relieved of the embarrassment of asking our visitors to change in a builder's hut. Although the building became 'operational' in February, the official opening took place on Whit Sunday, 6 June, and fortunately it was blessed by (relatively) fine weather. Mrs Celia Reiss graciously consented to perform the opening ceremony, which was kept short and simple, and afterwards the 100 or so guests availed themselves of the refreshments that had been provided.[395]

Other new sporting clubs, formed during the war or afterwards, included archery and darts clubs, and a variety of other minor sports groups captured in oral history recordings by the Welwyn Garden City Heritage Trust. Whether established or relatively new, competitive sports integrated the garden city into local and national leagues and competitions, and international sporting events. They helped WGC engage with the wider world.

## Young People in Post-War Welwyn Garden City

Despite successes in both social development and the ongoing vibrancy of its social scene, WGC was not immune to a social problem that increasingly caught the national imagination during the later 1940s and the '50s. A moral panic about so-called juvenile delinquency had emerged when petty violence, theft and vandalism increased during those years. Psychologists argued that many young children, torn from their parents, and especially their mothers, by wartime evacuation, were now, as teenagers, misbehaving as a consequence of their anger at 'maternal deprivation'. This gendered analysis is now viewed, in our more mixed household society, as out of date, but it was then viewed as a serious problem, particularly in the inner cities.[396] So when delinquent behaviour among the young occurred in WGC during the mid-1950s, warning bells began to sound. This was an embarrassment to the town, and it is puzzling as to why the Development Corporation alerted the Minister anyway:

It is with a sense of shame that one sees the children's playgrounds, presented so handsomely by Fine-Fare Ltd and opened by Lady Balniel [wife of the

Conservative MP for Hertford, within which part of WGC fell] in June, 1955, suffer the same fate of most playgrounds of this kind which have been presented and opened up and down the country, namely, smashed to bits within a matter of weeks. It is hoped that the public-spirited action of Fine-Fare will be followed by others despite in this case a lack of appreciation.[397]

When recalling their childhood or adolescence in Welwyn during the latter 1940s and '50s, quite a few interviewees for the WGCHT's *Where Do You Think We Played?* mentioned a dearth of organised leisure and a lack of spaces for younger people to gather together. This is perhaps surprising given the Company's previously much-vaunted record of providing and sponsoring leisure facilities, and of the corporate paternalism of the Development Corporation, but it also reminds us that 'bored youth' are a constant phenomenon in British society. So too is the fear of young people enjoying themselves and being viewed as a threat by elderly people. As Margaret C. recalled:

In the, well, '40s, '50s we just had to make our own play really, there wasn't anything, clubs to go to. … There was the Girl Guides and Girls' Brigade, to which I did belong. The Girls' Brigade for quite some years to a point of being an officer. I was born in Knella Road and on one part where Cranbourne Gardens goes off were four very nice trees … and we used to play rounders. And that was absolutely wonderful because the cars, well they were very few and far between. In fact the only person who had a car when I was a child was Mr Pickering of Pickering & Hale Funeral Undertakers …

We had one neighbour, an old grouch who used to hang his head out of the window with his top hat on telling us to shut up, to which we took no notice! Tried to tell us he was in bed with his top hat on.

We used to do a lot of play acting. We would make up plays and then perform them to the parents when we were ready, so that was something we did a lot of as well. Kept us all quiet, you know. It could be a play about doctors and nurses or it could be … anything that we dreamt up you know and we used to do those mainly in Shirley Austin's garden.

Sherrardspark Woods was another great place we used to go … there was a stream. I don't know if it still runs through. It was a silly little thing but when it was wet you would slip in it and, gosh, we would then take off home via the Welwyn Stores with our wet shoes and socks in our hands and get chucked out because it really wasn't the done thing was it? So that was something else. We usually had a big bundle of bluebells in our arms, which, of course, as soon as you pick a bluebell they die. We thought it was good to take them home to Mum.

And, of course, the grass verges are one of the main things of Welwyn Garden City and the boys used to make a trench in the grass verge down which we would play marbles. Always playing, mainly the boys, and occasionally they used to let us girls join in. Roller skating was another thing. We skated all over the town from one friend to another. As we got older one friend in particular lived in Longcroft Lane and I would skate there from Knella Road. I cycled a lot. I had an aunt who lived in Palmers Green. I used to cycle there and back.[398]

As Francesca H. stated, 'Welwyn has always been an old people's city', and it followed that occasional inter-generational tensions were by no means absent there.[399]

Osborn was certainly sensitive to criticisms made by Frank Schaffer, of the Ministry of Housing and Local Government, and by Elizabeth Denby, that WGC was not doing enough to meet the needs of young people and of newcomers. Referring to the 'adolescent problem', Osborn argued in correspondence to Schaffer that this was a countrywide crisis. He also defended the new town Development Corporations, and Welwyn in particular, against the prevailing criticisms of 'social provision in new towns', arguing this was merely a 'parrot cry' from newspapers and a vote-catching tactic of politicians. Enclosing a list of all the associations, clubs, groups and societies to Schaffer, Osborn argued that arrivals work and the supportive strategies of social development in encouraging groups to establish themselves were largely successful. That success was ignored, however, by critics of the new towns:

Although there existed in Welwyn Garden City by 1948 a very large number of societies and clubs – dramatic, musical, artistic, horticultural and sporting – there was no co-ordinating Council of Social Service. Energetic action in the last three years, initiated by a leading organisation of ladies and encouraged by the Corporation, has resulted in the establishment of such a Council, which has begun to take its part in the social life of the town and has fostered the organisation and location of a Citizens Advice

Bureau in premises close to the town centre generously made available by ICI Limited.

In 1948 eleven churches or religious meeting places existed in the town and one more was nearly completed. Since then sites have been made available for two more Church of England churches, one more Roman Catholic, one Baptist and four buildings for other denominations. In helping these religious bodies to have the opportunity to build their own premises, the Corporation has been in close touch with the Diocesan Board of Finance at St Albans and the appropriate co-ordinating committees or offices of other denominations. In general the aim that there should be at least one group of church buildings at each unit centre has been achieved. Some of the other church buildings in residential areas have played a significant architectural part in addition to meeting the people's religious requirements.[400]

The provision of play spaces and meeting places combined to facilitate the organised social life of young people. Church halls, the boys' clubs and the family centres all held functions for young people, and the Boys' Brigade, Cubs and Scouts, Brownies and Guides and other organisations for young people all continued to thrive in post-war WGC. In 1950, moreover, the 20–35 Club was established by WGCDC for those who, while no longer in their youth, sought the company of fellow relatively younger people.[401]

## Garden Citizens of a Certain Age

As the initial generation of settlers to the garden city grew older, some of them realised there were very few clubs or societies catering for elderly people. Again, collective self-help remedied the situation. A good example of this was legacy of the Rotary Club, established in WGC between the wars by Charles Purdom. The 65 Club for those aged 65 and over was first mentioned in the *WGC Directory* in 1962. It described itself as a 'meeting point' for people from the Handside and Sherrardswood area, and was still arranging meetings during the 1970s.[402]

An 'Over Nineties Set' was around in WGC by the 1960s and the Women's Luncheon Club, set up in 1929, was a mixture of women of various ages, but increasingly of advanced years. There was little for men of a certain age, however, so at an 'Over Nineties Set' meeting one day, Fred Carnill proposed a luncheon club 'for men of a similar age and background'. This following quote suggests a level of class discrimination, possibly a symptom of continuing segregation in the garden city, but more importantly it was a new departure in the social life of WGC:

> Fred, as he was generally known, canvassed those with him at the time and phoned up thirty further friends that same day, receiving an enthusiastic response.
>
> A long-standing Rotarian, Fred sought Rotary support, which he received from the chairman Dr Goss. The first meeting was held on 6 May 1965, in the Masonic Suite in Parkway, attended by thirty-three members and six Rotarians. Dr Goss was the first chairman. They chose to name it the Campus Club because of the location, overlooking The Campus.
>
> Despite membership levels being set at seventy, the group had already doubled by the following month when Fred Carnill was elected chairman and members got down to business. Subs were set at a nominal 5/- per annum and only reluctantly raised to 10/- (50p) in 1973.
>
> The most notable aim was 'The promotion of Good Fellowship'. Permission was given to use WGC UDC's armorial bearings on club stationery. Monthly lunches were held on the first Thursday each month, with a New Year's Ladies Night dinner at £1 per head at the Parkway Restaurant. The club aimed not to get bogged down by bureaucracy, but to hold events to entertain its members.[403]

The Campus Club later morphed into Probus, an abbreviation of *professional* and *business*. At the time of writing it boasts about 100 members who meet for regular lunches at a hotel.[404] This ongoing culture of community and association was more permanent than the governing organisations of post-war WGC.

## The End of the Development Corporation

During the 1950s, as the new towns expanded, the Conservative governments increasingly viewed them as a heavy burden on the Treasury. This was one aspect of a wider suspicion among many in the Tory Governments, especially on the right, that the new towns were leeches on the public purse. This perspective needs some wider context, however.

An important reason why the Conservative governments of the 1950s and '60s, and many local Conservative branches were suspicious of the new towns, was their association with socialism. Not only were they intrusions into the rural nirvana of county life, but left-wing intrusions. As we saw in the previous chapter, WGC set the trend here. The garden city may be viewed as something of a harbinger for the voting behaviour and local politics of the post-war new towns. Most were dominated by Labour during the 1940s and '50s. When the Jubilee of WGC was celebrated soon after the war, the UDC was comprised of fifteen members, namely seven independent and eight Labour.[405] To a degree this represented the national swing towards Labour in the General Election of 1945. The result of that election, declared in July 1945, was a majority for the Labour candidate Cyril Dumpleton of just 1,879. He polled 24,241 votes in the St Albans Division, as opposed to 22,362 for the Conservative hopeful and a miserable 5,601 for the Liberal outsider.[406] This slender majority was partly explained, as between the wars, by the wider local influence of the Conservatives in the constituency. And in early post-war local elections, it was also symptomatic of the manner in which a number of active Conservatives had formerly cloaked themselves as independents to negotiate the Labour-orientated culture established by Osborn and others. Nearby Stevenage in Hertfordshire, moreover, the first of the new towns to be designated following the 1946 New Towns Act even had a communist-sympathising 'Chairman' in Monica Felton by 1951. A Labour politician, she was a secret supporter of the Communist Party of Great Britain, or a 'fellow traveller'. When she walked off the job to support Soviet-backed forces in the Korean War in 1951, the Conservative press and politicians, local and national, were outraged. Her position was abruptly terminated by the Labour Government of Clement Attlee. Not only that, she was having an extramarital affair with none other than Lewis Silkin during the latter 1940s.[407] None of this did the Garden City Movement and new towns any favours, and the association of new towns with socialism endured long into the second half of the twentieth century.

The New Towns Act of 1946 had certainly time-limited the new town Development Corporations, intending their assets to be transferred to the local authority once the corporation was wound up. The 1950s and '60s are often looked back on as a 'golden age' for the British economy, as full employment returned, post-war rationing was mostly lifted by 1955, and real wages began to increase. Unfortunately the British economy grew more slowly than its major Western European competitors, and income to the Treasury was lower than hoped for. This economic insecurity explains why the Conservative Governments of the 1950s were increasingly concerned about the financial costs of the new towns. The programme had been rolled out quite quickly, and was proving to be extremely costly, as well as unpopular with Conservative voters living in rural areas where the new towns were built.

The new town Development Corporations were also many years from completing their work and repaying back their debts, or from transferring their assets to local authorities.[408] Moreover, they were almost completely associated with the public sector. Silkin had been opposed to the development of new towns by private enterprise financiers and construction companies, as evidenced in his 'much-criticised nationalisation in 1948 of the most successful extant example – Welwyn Garden City Ltd'.[409] As the planning historian Michael Hebbert argues, however, the tide was flowing increasingly in favour of more private investment into new towns during the 1950s. Some wider context is required here. Historians used to make much of the so-called post-war 'consensus' after 1945, as the Labour Governments of 1945–51 set a political agenda for increasing state involvement through a 'cradle-to-grave' welfare system and nationalisation of key industries. The 'consensus' was the apparent willingness of an opposition Conservative Party to accept this new dispensation in order to win back power. But that consensus was fragile.

Once in power from 1951, Tory Governments became increasingly hostile to what they viewed as an expensive and overweening state, and suspicious of ostensibly undemocratic local bodies such as Development Corporations, and to monopolies or near-monopolies in other areas of the society and the economy. Hence in 1951 the nationalisation of British Steel was reversed, while in 1954 the dominance of the BBC was broken by the introduction of ITV by the Independent Broadcasting Authority Act of 1954. Coming between the two events was the memorandum by the Chancellor of the Exchequer, R.A. Butler, in May 1953 entitled 'Can We Afford the New Towns?'[410]

The Treasury wanted less money to emanate from Government coffers, more private involvement to achieve that, increased capital returns from the new towns, and of course, a weakening of the Development Corporations, which were often popularly, and mistakenly, viewed by grassroots Conservatives as socialist and staffed disproportionately by left-wing bureaucrats. Thus, 'consensus' was always up for challenge and negotiation, and this had an impact on the new towns programme at both local and national levels.

Perhaps the Tory governments of the 1950s were more 'Howardian' than they have been given credit for, however. After all, Howard had been impressed by many small-scale company towns and worker villages financed by philanthropic employers.[411] He had also been suspicious of the notion that the state should play a major role in the development of planned new communities, a consequence of his self-description as a 'gentle anarchist'.[412] If this term is reinterpreted as 'gentle believer in more free-enterprise' then it is not a million miles away from Howard's initial prospectus. For these reasons, Harold Macmillan began to suggest in 1954 that the new towns might collectively be more efficiently and economically run by one public corporation, which was independent of the local authorities, to which the assets could be transferred. The New Towns Act of 1959, passed when Macmillan was Prime Minister, established the Commission for the New Towns (CNT). As a leading historian of town planning argued, quoting the 1959 Act:

> The Commission are charged with the duty 'to maintain and enhance the value of the land held by them and the return obtained by them from it' while at the same time 'having regard to the purpose for which the town was developed and to the convenience and welfare of the persons residing, working or carrying on business there'.[413]

Its basic rationale, in sharp relief, was to increase the financial resource from new towns. Given powers to make financial contributions to the amenities of the new towns, to provide and manage sewage disposal and water supplies, to promote business, and to manage residential properties under its auspices, its remit was wide. The first two new towns to be transferred to the CNT were Crawley and Hemel Hempstead in 1962, while Macmillan was still Prime Minister. It would take until 1966 for the CNT to take over WGC. In the meantime, the Development Corporation had a number of difficulties to deal with, and goals to meet. In its 1959 report to Henry Brooke, the Minister of Housing and Local Government, WGCDC recorded its sadness at the death of Reg Gosling in July the previous year, and the appointment of C.G. Maynard J.P., who succeeded Gosling as Chairman of the corporation.[414]

By the beginning of the 1960s, however, the Keynesian principle of long-term investment for long-term capital returns was paying off in the new towns. WGC and Hatfield were two of the seven new towns showing a surplus on the general revenue account for the year ended March 1959. *The Guardian* viewed this a signal of the 'progress' being made by the new towns, and of the invest-ment made in the Development Corporation by the Government.[415]

WGC continued to make a positive contribution to Treasury coffers. In 1985, as the Conservative Government moved full steam ahead with its privatisation of public assets, the *Observer* reported on the 'considerable suc-cess' in the work of the Commission for the New Towns to dispose of its property assets. WGC was one of the more successful new towns whose CNT properties were sold off to the Urban District Council. The Chairman of the CNT, Sir Neil Shields, viewed this not so much as 'privatisation' but as 'normalisation' as local authorities took over greater levels of resource and control in the new towns.[416] This was further proof of the strategic impor-tance and ultimate profitability of long-term public sector investments.

The story of the financial viability of new towns was not uniform, however, although WGC stands out as one of the most successful, mostly due to its unique provenance by Welwyn Garden City Ltd. In 2002, the *Financial Times* reported on the 'cash cow' of the new towns to the Treasury, which made a profit on them, but noted that in some new towns, even those built following the 1965 New Towns Act, a 'spiral of decline' might set in without further investment. Because new towns were built from scratch mostly over a relatively short period of time, as the infrastructure of many of them deteriorated, the scale of renewal was large and expensive.[417] WGC, however, was not one of those requiring large injections of capital. It had been built during the 1920s and '30s, rebadged and replanned during the 1940s, and expanded in the decades since. While there were problems with some roads, buildings, and housing estates, these were minor compared to the traffic built-up in older town and city centres.

On 1 April 1966, under the Labour Government of Harold Wilson, the CNT had taken over over the administration of Hatfield and WGC. The Development Corporations were dissolved soon afterwards. Although the Labour Party while in opposition had been critical of this new emphasis on economics, which they felt might overshadow social development, in power from 1964–70 they now understood the importance of new towns to the Treasury.[418]

Osborn observed both the birth of the WGCDC in 1948 and its termination in 1966 from his home in Guessens Road. Writing with Arnold Whittick, he argued that: 'Welwyn Garden City is now substantially completed for it reached a population of approximately 42,000 by the end of 1967. There will probably be no further intake of industry or population, and future building will be for the increase in natural growth.'[419]

He was only partially correct in his analysis and predictions. Understanding the past and present is a less dangerous project than predicting the future. The garden city was indeed substantially completed, but the CNT would have to handle 'natural growth' quite carefully. Later during the twentieth century, moreover, population growth in the south-east of England and London would also require further expansion of WGC, and further phases of planning.

## Assessing the Commission for the New Towns Era in Welwyn Garden City

Under the auspices of the CNT, WGC and Hatfield were to be partly managed by two local committees, one for WGC and one for Hatfield. The CNT now owned the freehold of the residential and commercial properties, including retail outlets, offices and factories, and also any undeveloped land. Unlike the Development Corporation, however, the CNT did not possess powers for the compulsory purchase of land. From September 1974 the two local committees were combined into one, which was wound up in June 1978. In November 1982, the Commission terminated its Hertfordshire Offices as a case of 'job done'.

During its lifetime the CNT mostly kept a lower profile in the life of the new towns than the Development Corporations. Nonetheless, it continued to manage and in some cases improve the social, cultural and economic resources and infrastructure bequeathed to it.[420] Housing at Panshanger and in the south-east of WGC remained a key priority.

Historians of the post-war new towns have pointed out that the Commission for the New Towns represented some key contradictions in the post-war new towns programme. The Commission was basically 'an amalgamation of all the separate Development Corporations, with staff continuing to work in their old offices' in the new towns.[421] As Meryl Aldridge argued, in a critical examination of the post-war new towns, they were basically a 'programme without a policy':

> The Commission for the New Towns, during those first fifteen years, could be said to symbolise all the contradictions of the new towns policy. Claimed by many to be the most dramatic evidence of the switch from a social to a financial rationale for new town development, it was staffed by people with a long history of involvement in new towns and with an intense belief in the concept.[422]

This was without doubt the case in both WGC and Hatfield. As the CNT stated in its Fifth Annual Report in 1967, in both towns 'the whole of the staff of the former Development Corporations' transferred to the CNT's operations, 'and no redundancy occurred'.[423] The CNT also retained Louis de Soissons and Partners as the planners for WGC, and Maxwell Fry for Hatfield.[424]

Most of Welwyn Garden City was completed or in completion when the CNT took over in 1966, thanks to both WGCL and WGCDC. This point was symbolised by the ongoing saga of health provision. Following many delays and obstructions after the war, the QEII hospital had been opened in 1963 by Queen Elizabeth II herself. The National Health Service, the Development Corporation and a variety of voluntary bodies contributed to the inauguration of the hospital.[425] The full story is told in Angela Eserin's history of the QEII.

In addition to repairs to infrastructure and improving retail and office space in the town centre, the CNT also oversaw the opening of Stanborough Lakes Park in 1970, and Campus West was completed in December 1973, just prior to the replacement of the CNT by Welwyn Hatfield District Council. This gave the town centre a new library and a theatre. Dame Flora Robson performed the opening ceremony, but as the theatre did not draw large audiences, it later became used as a cinema.[426]

Yet a larger task was to pour money and resources into the Panshanger district. Panshanger had been established by the Development Corporation, but it was left to the CNT to develop it. The CNT record on housing was mixed, however. Of the 2,500 houses the CNT aimed to build at WGC, most of them were intended for Panshanger, with the rest targeted for the Digswell Lodge area. The tenure of the new homes reflected the transition away from building most homes for rent, and instead aimed for both houses for sale and 'superior rented accommodation':

> In Panshanger I scheme 239 houses and 22 flats for sale were completed in 1966/67. In Panshanger II scheme 77 out of 228 dwellings were built. These houses for weekly rent to tenants of the Commission and the UDC and to their sons and daughters, were costing from £3,300 to £4,475. The first Panshanger residents had moved into their houses in April 1966. Now there were 140 families there, and as one of them wrote to the Welwyn Times, there was 'an extraordinary lack of everyday facilities for a modern town'. There were no shops, no phone box and even no letter box. Two hundred Panshanger residents met to form a resident's association to press for some swift action to remedy the situation.[427]

Both positive and negative conclusions can be drawn from this. On the plus side, most if not all housing targets were being met. Yet the lack of provision for the new neighbourhood was a betrayal of the town and country synthesis of Howard. A garden city that had supplied services, shops and leisure facilities as soon as was possible, and often when it was still uneconomic to do so, now failed to carry this tradition through while under new management. Yet the formation of the residents' association demonstrated that the collective spirit of self-help, no oxymoron intended, was still alive in WGC.

A further example of the community spirit at Panshanger was the introduction of 'Panshanger Village Day' during the early 1970s. Here was proof that long since the Company had folded, and in the aftermath of the Development Corporation, spontaneous local action continued to characterise WGC. As John S. recalled:

> Panshanger Village day was started by the Residents Association as a means of getting to know anybody and everybody there was and there still is in the middle of the area of Daniels and Wren Wood and Westly Wood, a large open space that the Residents Association were determined should not be built on. So Village Day was created in the very early 1970s, probably about 1971 or thereabouts, and it was organised by the

Residents Association with people like Fred Pilkington, the Chairman of the Residents Association, and the various organisations that existed at that time: the Scouts, the Guides, the Church, the Women's Institute. You name it, we had organisations in a typical village fashion and the Village Day was always held in brilliant sunshine. In fact, I can remember only twice in how many years it got rained off and when it did we just carried on until we got drowned. However, we used to have a number of organisations with their own stands. They paid a small fee and kept the profits themselves. There was keep fit with the very young ladies leaping up and down, and the children were involved in all sorts of activities, particularly of course a tug of war, and there were the parents having a tug of war as well, which was always hilarious as people kept joining to make things easier.

I remember that on at least one occasion we had a pony ride going along the length of the thing and we always seemed to have a large coconut shy stall. Where the coconuts came from was anybody's guess but two sacks full of coconuts used to be rapidly won by the children and the adults and we used to have to fetch the balls, sometimes from the gardens in the back of the surroundings. There would always catering, hot dogs and so on, and after a while the Residents Association seemed to lose steam so the Church took it over and we remember that most of the activities then were organised through the Church.[428]

What types of accommodation were built at WGC by the commission? The rise and rise of the motor car led some architects, who favoured higher densities, to design modern houses with more garage provision. At Panshanger this can be seen today in the housing built during the 1960s. The growing delivery of flats for older people and smaller families, often childless couples, also expanded during the CNT era.

In 1967, the Ministry of Housing and Local Government cut back on subsidies for housing not conforming to Parker-Morris standards, meaning that poorer-quality construction would not be financially supported. This led to higher densities in housing to recoup costs, and the use of cheaper building materials.[429] It is also interesting to consider that a Labour Government, headed by Harold Wilson, a staunch advocate for egalitarianism, was encouraging higher densities and poorer construction materials than had been envisioned by the Conservative Government that introduced the Parker-Morris guidelines in 1961.[430] The CNT had other challenges to meet, moreover.

## Cars and Roads: A Major Challenge

There were further trials ahead for the Commission, mostly inherited from the Development Corporation era. These were the rapid rise of motorisation nationally, and the related impact of cars and motor transport on the road system in WGC. The interwar years had witnessed the expansion in ownership and usage of the motor car, particularly among the middle classes. During the 1950s and '60s, however, motor-car ownership was in a sense increasingly democratised as growing numbers of working-class households bought a car. The achievement of near full employment and of rising real wages for most in full-time work underpinned this democratisation. The official report to the Ministry of Transport by the consultant Colin Buchanan on *Traffic in Towns* (1963), called for more roads to be laid down in town and city centres, and for the widening of many existing streets. The reduction of the national railway network from the same time, the so-called Beeching Cuts, justified by the belief that roads not railways were the future, are widely viewed as misjudgements today, but the 1960s witnessed higher levels of private car-borne mobility than ever before.[430]

Britain experienced a remarkable rise in the number of motor vehicles between the long-drawn-out ending of wartime austerity during the early 1950s and the beginnings of the 'Swinging Sixties'. As *Traffic in Towns* demonstrated, in 1952, there were slightly fewer than 5 million motor vehicles on the roads, of which almost 2.5 million were cars. Ten years later the total number of vehicles had more than doubled to 10.5 million, and the number of cars had risen to almost 6.5 million.[432]

What Buchanan called the 'onset of the Motor Age' posed problems for all towns and cities in Britain. The authors of the report felt that new towns were slightly better positioned to accommodate the imminent escalation of car ownership and the pressure on roads. They were relatively recent, had incorporated Radburn-style planning, and had a newer road system:

> We found the New Towns not unimpressive in their arrangements for deal-
> ing with traffic, though it was quite obvious that in most cases there had
> been a serious under-estimate of the rate of growth of car ownership. Most
> of the towns seemed to start off with a garage ratio of about one to every
> four dwellings, a figure which is now generally being altered to one to one.[433]

By implication, the planners at WGC were culpable of underestimating the
rise of motorisation and therefore of not fully comprehending its impact on
the overall composition of the town. Yet the problem was not intractable.
Building upon the interwar roads in WGC, the de Soissons Plan of 1949 had
called for improvements to the transport infrastructure. The road bridges
over the railway were to be widened, as was the north–south industrial traffic
route, the B1000, which cut through WGC from the orbital road in the south
to the Hertford to Welwyn Road in the north. North–south 'spine roads'
were to be enhanced, and 33 miles (53km) of roads would be added to the
existing 32 miles (51.5km) in the city.[434]

During the 1950s the Development Corporation had extended the provision of roads as it added to the housing stock and improved the industrial,
commercial and retail offer in WGC. Roads could, of course, not be isolated
from wider patterns of growth. Yet by the 1960s, there were still logistical
problems for WGC from the growing number of motor vehicles, private and
commercial. The town centre bore the brunt of that pressure. By the mid-
1960s, inadequate parking spaces and overcrowded roads were a common
complaint, one the outgoing Development Corporation intended to remedy
with upgraded roads and a number of multistorey car parks. Many living in
WGC were aghast at the latter proposal. The number of garages built was
also inadequate. In the year 1964–65, 384 new garages were built, despite a
waiting list of 550. The problem was particularly acute in the south-east of
the city.

The centre of WGC continued to bear the brunt of heavy motor traffic,
however. As newer retail facilities and office spaces were opened up,
shoppers and workers commuted locally by car as well as by bus, increasing
road usage and pressure for more car parking spaces. Yet whereas in older
towns and cities, which had grown haphazardly, it was easier to knock down
streets and houses and drive new wider roads through, the site plan of WGC
was protected. Hence the town planners had to be very careful how they

managed traffic flow and parking provision. In 1962 the first multistorey car park was proposed, in addition to further parking on The Campus. Many residents objected. The Development Corporation and later the CNT and the UDC struggled for many years to meet the demand for car parks with opposition to them from WGC citizens, many of whom may well have possessed cars themselves.[435] Nonetheless, the Church Road car park was opened in 1959, and from 1973 a multi-storey car park eased the problem in the town centre.[436] (A later multi-storey car park was provided with the opening of the Howard Centre in 1990.)

## Welwyn Hatfield District Council

Following the nationwide reorganisation of local government under the Conservative Prime Minister Edward Heath, Welwyn and Hatfield Urban District Councils were merged in 1973. In 1974, in one of its first major strategic moves, WHDC announced a £30 million development in Panshanger.[437] The *Welwyn Hatfield District Plan*, initiated in 1980, was the first statutory land use plan for the local authority since its formation. It followed an 'extensive public participation programme' in the autumn of 1980, and a draft plan of 1981.[438] The plan had to be certified by Hertfordshire County Council in accordance with the HCC Structure Plan. Its most important items for development followed on from the work of the Development Corporation and the CNT: the need for more housing; the continuing need to attract inward investment and new employers; improved retail facilities while addressing the relationship between declining neighbourhood shops and the town centres; the preservation of the green belt, and the conservation of older buildings and landscapes; continued provision for leisure and recreation; and the ongoing problem of traffic congestion, including the lack of parking spaces in both the centre and on the housing estates. The needs of cyclists were also noted.

The need for at least 2,000 more houses meant planned and focused new development or redevelopment within targeted areas of Welwyn Hatfield. In WGC this was within a couple of areas of land adjacent to schools: Peartree, Ascots Lane, Boundary Lane and notably Panshanger Airfield.[439] The district plan emphasised the commitment by WHDC to 'constrain' the amount of housing development by maximising the potential of 'existing housing stock'. However, this task was made more difficult by the decline in the number of houses in public authority control, even though tenants voted to stay under it. This was only partly a consequence of the Housing Act of 1980, and the so-called 'Right to Buy', because the Development Corporation and the CNT had previously begun to sell on rented housing to their tenants.[440]

The district plan also acknowledged the proliferation of the number of smaller households, and whilst not providing the reasons for this phenomenon, it claimed it would encourage developers to build more homes for one-, two- and three-person households.[441] Welwyn and Hatfield were, of course, part of the wider trend of secular legislation and its consequences. The Family Planning Act of 1969 had limited family sizes among many younger households, and enabled working-class families, and single people, to access free contraception. This meant smaller families. The Divorce Act of 1969/70 also made it easier and less expensive to terminate marriages, leading to more divorcees, fragmented families and the need for more housing. The ageing of the population also meant smaller units for elderly people were required, both couples and singles. WHDC pursued the following housing programme between 1981 and 1986, namely to maintain a five-year supply of land to meet housing demand; to encourage more smaller homes; 'to seek ways to maintain the balance between council owned and privately owned property to provide a choice of tenure for local households'; and also to consider converting larger older residences into smaller dwellings.[442] The ageing of the population also required further construction of dwellings for elderly people.[443]

With the sphere of employment and inward investment, the Council noted that the 1950s and '60s had witnessed a rapid growth of the economically active population as a consequence of migration to the new town, but since the early 1970s an ageing population had reduced the number of younger economically active people. This was, to a degree, counteracted by the decline in out-commuting, a further if qualified affirmation of the principle of self-containment. The Council allocated a number of reserve sites for industrial development within or nearby the trading estates of Welwyn Hatfield, and called for new office development to be completely focused within 'Welwyn Garden City Central Area' and 'Hatfield Central Area'.[444]

The provision and viability of shops in Welwyn Hatfield centred upon the important role of retail in the local economy, the practical needs of people living in neighbourhoods, some of whose local shops were in difficulty, and a desire for further provision of retail choice. WGC contained eight local centres: Woodhall; Panshanger; Handside; Peartree; Hollybush; Hall Grove; Shoplands and Haldens. Hatfield also contained eight local centres and 'others' included Old Welwyn and nearby villages.[445] Protecting the viability of neighbourhood shopping centres meant preventing the construction of out-of-town shopping districts, engaging with expanding car use and parking needs while negotiating this with 'environmental impact' factors, both in local shopping areas and in the town centre.[446] As for WGC and Hatfield town centres, the Council could report fewer problems than older unplanned town centres. Thanks to the de Soissons Plan there was less pedestrian–traffic conflict due to the walkways (although no mention of Radburn was made). WHDC called for more pedestrianisation of certain streets, and the restriction of traffic flow, where possible, through traffic management schemes.[447]

The conservation of historic buildings, and of cherished and beautiful outdoor spaces such as Sherrardspark Wood and the parks, were also attended to in the district plan. The fact that Sherrardspark Wood was protected was a consequence of the long-standing 'Save the Woods' campaign that had initially begun during the 1930s in opposition to plans by Welwyn Garden City Ltd to build over some of this cherished outdoors space. The Urban District Council published an alternative plan that spared most of the woods from development. During the latter stages of the Second World War, both the UDC and the WGCL began to draw up plans that would have eaten into the woods, so the Save the Woods Campaign was rebooted, sponsoring a large-scale petition that successfully opposed further development. Once the assets of the Company were transferred to the Development Corporation many feared development on Sherrardspark Wood, but as a 'Woods Warden' recalled in 2016:

A Public Enquiry on the question of building over the woods for the most part secured the woods from housing development. By 1953 Volunteer Wood Wardens were appointed, many 'old-soldiers' from the Save the Woods campaigns, to be the eyes and ears of the Corporation in the woods. [In] 1966 Sherrardspark Wood Wardens Society was formally established with a constitution.[448]

As initial post-war plans were being publicly aired, the love of the great out-doors and access to the nearby pleasant countryside of Hertfordshire was also evident in the formation of the Mid-Herts Footpath Society on 21 March 1947. In 1949, the National Parks and Access to the Countryside Act in effect legitimised the ploughing of cross-field footpaths in the interests of 'good husbandry'. This led to many landowners removing cross-field routes 'regardless of whether they could avoid them and then failing to comply with the restoration requirements' [449] On 27 April 1951, the *Welwyn Times* noted a preliminary meeting to re-form MHFS to serve the district in three distinct ways: 'To take an overall view of disputed paths; get help from various youth organisations to see that the paths were walked and kept open; press for sign-posting of paths.' The meeting was convened by Charles Dalton, the editor of the *Welwyn Times*.

Preservation of the Metropolitan Green Belt also remained a priority for both the District Council and the County Council, requiring housing con-struction to be concentrated in WGC and Hatfield so as to preserve the *cordon sanitaire* between the two towns as well as the rural qualities of the vil-lages in their hinterland, for example Ayot St Lawrence (where the National Trust manages George Bernard Shaw's old house). [450] Yet the plan also unwit-tingly paid tribute to the original work of the Welwyn Garden City Co. and its successors, who had worked with earlier iterations of the Urban District Council to 'conserve and enhance' the centre of Welwyn Garden City, namely the conservation area. And WHDC also unwittingly admitted that it did not know about Nikolaus Pevsner and his compendium of the historic and significant buildings in WGC. The first volume of *Buildings of England: Hertfordshire* was published in 1953, and the second updated survey in 1977, when it was revised by Bridget Cherry:

> The main difficulty facing the District Council in carrying out its devel-opment control functions in conservation areas has been the lack of a comprehensive record of their architectural and historical character. Places like Welwyn and Old Hatfield have seen considerable changes to their physical fabric over the past few years and continue to experience pres-sures for further change. The District Council hopes to carry out a detailed architectural and historical survey of Welwyn Hatfield's conservation areas as and when the necessary resources are available. Such a survey will take

some considerable time and the areas will be surveyed in the following order: Welwyn [Garden City]; Old Welwyn [Village]; Hatfield; Essendon; Ayot St Lawrence; Ayot Green and Northaw. Welwyn Garden City conservation area is somewhat different to the rest. The Council's powers of control over development here are much more comprehensive than the powers available under planning legislation alone.[451]

Essentially, the conservation policies of WHDC sought to promote high quality in new developments, to ensure that proposals for new buildings or extension to existing buildings harmonised with the scale, siting and materials of adjacent properties and streets, and all applications would be scrutinised to this effect.[452] That the present centre of WGC and many of its older residential areas are so well preserved is a testament also to the work of WHDC, despite that certain naivety mentioned above. This conservationist approach was also evident when the Howard Centre, a covered shopping mall, was mooted in the 1980s.

The Centre was opened in October 1990, in a prime location near to the railway station, and close to the shops, pubs and restaurants of the town centre. As noted above, a multistorey car park also provided convenient access and parking for shoppers. While it did not really achieve the architectural qualities of the 'Crystal Palace' envisioned by Howard, the Centre did fulfil, to a degree, some of its functions. It was indoors, and offered goods for sale and opportunities to socialise. WGC had needed further retail facilities to meet the aspirations and demands of its increasingly affluent citizens, and also the surrounding area, and the Howard Centre augmented choice within the context of an enclosed shopping mall that also kept the weather at bay. The first anchor stores, those retail outlets that are the largest and attract most customers, included Marks and Spencers, the pharmacist Boots, the stationer WH Smith, and the clothes shops Monsoon and Next. Most anchor stores tend to be located at the end of the mall. They have a multiplier effect in the sense that they bring in shoppers, who then go into adjacent stores. From its opening until 2009, the Centre was owned by Land Securities, which sold it to La Salle for £48 million. According to Nikolaus Pevsner, the location of the Centre and its car park did not spoil the original composition of the town centre.[453]

Howard Centre, Howardsgate, September 2019. *(Photographer Vanessa Godfrey)*

## Party Politics in Post-War WGC

The Conservative and Labour parties continued to dominate party politics in WGC and the Hertfordshire hinterland after the war. The Liberal
Party had made little impression in interwar WGC. Yet during the early
years of the Development Corporation, from 1948, the 'Liberal Association'
appears in the WGCDL-supported *Welwyn Garden City Official Handbook
and Directory*. (This may reflect a more systematic gathering of information
by the Corporation compared with the Company, but that is a long shot.)
The twinning with Hatfield from 1948 may explain this weak ascendancy
of Liberalism, as there was a Liberal Association there, alongside Labour and
Conservative organisations. The Hatfield Liberal Association was probably
instrumental in establishing the Liberal Association in WGC, headquartered
at Roundwood Drive, by the early 1950s. More research is required into the
Liberal Party in Welwyn Garden City in particular, and in the new towns
in general.

The new constituency of Welwyn and Hatfield came into being in time
for the two General Elections in 1974. This makes it easier to grasp the
increasingly conservative nature of politics in WGC. Of the thirteen General
Elections since 1974, Labour only won three. These elections thus reflect
more accurately the political preferences of the new town voters than previously, when the Conservative Government of Edward Heath had been
wracked by industrial strife and forced to make significant cuts to public
expenditure as a consequence of the Oil Crisis of 1973. At the first election in February 1974, the Conservative candidate Robert Lindsay won
by a tiny majority over Labour, polling 22,581 votes to Labour's 21,166.
As had long been the case in WGC, the Liberal Party came third. But in the
October election the Labour candidate Helene Hayman squeaked to victory,
winning 23,339 votes to Lindsay's 22,819, a majority of just 520 votes. The
Liberal vote declined from almost 13,000 in February to 8,418. In Welwyn
Hatfield the major issues were national problems, namely the apparent weak-
ness of the Conservative Government to confront militant trade unionism,
public expenditure cuts, and the looming referendum on membership of the
Common Market (now the European Union).

At the General Election of 1979, which brought Margaret Thatcher to
power, WGC mirrored the national trend by returning a Conservative to
Westminster, Christopher Murphy, who would also win in 1983. In addition to
the Conservative, Labour and Liberal candidates, there was a fourth name and
political party on the ballot paper in 1979, namely a J. Ruddock of the neo-
fascist National Front, who polled 459 votes, less than 1 per cent of the total
number of votes cast. In some constituencies that had witnessed high levels of
immigration and sizeable populations of people of colour, the National Front
had beaten the Liberals into fourth place. Not so in WGC, which proved it was
mostly opposed to the extreme right. This may also reflect the predominantly
white British demographic at that time. That WGC's population hardly grew
during the 1970s is also a possibly connected factor.

At the following two General Elections in 1987 and 1992 the Conservative
candidate David Evans successfully defeated Labour, as WGC and Hatfield
again reflected the national trend, something proved even more spectacularly
in 1997 when eighteen years of Conservative dominance both nationally
and locally came to an end. The national swing to Labour in 1997 was clearly
evident locally, as Melanie Johnson defeated David Evans, standing in his

third and final General Election in Welwyn Hatfield. In 1997, Johnson polled 24,936 votes to Evans' 19,341, a margin of victory of over 11 per cent. As ever the Liberals came a poor third, but also on the ballot paper was a candidate for the Residents Association, and for Pro-Life, an anti-abortion party. Both lost their deposits. Labour held on to power in the 2001 poll.[454]

In 2005, as part of the national swing against Labour due to the Iraq War, Grant Shapps was elected as MP for Welwyn and Hatfield. He had unsuccessfully contested the constituency in the General Election of 2001, and has been elected as Tory MP in each poll since. Shapps was Minister for State at the Department for Communities and Local Government from May 2010 to September 2012, and following a three-year period as Minister Without Portfolio, he indirectly represented WGC on the international stage as Minister for State at the Department for International Development in 2015, and then as Parliamentary Under-Secretary at the Foreign and Commonwealth Office.[455]

And so to the referendum on membership of the European Union on 23 June 2016. The turnout at the referendum was a little over 75 per cent, lower than in a number of General Elections, which usually had a participation rate of at least 80 per cent. Some 31,060 people (53 per cent) voted to leave the EU, while 27,550 (47 per cent) wanted to remain. This was a slightly wider disparity than the 52 to 48 per cent in the national vote.

As the almost interminable process of Brexit ran on, there was evidence that many people living in Welwyn Hatfield had changed their minds. A poll for the *Welwyn Hatfield Times* in June 2018, exactly two years after the referendum, found that 70 per cent of voters asked preferred to remain in the EU. In an interesting reversal of the local trend, however, Grant Shapps, who had voted to remain in 2016, stated he was now in favour of leaving. WGC was also, in common with the country in general, divided. 'Regardless of how people voted,' stated Shapps, 'I happened to be remain. I think the majority of Brits just want us to get on with it now.' Welwyn Hatfield Chamber of Commerce chairman, Nick Brown, who voted Leave, also said the country should not waste time on another referendum. 'In the words of Michael Caine,' he added, 'I would rather be a poor man in charge of my own destiny than a rich one controlled by somebody else.'

However, a significant chunk of residents claimed such a momentous decision should not be based on the negligible details available two years ago.

The Liberal Democrat Parliamentary candidate Barbara Gibson – who would back Remain in a rerun – said everyone would agree that voters lacked an 'honest and realistic picture' of what they were voting for. 'Had it been clear that the referendum was merely advisory,' she added, 'then our MPs – the majority of whom now believe we should remain – could do the right thing and reverse Brexit.' Welwyn Hatfield Labour leader Kieran Thorpe said he would vote Remain 'with reservations', adding the Brexit chaos had stemmed from 'boiling down a complex issue into a simple binary choice'.[456] Shapps was re-elected to Parliament in the 12 December General Election. The Withdrawal Amendment Bill was passed in January 2020 and Britain began the process of exiting the EU on 31 January.

One of the major concerns triggering the Brexit process, and the majority for Leave, was the fear of unfettered migration and the free movement of labour that accompanied the free movement of goods and services within the European Union. So how diverse was WGC, and to what degree, if at all, had migration to the town influenced the vote?

## Diversity and Change in Welwyn Garden City

Writing in 1969, Osborn and Whittick were partly correct in their analysis that Welwyn Garden City was 'substantially completed' by then. They implied low levels of 'natural growth' in the coming decades, and for some time that appeared to be the case. The population rose from 42,000 in 1967 to a little over 46,000 by the Census of 2011. Yet the present century witnessed a faster rate of population growth than the garden city had experienced since the Development Corporation was wound up. The population increased by more than 6,000 to reach 51,000 by 2017.[457] Together with Hatfield, the total number of people living in the Borough was in excess of 122,000. This was one of the highest rates of population increase in the east of England.[458]

Until the 1960s, WGC was predominantly white. There were differences along religious affiliations, of course, and this book has attended to the class structure of the garden city. During the 1950s and since, however, mass immigration into Britain from the Caribbean, India and Pakistan began to change the character of many urban neighbourhoods, a social history that has been extensively covered elsewhere. In WGC, the impact of immigration of people of colour appears to have had a lesser impact upon the demographic profile.

The continued growth of WGC was also a consequence of internal migration from other areas of Britain, as the prosperous South-east of England had long attracted active and ambitious workers from elsewhere. The accession of Eastern European countries into the European Union from May 2004, namely the Czech Republic, Estonia, Latvia, Lithuania, Hungary, Poland, Slovenia and Slovakia, also meant that many younger and ambitious Eastern Europeans came to work and live in Welwyn–Hatfield. Economic migrants from India and China also began to appear in greater numbers. WGC has remained predominantly white, and Christian, but is increasingly characterised by ethnic and religious diversity.[459]

Bearing in mind these statistics are for both Hatfield and WGC, Welwyn and Hatfield Borough Council estimated the population of the new towns was, as noted, more than 122,000 in 2017. Of these, 62,000 were women, while a little more than 60,000 were men. There was no category for those self-identifying as non-gendered. Over 80 per cent were white, 76,000 being white British, others coming mostly from the Republic of Ireland and Europe. Those described as 'mixed or multiple ethnic group' numbered about 3 per cent, and were comprised particularly of African-Caribbean and white households, and about 7 per cent of the combined population of Hatfield and WGC was Asian, a group including Bangladeshis, Chinese, Indians and Pakistanis.[460]

Religion reflected the more diverse demographic profile of WGC and Hatfield. A town whose foundation during the 1920s was strongly influenced by Christianity was becoming less Christian. The 2011 census found that 57 per cent of the population was Christian; 2.75 were Sikhs; 2.54 per cent were Muslims; and fewer than 1 per cent were Jewish. The synagogue is still active in WGC, however.[461] Almost 28 per cent had 'no religion' and 12 per cent were 'religion not stated', reflecting growing secularisation in British society. The new towns also reflected the ageing of the wider population of Britain, with a growing number of people aged 60 and over.[462] There was little substantive difference between the demographic profile of Welwyn-Hatfield and the county of Hertfordshire, although less diversity than in the major metropolitan regions.

De Soissons memorial, The Campus, October 2019. *(Photographer Vanessa Godfrey)*

A combination of natural population increases and inward migration has exerted further pressure on the garden city during the present century. This has required new plans for more housing. So too has the emphasis from Government for higher densities and more mixed use streets as a consequence of Planning and Policy Guidance, first introduced in the late 1990s under the first New Labour government. Subsequent governments, Labour, Coalition and Conservative, continued the policy. As we will see in the concluding chapter, this meant that many newcomers who moved to WGC were not able to enjoy the more spacious detached, semi-detached and terraced homes with gardens into which earlier generations had moved.

Following the difficult and prolonged interruption of the Second World War, there was continued population growth during the latter 1940s to the late '60s, leading to greater levels of housing provision but often in difficult circumstances. The segregation in the garden city that was the subject of critical observation between the wars was never fully removed, but the population became more mixed as working-class households moved in under the Development Corporation. The ethnic profile of WGC became more diverse. Furthermore, tenure patterns also became less solidified as a consequence of the legislation of the late 1960s, and more famously by the Conservative Housing Acts of the 1980s.

Public transport links between the east of the city and the centre improved, and the huge increase in the number of private cars also broke down some of the earlier spatial inequalities. Along with transport infrastructure, employment, commercial and leisure facilities also expanded to meet the needs of a growing and mostly more affluent population.

The top-down provision of enhanced leisure facilities helped, but the impressive level of organised sports, and the cultural, social and political societies in WGC, was mostly due to the efforts and aspirations of its citizens. Most clubs and organisations begun between the wars continued to adapt and thrive. Some folded, while new ones came into being. Sports and other free-time activities were not only important as expressions of participation, they also wove WGC into the wider regional, national and international contexts of active involvement. From Dame Flora Robson to the many relatively unknown organisers of the clubs, groups and societies, the garden city reached outwards to make it a place known to millions.

Yet that attractive townscape designed by Louis de Soissons, originally laid out by Welwyn Garden City Ltd, and extended and maintained by the Development Corporation, the Commission for the New Towns, WGCUDC and lately Welwyn-Hatfield Council, has mostly weathered well. There have also been many political changes in the composition of the local councils, but few sought to dismantle the heritage of one of the world's most famous and influential garden cities. WGC mostly retained its environmental qualities, an enduring and essential reason why it continued to attract international attention.

# 6

# THE GARDEN CITY IN
# THE WIDER WORLD

As we have seen in previous chapters, global events such as war brought thousands of people to WGC. In sports, film and the arts, successes on the pitch, in the field, on screen and stage also raised awareness of WGC to millions of people nationally and internationally. Yet the greatest export of the garden city was its built environment. It could never be copied entirely, and some of its planning and environmental qualities would be diluted when applied elsewhere, but as a set of guiding principles and a working model for new communities WGC had no equal in twentieth-century Britain.

## The International Diffusion of WGC
## as a Model of Town Planning

The town's historic significance in the field of town and social planning is global, attracting study and visits from tourists and representatives of civic organisations from abroad. Its success led directly to the creation of other new towns such as Harlow, Stevenage and Milton Keynes. It is often held up as the best example of civilised, sustainable new settlements and a model for others to follow.[463]

When Ebenezer Howard went ahead and purchased the land for his second garden city he was well aware that if it became a success it would become, in common with Letchworth, a town of national and international attention. He was right. Although Letchworth came first, WGC extended the garden city ideal across the country and across the world. Arguably, WGC is historically more important than LGC. Its designation as a new town in 1948 crystallised and symbolised its significance in the application of garden city planning principles and practices to many of the largest planned new communities of the twentieth century.

Between the wars, the national reputation of WGC was nuanced, and many were sceptical of its nature and claim to be a proper town. The garden city had its enemies, as Chapter Two made clear. Yet during its first two decades many in the media, and professionals in architecture and town planning, looked more favourably upon the garden city. The *Daily Mail* Exhibition in 1922 was an early declaration that the amenable environment and the housing styles at WGC appealed to popular tastes in domestic architecture, and that not everyone wished to live in the busier streets of larger cities. Howard and his followers had understood that. Now thousands of people moved to WGC to live the dream of an attractive home and garden.

So increasingly did architects, town planners, housing experts and social reformers in other countries. As a medium-sized, well-planned, attractive but unboastful low-rise built environment, the casual visitor, and even many residents of the town itself, may be unaware of the global impact on town planning that WGC had during the twentieth century. As Richard L. Reiss argued in 1959:

The influence of Howard's ideas, together with the practical embodiment of those ideas at Letchworth and Welwyn Garden City, has profoundly affected town planning throughout the world. It is worth recording that the Leningrad Architects' Society elected Sir Ebenezer Howard an 'Honourable member', and in a letter the President of the Society wrote: Even now you command here, in our remote land that has sustained so many disasters, fervent adherence of your great idea. We wait for the day to come when it can be put into practice.'

In 1936, when President Roosevelt established the first 'Green Belt Towns' in the United States, the official literature explained that the projects were based on the successful experience at Letchworth and Welwyn, and a photograph of Welwyn Garden City was included with the caption 'a model of scientific planning'.[464]

Ultimately the USSR opted for large-scale modernism rather than the garden city model. Morover, Reiss bypassed the influence that Howard and WGC had on Radburn, New Jersey, in the USA between the wars, as we will soon see. But his general argument remains valid. And professionals in European and Scandinavian countries, Australia, Canada, Israel, New Zealand, and Japan all looked to the British Garden City Movement for inspiration and for guiding principles in new town design during the twentieth century. And in this century, China has seen a raft of planned new communities where the imprint of Letchworth and WGC is undeniable.

There was, however, a greater significance to the Anglo-American connection for WGC when compared with other international links. This was partly because of the shared English language, and also to the transatlantic networks established during the Progressive Era. Yet it was also down to the work of Osborn himself. As his personal papers and cuttings reveal, Osborn went to many countries across the world. In his role as Secretary of the Town and Country Planning Association, for example, Osborn visited Austria (1959); Czechoslovakia (1961); Denmark and Sweden (1947); France (1953); Germany (1950); Holland (1948); Italy (1949); Netherlands/Ruhr-Rhine (1955); Norway and Sweden (1954); Portugal and Southern Spain (1957); Spain (1952); the USSR (1958) and Yugoslavia (1958).[465]

With the International Federation for Housing and Planning (IFHP) he spoke or participated at twenty different international Congresses between 1946 and the later 1970s.[466] And in his personal tours abroad, usually undertaken with his wife Margaret, he visited many European countries, Japan, the Caribbean and Central America. Nonetheless, the prominence of North America in his travels and his proselytising about WGC and the garden city cause is pronounced. This was also symbolised in his relationship with Lewis Mumford. And many planners and housing reformers in the US were certainly interested in Osborn. In October to December 1947 he visited the US and Canada, giving lectures and talks, and enjoying guided tours of planned new housing developments. He was back again in both Canada and America between September to December 1950, and returned to the US in 1960.[467]

# The Anglo-American Connection

In the USA, the impact of the British Garden City Movement from the early twentieth century was strongly evident. As the planning historian Carol Corden has argued, the most important British and American experiments in planned new towns before 1939 were by companies, for example Saltaire, Bournville and New Earswick in Britain, and Pullman near Chicago, built by the railway company during the 1880s.[468] She also views Letchworth and Welwyn Garden Cities as company towns, which was true for WGC until 1948, when it came under the auspices of a public Development Corporation.[469] However, it is important to distinguish between company towns whose housing was intended for the workers of the enterprise, such as Port Sunlight and Bournville, and towns built by companies who existed only to build garden cities, namely the First Garden City Co., and Welwyn Garden City Ltd.

During the Progressive Era of 1880–1940, urban and social questions were key themes at the heart of transatlantic debates and initiatives to address the problems of the overgrown industrial city. Housing reformers from the USA visited Britain and Europe to examine planned new communities, and as noted in the first chapter, Ebenezer Howard drew upon some radical ideas in the USA to develop his schema for the garden city. In turn, prominent American urban reformers and writers such as Catherine Bauer and Lewis Mumford, and lesser-known activists such as Louis Pink and Charles Forrest Palmer, visited Britain between the wars to draw inspiration from municipal reform and garden city experiments.

Pink was impressed with many aspects of WGC. In *The New Day in Housing*, published in 1928, he waxed lyrical about 'the close' or 'cul-de-sac' in the residential areas, for which Louis de Soissons 'deserves credit':

These are private and quiet; they lend themselves to embellishment with trees and shrubs and gardens; they are safe for children and are inexpensive to build as the roads are narrow, carry no through traffic and are of less costly construction. The variety of these 'closes' is one of the most charming features of Welwyn, and the many huge trees which remain, as well as the new ones planted add greatly to the setting. This feature is also distinctive of Radburn, the model town now in its beginnings near Paterson.[470]

Radburn threw into relief the influence of the British Garden City Movement on town planning in interwar America, particularly the working examples of Letchworth and WGC. As Nicholas Dagen Bloom argues, in the New York Region the planner Clarence Stein, a leading member of the Regional Planning Association of America (RPAA), adapted Howard's ideals for American suburbia. In fact, Stein visited WGC in 1924, and recalled 'walking about Welwyn and talking with old Ebenezer'.[471] Although the self-containment of the garden city was not a particular aim of Radburn, it rigorously separated cars from pedestrians in its road system, and introduced the 'superblock', which was a shared landscaped public space adjacent to housing, rather than a mish-mash of gardens and alleyways. The influence of garden city principles in general and of WGC in particular is clear:

> the designers made schools the focus of neighbourhoods, developed a mixture of housing types, offered grade-separated walkways, pioneered cul-de-sacs [sic] and organised a community association with extensive recreational facilities.[472]

Radburn was the first flowering of the RPAA, whose members also included the architect Henry Wright, and the writer and critic Lewis Mumford, the friend of Frederic Osborn. Radburn is historically significant as the first planned 'town for the motor age' and one that 'exemplified the balance and self-containment that Howard had originally sought'.[473]

Unfortunately the expansion of Radburn was curtailed during the 1930s by the Great Depression, although it would in turn influence new town urban design in post-war Britain. Clarence Stein further developed Radburn principles in the so-called three green belt towns built in the USA under President Franklin D. Roosevelt's New Deal during the later 1930s. These were Greenbelt, Maryland; Greenhills, Ohio; and Greendale, Wisconsin. As noted above, Reiss drew attention to the influence of WGC on the green belt towns, and a history of these New Deal housing and community programmes described them as 'the culmination of the Garden City Movement in America' before the Second World War.[474]

A key figure here was Rexford G. Tugwell, a Democrat who admired both Roosevelt and the British garden cities. He worked for the Resettlement Administration, a New Deal agency dedicated to the rural and suburban resettlement of thousands of poor migrants who left the failing farms and impoverished countryside to find work in towns and cities. His three green belt towns were bitterly opposed by conservative Republican critics, who viewed them as intrusions into the rural domain, and given their emphasis upon planning and racial integration, as 'un-American', even communist-inspired.[475] Similar sentiments had been expressed about Letchworth, WGC and Stevenage, as we have seen.

Further south, in Atlanta, Georgia, there was some Republican support for the New Deal's housing programmes, personified in the larger-than-life figure of Charles Forrest Palmer. A businessman with a humanitarian sentiment, he would use New Deal funding to develop the housing scheme of 'Techwood'. This was basically segregated rental housing for African Americans in Atlanta, a city where segregation was almost total.[476] A housing reformer, and self-declared 'slum fighter', Palmer had visited Britain and other European countries to audit the possible application of housing and planning experiments for the USA. He was a leading light in the Atlanta Chamber of Commerce, and sought to inspire slum clearance and housing improvements there, setting an example for other American cities.

Palmer had been present when British town planners including Sir Raymond Unwin and Theodore Chambers visited Atlanta in 1934. Two years later, while touring British towns and cities with his wife Laura, Palmer took up a suggestion by Henry Wright of the RPAA to visit Welwyn Garden City. The intention was to see for himself how WGC had developed thus far, and to learn potential lessons valuable to American businesses interested in building profitable new garden cities. Palmer was impressed with Chambers, whom he met just prior to visiting WGC. Chambers likened the achievement of WGC to the Greeks and Romans who had built great cities 'from nothing'. Playing to Palmer's American profit-making instincts, he argued earnestly that Henry Ford and other successful and wealthy Americans could make enormous amounts of money from planned new towns while engaging in 'great public service'. WGC was by no means capable of generating such wealth in the mid-1930s, but Chambers impressed upon Palmer the humanitarian need to keep rents low for the working classes, as 'most of the money was made from the middle- and higher-income groups, the shops and the factories.'[477]

Palmer expressed no qualms at such a financial and social redistribution. He and Laura visited WGC the day after their meeting with Chambers: 'It lived up to our expectations in every respect. A modern town, it was

operated like any well-run profit-making business.'[478] Charles and Laura were
driven around WGC by the manager, John F. Eccles, who explained that the
empty land in the town centre was still to be developed as the population
grew. Palmer may have been exercised by the previous monopoly of Welwyn
Stores, which he described as 'an attractive low-gabled shop with one or two
other neighbourhood stores adjoining it'. Referring to the exodus of female
shoppers due to prices, discussed in an earlier chapter, Eccles explained that
the grip of the Company over retail had weakened, and now 'a parade of
shops downtown and in each quadrant of the city' meant that local residents were once more shopping in the town.[479] This was music to the ears of
Palmer and his belief in competition between businesses.

   While not quite as prominent as Osborn, Richard Reiss also played
his part in engaging WGC with the wider world. His *The New Housing
Handbook* (1924) and *The Town Planning Handbook* (1926) were well-known
guides to housing and the garden city idea. In 1937, he was invited by Miss
Helen Alfred, Executive Chair of the American National Public Housing
Conference, to make the first of three visits to the USA. The other two
were in 1938 and 1939. Alfred had visited Welwyn Garden City on a
number of occasions and was known to Reiss and others in the Company.[480]
Alfred's invitation was strategic. Reiss was to give speeches and interviews
across the US in support of planned new communities, and to bolster the
legitimacy of the New Deal federal housing programme that was then
beginning to produce such tangible new communities as the green belt
towns. Reiss visited many American cities and met many public officials,
housing reformers, journalists, business people, and also members of the
American public. His tours took in New York, Washington DC, Boston,
New Haven, Richmond, and Atlanta, to name just a few. Newspapers across
the country reported on his visits and his support for planned new communities to help relieve slums and rural poverty.[481]

   In 1938, Palmer and the Atlanta Chamber of Commerce invited Reiss
to Atlanta while he was on his second tour. This was a tactical move by the
American reformers, to encourage the city council to 'see the light' of slum
clearance rather than view it and government-funded planned new communities as a socialist intrusion into the free market. At a 'large civic luncheon'
on 18 February, Reiss appears to have earned his dinner. To quote Palmer:

'Public housing authorities do not interfere with private enterprise,' Reiss declared, and 'Government-financed public housing saves money in the long run.' This was exactly what Atlantans needed to be reminded of. They had heard it often enough, but locally the same old crowd was still shouting 'socialism'. It took on a different meaning when refuted by such leading businessmen as Captain Reiss, who had helped put Welwyn Garden City on the map financially.[482]

Reiss went on to describe Techwood as 'the best public housing in America', an assist that Palmer acknowledged in his partly successful efforts to gain subsidy from Washington for further homes in 1938 to 1939.[483]

The Second World War interrupted this transatlantic interchange of town planning ideas, but within the context of urgent wartime prerogatives, it also intensified it. Following American entry into the war after the bombing of Pearl Harbor in December 1941, military co-operation between the Allies was paramount. But the American President and his government also looked to the British home front. The destruction wrought by the Blitz, the consequent housing problems, and the pressure on emergency and public services, provided something of a laboratory for the Americans to draw lessons from in the event of attacks on the contiguous mainland. To this end, Roosevelt established the Special Housing Mission (SHM) to Great Britain in 1942. Headed by a Democrat social reformer, Eric Harbeson Biddle, from Pennsylvania, and the aforementioned Charles Forrest Palmer, the SHM team visited London and other towns in Britain during the war. They made observations on Civil Defence, emergency housing provision and problems with it, interviewed leading politicians and professionals about post-war planning issues, and reported back to the President. The cast list of the people the mission met was impressive, including Sir Patrick Abercrombie, Sir William Beveridge, the historian G.D.H. Cole, Elizabeth Denby, the architect-planner Philip Sargant Florence, the town planner William A. Robson and many others. Whether the mission met with Osborn it is difficult to tell from the SHM materials held at the National Archives near Washington DC, but Osborn and Palmer struck up a correspondence soon after the Second World War, suggesting they had at least made some contact during the conflict. The Osborn collection held at Hertfordshire Archives and Library Services

contains a file of the correspondence between Osborn and Palmer, and some
accompanying materials about the American and British experiences of new
towns and urban issues.

Palmer was clearly impressed with Osborn and the British new towns programme, and became a tireless advocate for such development in the USA
after the Second World War. He might be viewed as a minor American disci-
ple of FJO. In his address to the Department of City and Regional Planning
at the University of North Carolina in 1948, Palmer spoke on 'What British
Planning May Mean to America'. He drew attention to the growing influence
of decentralisation as a tool to remedy the pre-war city, the acceleration and
expansion of town planning in Britain during the Second World War, and the
town planning legislation of 1946 and 1947. He argued, mostly in vain, that
the USA should adopt a similar system.[484] In 1949, while Palmer was visiting
Britain, Osborn invited Palmer to WGC. Some years later the compliment
was returned, as Frederic and Margaret Osborn were invited to Atlanta during
one of Osborn's overseas tours. Palmer was certainly an important figure in his
home city. As the *Atlanta Journal* reported in May 1960:

> Receiving a warm welcome here are Sir Frederic and Lady Osborn of
> Welwyn Garden City, Herts, England, who arrived Wednesday as guests
> of Mr. and Mrs. Charles F. Palmer. The Piedmont Driving Club will be
> the scene of the dinner to be given Friday evening by the Palmers in a
> compliment to the British visitors, who are at the Biltmore Hotel. They
> arrived here from Mexico and plan to go on to San Juan, Puerto Rico. Sir
> Frederic, a noted author and lecturer, is an authority on planning. He was
> instrumental in planning the rebuilding of England after the World War 2
> bombings. His latest book is *Can Man Plan?*[485]

Palmer was both a businessman and a long-standing advocate of dispersal to
solve housing problems in the overcrowded city. He was not alone. During
the 1960s, the idea of planned new towns in the USA became increasingly
popular with a couple of businessmen who can also be viewed as philanthropists, namely Robert E. Simon and James L. Rouse. Like Howard, they shared
a vision of a planned new community, socially integrated and economically
self-sufficient. Robert E. Simon established the eponymous town of Reston
in Virginia from 1961, and Rouse financed the building of Columbia in

Maryland from 1963. Both towns drew upon British garden city principles and practices, and eclectically from planned new communities in Europe and other parts of the world.

Rouse and Simon, and members of their architectural and planning teams, undertook tours of planned new towns overseas during the early 1960s, including lengthy visits to Britain to look at the post-war new towns programme, and the lessons that could be learned and applied to their future new towns. Rouse and his team were critical of some of the repetitive row housing, and the size and scale of the neighbourhood units, but admired the more traditional-looking homes that were inspired by the Garden City Movement. He was inspired by Lewis Mumford 'and the English garden city tradition', arguing against suburban sprawl in the USA, and the need for satellite towns constructed to neighbourhood unit principles.[486]

Before Reston began, Simon visited England in 1961, arguing that 'we can learn a lot from British experience'.[487] He devolved social planning matters for Reston to Carol R. Lubin, a stalwart of the New Deal, who was associated with the Ford Foundation and the promotion of social science in Europe after the Second World War. During her visit to England in 1962, Lubin was impressed with the arrivals and social development work in the London new towns, arguing that they had produced a large and invaluable body of knowledge. Social planning materials for Reston during the mid-1960s demonstrated many of the impressions and influences on Lubin from her visit to the UK. Reston aimed for neighbourhoods with community facilities to encourage social interaction and community spirit, and an American-style version of interest groups and civic associations.[488] And both Columbia and Reston aimed to create racially integrated and balanced communities in common with the aim of social mixing inherent in the Garden City Movement.[489] In words that were redolent of WGCL publicity materials and the writings of Ebenezer Howard, a 1970s promotional brochure for Reston emphasised a key goal: 'To build a community, a place where people can live, work and play without leaving their community. Where cultural, educational and recreational facilities are within easy reach of all residents'.[490]

Despite this claim, it appears that neither Mumford nor Osborn were convinced that Reston would become a socially mixed community, rather a 'new upper-class new town', as Mumford described the proposal to FJO in a letter in August 1964.[491] They appeared to be more impressed with the

Rouse experiment in Maryland, as it drew in some disparate settlements into a planned whole. Mumford still felt that Columbia would become predominantly middle class, however, with poorer groups having to live elsewhere. Nonetheless, Osborn suggested that in its golden jubilee year, WGC should be twinned with Columbia rather than Reston, for reasons that, in the correspondence between Mumford and Osborn, are not particularly clear.[492]

Yet both Columbia and Reston symbolised the ongoing etiolation of original garden city principles during the twentieth century as they were adapted and applied overseas. While partly inspired by Letchworth and WGC, most experiments became either garden-suburb-style satellites around major cities, class-segregated or exclusive communities, or both. It is interesting that there is no entry for 'Reston' in Osborn and Whittick's *New Towns: The Answer to Megalopolis* (1970) and 'Columbia, Maryland' is given one entry, but no page number! This was an unwitting oversight that leaves the reader to scour the book for its inclusion. Such omissions were perhaps surprising given the recent beginnings of these two American new towns during the 1960s, and Osborn's knowledge of them. It may also reflect a wider disappointment that new towns often were not really answers to megalopolis or metropolitan sprawl. The two British garden cities had inspired so many and so much, but their fullest realisation still lay in Hertfordshire. Ultimately, Columbia and WGC were not twinned with each other.

Along with the other 1960s new town of Irvine in California, which was unfortunately gobbled up by suburban sprawl, Columbia and Reston did, however, stimulate both political and professional interest in reviving the new towns concept in America. Palmer had continued to lobby for new towns in the USA in the British garden city mould. As his correspondence with Osborn shows, he was invited to participate by the Department of Housing and Urban Development (HUD) in the early debates that led to the New Communities Act of 1968, and to subsequent legislation aiming to create racially integrated new towns in the United States.[493] The American Institute of Architects (AIA) also lobbied HUD, and like Palmer, looked to the British example. The AIA got a few facts wrong, however. Arguing that 'since 1946 England has completed or started 28 new towns', it stated that 'the term new towns originated in Labour Government laws enacted by the Churchill–Labourite coalition', new towns that owed a significant debt 'to the Garden City theories popularised around 1900 by Ebenezer Howard'.

The AIA then went on to endorse Columbia and Reston as models of successful social mixing.[494]

In 1969, officials from HUD, and a number of researchers in urban affairs, undertook a 'New Towns Tour' in Britain, in association with the Ministry of Housing and Local Government, where the London new towns were visited. On the tour was Betsy Levin, a project officer based at the Urban Institute in Washington DC. Her notes, which she forwarded to HUD officials, included the importance of the ideas of Howard and their realisation at Letchworth and WGC, but she also critically pointed out that despite some impressive social development work, the post-war new towns around London were dominated by working-class households, thus failing to achieve the goal of mixed communities.[495]

The American new towns programme initiated by the New Communities Act ultimately proved disappointing, mostly because of a lack of strategic government intervention, and the withdrawal of sufficient funding under the Republican administration of Richard Nixon during the early 1970s.[496] Correspondence between Osborn and Palmer articulated hopes that planned new communities emulating the British garden city might ameliorate ethnic tensions in the United States. But both were realistic enough to view those tensions as incredibly difficult to solve. [497]

## Beyond the Transatlantic Connection: WGC and Garden Cities Across the World

It is often easier to identify the influence of Ebenezer Howard and of the post-war new towns on overseas experiments in planned new communities than to identify the specific impact of WGC itself. Yet teasing out the contribution of WGC, and of its resident tireless exponent Frederic Osborn, is a fascinating exercise. As many historians of town planning have shown, particularly Gordon Cherry and Stephen V. Ward, the British Garden City Movement exercised significant inspiration for new residential developments and new towns across the world during the twentieth century. As we have seen, the United States was probably the most significant importer of Howard's visionary proposals, but Scandinavian countries, the Netherlands, France, Germany, Australia, Japan and more recently China have all imbued their new satellite towns and planned residential suburbs with British garden city principles.[498] And Osborn visited or wrote about most of them, with the exception of China, because he died before the Chinese began their long march of planned urban development.

In Scandinavia, two key examples of the influence of British garden cities are Tapiola in Finland and Vällingby in Sweden. Tapiola was begun in 1946 and incorporates some key aspects of garden city planning to this day. Its similarities with Welwyn Garden City and new town are strongly apparent. Although it was initially intended for 15,000 residents, it used the term garden city, and was generously endowed with open parks and woodlands. It is close to the capital city of Helsinki, closer than the satellite town of WGC is to London. Its residential areas were designed to neighbourhood unit principles, and while blocks of flats as opposed to private houses predominated at Tapiola, the height and scale of these was low to medium rise.[499]

Two notable post-war Scandinavian experiments in satellite towns were Vällingby and Farsta, in Sweden, both new towns for Stockholm. Swedish planners drew less closely than the planners of Tapiola on British experiments, but were influenced by Sir Patrick Abercrombie's *County of London Plan* and *Greater London Plan,* and the professional debates over the post-war British new towns programme. Swedish planners generally absorbed key principles, notably the need for decentralisation itself, the neighbourhood unit, residential zoning with convenient access to places of employment, the importance of a distinct town centre, and the provision of parklands. Vällingby was initiated in 1946, the same year as Stevenage. There was much interaction between the British and Swedish planners of these towns. Farsta began in 1958, and by 1966 its population was greater than the 55,000 living at Vällingby. As Ward shows, there was less a commitment to economic self-containment than in the London satellite towns, as out-commuting was expected to be, and was, higher than purists following the Howardian agenda might have liked. Many more high-rise blocks were built than in British new towns.[500]

In Denmark, the so-called 'Finger Plan' of 1947 for the decentralisation of post-war Copenhagen was also inspired by the need to disperse population from the capital, and to house the growing population in attractive residential zones. The 'fingers' referred to the elongated corridors of housing alongside the railways built to encourage movement between Copenhagen and residential areas. The environmental value of parks or 'green wedges' was taken on board by Danish planners, but suburban infill weakened the overall vision.[501]

In the Netherlands, and Belgium, small garden suburbs had been built during the first half of the twentieth century. During the early post-war years, however, as the population of Holland grew rapidly, Dutch planners looked to the British new towns and garden cities, and the experience of decentralisation, to inform a large-scale programme of decentralisation. Zoetermeer, Lelystad and Almere were sizeable new communities built on land reclaimed from the sea by the Dutch polder system, the first two being completed during the 1960s, and Almere during the 1970s.[502]

A number of garden suburbs to a small degree inspired by Howard, though lacking his overall vision of self-containment, were built in twentieth-century Japan. Prior to the Second World War, as Japan modernised, and even taking into account the ascendancy of a militaristic nationalism, more liberal-minded and Western-orientated Japanese professionals admired the British garden city, and American garden suburbs. Within the orbit of Tokyo, the Toshi Co. built Den-en Chofu from 1918 to 1928. Hence it was initiated just prior to WGC but after the early growth of Letchworth. 'Den-en' means 'garden' in Japanese and 'Chofu' refers to the area in which the garden suburb was built. Like so make American developments, and in common with Letchworth and pre-1948 WGC, it was a company town. Although it absorbed a number of Howardian principles, it was never a true garden city because it was a middle-class commuter suburb served by a purpose-built railway line. In that sense it was both a railway suburb and a company town, rather than the mixed and self-contained new town envisioned by Howard.[503]

During the Second World War, Japanese cities were devastated by Allied, and particularly by American, bombing. The conventional air raids on Tokyo in 1944–45, and on other great Japanese conurbations, devastated more than 70 per cent of the built environment. The atomic detonations over Hiroshima and Nagasaki in 1945 also wiped out most of these cities' buildings. Post-war Japan required a massive project of reconstruction.[504]

In his co-written tome with Arnold Whittick, *The New Towns: The Answer to Megalopolis* (1963), Osborn lamented that, despite its industrial progress, town planning in Japan was 'strangely backward'. The authors observed that 'advanced Japanese planners' agreed with a decentralisation and new towns policy analogous to the British model, but that national policy lagged

far behind.[505] The list of Japanese garden cities and new towns was not
lengthy: it included the aforementioned Den-en Toshi (aka Den-en Chofu)
and those being constructed around Tokyo, Osaka and Nagoya. But how far
were Japanese post-war new towns really an 'answer' to the accelerating and
expanding Japanese conurbation? This is a question Osborn and Whittick
do not fully address. Listing the fastest-growing and most populous cities
of the world during the early 1960s, including the Tokyo–Yokohama and
Osaka–Kobe conurbations, the authors suggest that 'correcting the existing
maldistribution' and over-densification 'will be a colossal and daunting task'.[506]

It was a task that the Japanese urban developers and town planners were
only partially able to address. The post-war new towns provided mostly flatted
accommodation, some low-rise detached, duplex or terraced family housing,
much-needed parklands, a central retail and leisure zone, and neighbourhood
facilities of schools, places of worship, and smaller shops. But they were much
closer to the garden suburb than the garden city model, relying upon levels
of commuting and on population densities that would have caused Ebenezer
Howard to turn in his grave. Japanese experiments ultimately did little to
contain urban sprawl. Tokyo is now one of the world's largest metropolitan regions, and Nagoya and Osaka are bristling modern cities hosting new
towns within their orbit.

Frederic and Margaret Osborn toured Japan in the summer of 1966 at
the behest and under the guidance of Issei Inuma, a leading Japanese town
planner and advocate of the garden city. The Osborns were availed with
upscale hotels, driven around in 'comfortable cars' and FJO himself was
given airtime on Japanese television to 'preach the New Towns gospel'.[507]
He also held a public lecture in Tokyo, and enjoyed a private audience with
the Crown Prince and Princess. Osborn was pleased that regional planning
and the decentralisation of urban populations into planned new settlements
were in vogue in Japan, but was also aware that Japanese town planning was
more in line with the American Institute of Planners, who advocated garden
suburb-style satellites, rather than the TCPA, and its vision of self-contained
new towns similar to those around London.[508]

Having visited a number of satellite cities in Japan during this century,
it was obvious to this writer that although the Japanese planners actively
embraced decentralisation, the post-war new towns were envisioned
mostly as high-density and often high-rise suburban developments,

connected to Tokyo or to large provincial cities such as Nagoya and Osaka, by railway networks. Tama New Town near Tokyo, Kosoji New Town in suburban Nagoya, and Senri near Osaka, are the most famous examples.[509] The appearance and atmosphere is unlike any of the post-war English new towns, although resemblances to the original principles of Howard and their application to the British new towns arc identifiable. Neighbourhood units, a distinctive shopping centre, retail sub-centres, public parks and preserved woods are noticeable.[510]

Further south in the Pacific, Australia had also experimented with garden cities and suburbs prior to the Second World War. Australian urban planners were strongly influenced by the British Garden City Movement. During the Second World War, despite the minor incidence of destruction compared with Britain, many Australian politicians and planners looked forward to a comprehensive programme of urban renewal, abolishing the slums and 'nasty inner suburbs' for garden cities, more accurately described as garden-city-inspired satellite towns.

Soon after the war, an Australian academic juxtaposed photographs of the grimy Sydney suburb of Paddington, 'with one of England's Welwyn Garden City'. Along with other researchers into urban problems he was 'convinced that WGC could be Paddington's salvation'.[511] The planning of the South Australian town of Elizabeth, a satellite of Adelaide, was one of a number of new planned towns that owed a great deal to British and American planning theories and practices. During the 1950s, Australian planners visited Letchworth, WGC and a number of British new towns. They adopted Radburn-style urban design, and the neighbourhood unit, both essential to the planning of the Mark 1 new towns in the United Kingdom.[512] As we saw in a previous chapter, the neighbourhood unit was already becoming out of date as it was rolled out during the 1950s, but Australian planners made the same mistakes as their British counterparts:

> Begun in 1950, with the first houses completed by 1955, it was created by the South Australia Housing Trust, the state's public housing agency. Planning closely followed the first-generation British new town model. By the mid-1950s, the British New Town 'tour' to Harlow, Crawley, Stevenage, Hemel Hempstead, Welwyn Garden City, Letchworth and Cymbran was well established for Trust officials.[513]

In common with the USA, Australia shared an English language connection with Britain, which also helps to explain the influence of the Garden City Movement there.

## Anniversaries and International Attention on Welwyn Garden City

During the post-war years, the architectural continuities emanating from the original master plan by Louis de Soissons ensured that as WGC became more socially mixed, it mostly maintained its neo-Georgian sense of space and style. Both the Welwyn Garden City Development Corporation, and also the Commission for the New Towns, deserve credit for employing de Soissons as the master planner for the new post-war iterations. And de Soissons deserves recognition for drawing up plans that have proven to be flexible yet steadfast in the manner WGC has handled such key social changes as increasing affluence, the acceleration and expansion of motorisation, and the increased demand for leisure and recreational facilities.

Four anniversaries in the history of Welwyn Garden City illustrate, in sharp relief, the global interest in WGC, and its influence overseas both as a garden city and a new town. These were the silver jubilee in 1945, the golden jubilee in 1970, and the seventy-fifth anniversary in 1995. The latest centenary celebrations in 2019–20 also demonstrate the national and international significance of Welwyn Garden City.

The twenty-fifth anniversary, or silver jubilee, in 1945 was a relatively low-key affair, as Britain was coming to the end of a long war, and was mired in rationing and austerity. In 1970, when Britain was still enjoying its post-war 'Golden Age' of economic growth and relatively full employment, the golden jubilee of Welwyn Garden City took place. The Commission for the New Towns came into greater public focus locally as it organised the celebrations, invited royalty to the garden city, and provided a permanent memorial to the work of Louis de Soissons. In its Eighth Annual Report to the Minister of Housing and Local Government, Anthony Greenwood MP, the CNT recognised, with a touch of corporate spin, 'the successful realisation of Ebenezer Howard's original Garden City concept, which inspired the present new towns movement' and the 'universal admiration' for the new towns. Yet the report also acknowledged the importance of the architect-planner who had designed Welwyn Garden City:

> Her Majesty Queen Elizabeth the Queen Mother has graciously consented to open on 30th May 1970, a floral garden in Parkway incorporating a memorial stone to Mr. Louis de Soissons, the planner and architect of the town. The occasion and the public celebrations will have a fitting international flavour, as the Town and Country Planning Association have organised an international study tour of the new town which will open with the celebrations at Welwyn Garden City and continue with a one-day conference in the town on 2st June and a banquet in the banqueting hall of the Old Palace of Hatfield House.[514]

This was spin on a different issue, however. In a letter dated 2 April to Mumford, Osborn highlighted the controversy surrounding the memorial to Louis de Soissons:

> The design for the memorial garden to Louis de Soissons at the top end of Parkway included a long wall about 4ft high, which was built, and roused a storm of local protest. The matter was referred to the Royal Fine Arts Commission, which supported the objectors, and the wall was instantly demolished and a new plan prepared, which has to be very quickly acted on, as the Queen Mother is opening the garden on 30 May.[515]

The use of Hatfield House for the banquet and conference was symbolic as well as practical, linking Welwyn and Hatfield. And the CNT went on to stress the global significance of the celebrations that linked the garden city tradition in town planning with the post-war new towns programme:

> The number of planners, sociologists, and others from all over the world who will be present will bear testimony not only to the success of Ebenezer Howard's garden city ideal in this town but to the universal admiration of the whole British new towns movement. It is not just a matter of academic appreciation of an interesting social experiment; indeed the surest tribute from overseas lies in the number of countries which have taken up, and are still taking, the British new towns as an

inspiration, and are asking for advice, drawn from British experience, on how to set about building them.[516]

Osborn made one of his last speeches at the banquet, tailoring his praise of WGC and its contribution to new community planning to the audience of 'tourists from all over the world'.[517] Twenty-five years later, the seventy-fifth anniversary celebrations in 1990 also witnessed the unveiling of a new memorial, this time to Captain Richard Reiss. His important role in developing WGC was accompanied by another significant and positive legacy, his efforts to save young Jewish refugees during the late 1930s.

## The International Legacy of Welwyn Garden City

From its unfavourable image between the wars, WGC has become a mostly highly regarded garden city overseas. This was partly a happy consequence of both the active citizenry who have participated in the arts, cultural activities and sports overseas. In the world of global philanthropy and reaching out to the oppressed and vulnerable during the darkest days of European history, it has little equal for a town of its size, particularly given its relative newness when compared with most other towns.

It is within the professions of architecture and town planning, however, that WGC has long provided an example and inspiration in other countries. The international diffusion of town planning ideas and practices is a key theme in planning history. It is absolutely no exaggeration to argue that Welwyn Garden City occupies a pivotal place in the history of the global spread of British garden city planning and in its influence upon thousands of planned new communities overseas. Yet despite the impressive role of the British Garden City Movement as a soft power export in British overseas influence, that influence was mediated by local, political and cultural factors in other countries. Transplanting a new garden city that looked and functioned like WGC onto foreign soil was not always a straightforward task. In his groundbreaking book, *Model Communities*, planning historian Robert Freestone summarised the influence and impact of the British Garden City Movement as 'the diluted legacy'. This was the history of how initial intentions and inspiring ideals became watered down simply by the realities of

social, economic and political changes and developments. This legacy of dilution works on two levels:

> The first is the gap evident between ideal and reality [...]. This is consistent
> with overseas evidence that the garden city tended to be elevated to an
> almost metaphysical ideal, yet regularly degraded in practice. Expectations
> built into most community plans have not been realised. This is perhaps
> inevitable, for life is simply more complicated than any single idea, image
> or goal. Yet explaining the gap is important. [The] degree to which alluring
> 'bird's eye' or other visions were fulfilled ultimately depended on con-
> siderations such as the location and timing of a project; attention given
> to the actual process rather than mere plan of development; the financial
> resources and commitment of the initiators; the nature of controls over
> long-term development; the strength of conservative 'anti-planning' forces,
> and changing institutional and political arrangements.
>
> The second most fundamental interpretation is the drift away from
> Howard's radical manifesto for 'a better and nobler society' through the
> physical reforms of liberal-progressive planning movements to actual
> schemes which compromised or even totally contradicted the original idea
> in economic, social and spatial terms. In effect, the peaceful path to social
> revolution splintered, changed and was trapped within the status quo.[518]

Freestone is mostly concerned with the overseas legacy of the British Garden
City Movement, and the complicated ways in which the original ideals of
Howard were compromised by social, economic and political factors, and also
because, in being transplanted to countries overseas, some of Howard's aspirations became lost in translation. As this chapter has shown, whether the garden
city was assembled in Australia, North America, Europe or Japan, they were often
more akin to garden suburbs. Ironically, the New Townsmen had been formed
during the First World War in part to protect the fuller vision of the Garden City
Movement from being watered down by garden suburb experiments.

Welwyn Garden City was the second major laboratory for Howard and his
team to put into practice the ideas of the founder. Applying Freestone's general approach, we can see its history has indeed demonstrated some dilution
of Howard's principles. This was consequent upon the complexity of social
and economic change; site-specific issues such as the railway line; political

infighting within WGC itself; changes of national Government and shift-
ing financial imperatives; and the history of its governance from the first
decades when Welwyn Garden City Ltd was in control, to the Development
Corporation, the Commission for the New Towns, and the relationship of
the Urban District Councils to the development of WGC.

Walking around Welwyn Garden City new town today, it would be evident to most informed observers that despite the changes and challenges it
has faced, the town reflects a great deal of the initial vision of Howard, and
has remained largely true to the attractive neo-Georgian urban design of
Louis de Soissons. This was also due, of course, to the unstinting work of
the key members of the Company that laid down the foundations for WGC
between the wars. The institutions responsible for the post-war development
of WGC largely maintained the environmental amenities of the town, adding
others where necessary. WGC, in common with Letchworth, remains the
least diluted of the world's garden cities, and the continuing interest shown
in it by academics, architects, planners, politicians and other professionals
from across the world is testament to that. The final questions for this book
have to be: as Welwyn Garden City celebrates its centenary, will it remain
such an attractive and influential exemplar for new community planning?
How – or will – its garden city qualities persist over the remaining decades
of the present century?

# 7

# CONCLUSION: FROM THE PAST TO THE PRESENT AND THE FUTURE

The origins of Welwyn Garden City stemmed from the eighteenth- and nineteenth-century intellectual and practical reactions to the problems of the unplanned urbanisation of the Industrial Revolution. Yet WGC was a child of the twentieth century. Born at the end of its second decade, it became an influential and forward-looking experiment in modern town planning. Yet the character of WGC is facing some significant changes now. In a sense, of course, it has always faced changes, and has managed them with greater or lesser degrees of success. The nature of the current changes, however, stemmed more from an architectural antipathy toward low-density suburbia, particularly in the United States. This provides a fascinating opportunity to assess the past, present and possibly the future of WGC.

## From Influencer to Influenced?

Since the 1990s, the architectural and planning philosophy known as New Urbanism has increasingly permeated British town planning. American in provenance, global in its impact, New Urbanism questioned the legitimacy of zoning, of residential areas consciously located separately from industrial and employment districts. It called for a retrofitting of housing areas, by inserting more accommodation and diverse amenities into low-density streets, a feat to be achieved by converting gardens and pocket parks into housing. Residential areas were, in effect, to become less 'residential', more populated, and increasingly mixed in land use and appearance.[519] Welwyn Garden City, for so long an influencer, now became an experimental laboratory, among so many others, for this new direction in domestic architecture and town planning.

The impact of New Urbanism in *fin de siècle* Britain coincided with an increasingly fashionable critique of new town and suburban living. In 1999, the Labour Peer Lord Rogers of Riverside, who was appointed by Tony Blair's New Labour government to chair the Urban Task Force, led the call for an 'urban renaissance'. The Urban Task Force was a group of professionals working on the regeneration of rundown areas in Britain's towns and cities. In his own words, Rogers wanted to 'cram' British cities by increasing densities.[520] He was scathing of zoning and low densities, and a protagonist for mixed-use cityscapes. In short, lower densities and spatially distinct areas of the city increase commuting and the use of the motor car, are wasteful of land, and therefore 'unsustainable'. The New Labour government only partially deployed his recommendations, but the emphasis in planning and policy guidance since has been to question the legitimacy of key garden city planning principles.

Rogers either fundamentally misunderstands or wilfully downplays the Garden City Movement and its popular appeal. There is no reference to garden cities or Welwyn Garden City in the index to *Towards an Urban Renaissance*, and Letchworth is listed as a 'garden suburb', which it palpably is not. To be fair, Rogers includes 'Howard, Ebenezer' in his index (he ignores Frederic Osborn) but the reader who turns to the relevant page for Howard will not learn very much. Acknowledging that much unplanned Victorian urbanisation had been ugly and insanitary, Rogers understood why Howard and other visionaries had called for an escape from the city. Yet the lower-density and spatially distinct environments of the Garden City Movement, and in the new towns that drew so much from them, were largely dismissed as 'suburban' in character, a worn-out trope we observed in previous chapters:

> At their best, our garden cities and new towns have provided a form of suburban living where the relationship between urbanity and country; between public transport and walkability; of work and residence, continues to hold significant implications for sustainable planning today.[521]

So WGC was not only charged with suburbanity but was also guilty of undermining the new sustainability agenda, which emphasised more public transport and a closer spatial connection between work and home. The report also went on to blame the small but significant role that garden cities and new towns had in eroding the viability of city centres during the twentieth century as a consequence of decentralisation.

Lord Rogers is a Labour Peer, but antipathy towards garden cities and new towns, and WGC was a paradigm of both, was increasingly evident among Conservative thinkers. At much the same time Rogers and his Urban Task Force were preparing their report, John Selwyn Gummer, a former Conservative Minister of Agriculture, and Secretary of State for the Environment from 1993 to 1997, decried the 'brave new world' of new towns and garden cities. He blamed them for creating new settlements away from urban centres, and for contributing to the decline of those established towns and cities:

> So the theories which had built Welwyn and Letchworth Garden Cities, and earlier had inspired Bournville and Saltaire, now created Stevenage and Harlow, Great Cornard and Milton Keynes, Runcorn and Thetford. These indeed offered conditions undreamt of by the inhabitants of the crowded cities of pre-war England. Yet they were created with no thought for their impact on the countryside, and no consideration of their effect on the old towns, which were left to decline.[522]

The rationale of the Garden City Movement is profoundly misunderstood by Gummer. They are not responsible for inner-city decline. The practical benefits of thinning out and replanning the overcrowded city centres were not seized upon by central and local governments of twentieth-century Britain. For example, the Abercrombie Plan for Greater London, in which WGC played a significant symbolic and practical role, was never fully implemented. Dispersal of population to the new towns certainly occurred, but a host of vested interests and practical difficulties meant that London was never remodelled in the way that Abercrombie, and Howard, in their different ways, had intended.

Hence WGC cannot really be blamed for any negative effects on London. And as we have seen, many Londoners who moved there were more than pleased with their new life, a point that Gummer is prepared to concede.[523] It is incorrect to argue, however, that the new towns were planned with no thought for their impact on rural Britain. WGC had proved an exemplar in synthesising the advantages of town and country. The original master plan and subsequent plans carefully preserved trees and areas of beauty. Later in the twentieth century, larger new towns, notably Milton Keynes, conserved trees, planted millions more, and preserved coppices, fields, watersides and woodlands within a grand vision for 'the city in the country, and the country in the city'.[524] New parklands were also created. Milton Keynes owes much to Howard's original ideas, and it remains a hugely popular city with its residents, many of whom love the urban facilities juxtaposed with wide open spaces.

Yet the growing influence of higher densities, smaller plots and the consequent tinier gardens (or no garden) represented a direct challenge to garden city planning principles. The sustainability agenda of the present century means that a 'green' garden city may well become more urbanised and packed with more people. How very different this all was to the promotion of WGC during the 1920s as a spacious garden city where incomers could enjoy a garden at the front and rear of their houses. This can be identified all over Britain but also in the built environment of WGC. Growing numbers of flats and small townhouses near the town centre, close to the old industrial zone containing the sadly dilapidated Shredded Wheat factory, represent the emphasis on densification and mixed use in planning and policy guidance since the late 1990s. To this writer's eyes, WGC is becoming a busier and untidier-looking garden city. To others, this is the future, but that future is very different to the original vision for Welwyn Garden City. The current plans to redevelop the Shredded Wheat site have proved to be controversial, providing higher population densities in a mixed-use environment that is far from what Howard envisaged.[525]

As a kind of postscript, in February 2019 the Government announced plans for 250,000 new homes in England. They are to be built in various regions, and Welwyn Hatfield, if the plans are initiated, could gain up to 12,000 new dwellings by the mid-2020s.[526]

In their oral histories of WGC residents, the Welwyn Garden City Heritage Trust heard some testimonies to the effect that WGC was losing its garden city character. Higher densities, at the heart of national housing policies since the late 1990s, were also at the heart of perceived notions of decline. One woman was critical of the higher densities and called for the funding principles of the garden city to be kept. Her testimony is worth quoting in full as a counter to the official orthodoxy of 'cramming' in current new-build policies:

> Very sad that they are squashing houses so close together, I would have liked to see them keep the original number of houses per acre. I think it is losing its Garden City, much of it is losing its original roots, I think they are still … putting grass along all the paths, because one of our big features was to have a grass verge next to the road, and they are putting some trees in but they are not putting in lovely little areas of flowers at the end of each road. They seem to be cramming things so close together and I think it has gone very sad. I think Ebenezer Howard would be very upset … I think the town centre is still pretty beautiful. I like the town centre, I don't think they've ruined that too much – they have kept the flower beds going, which are nice …[527]

As Gladys A. put it, when asked by the WGCHT whether the garden city had changed:

> Yes – well obviously the size and the expansion of it and I think it has become as you go out further and further – especially over the last ten years – it has become much less of a garden city because Ebenezer Howard's theory was I think fourteen people to an acre or something like that – and now it looks as though it is 140 houses! It is no longer really a garden city. I feel it has become a bit of a town without a heart now and I am sorry to have to say that …[528]

Gordon A. lamented the increasing untidiness and busyness of the town centre:

> I liked a lot of what we had and I don't like a lot of what we have at the moment … I have parked in the Howard Centre car park, came up Howardsgate and along Parkway and a rather garish frontage to an establishment along there, which is the first time I have had a good look because I have always been driving, and I was not impressed. And various other bits;

it is hard to pin down anything specifically but it just the way the town is being allowed to develop in some ways, which is not quite right for me – I think we could do without that. It is difficult to stress any particular point. The town centre has unfortunately gone down a wee bit – hopefully it will be allowed to recover depending on other pressing circumstances at the moment.[529]

Similarly, Ann W. felt that WGC 'is still lovely but it is changing not for the better – I feel it has become quite scruffy' and she expressed her concern that it might become like any other town if it lost its environmental qualities.[530] Another woman felt that WGC had recently 'changed so completely that the garden city it was meant to be has gone. There's no garden city here. It's all houses. Different nationalities. We were a village.'[531] And she went on to lament the loss of community feeling, and as she saw it the growing disaffection of young people who felt they did not belong: 'That sense of belonging has gone.'[532]

Not just higher densities, perhaps, but also nostalgia for the early days of WGC informed her memory. But some still loved the garden city, as did others from 'the wider world' beyond both WGC and England. As Mary A. stated with some pride in her voice:

Whenever I bring friends to the garden city, particularly friends from abroad, whether Australia or from Europe or whatever, they think it's *marvellous* … and we all stand on the White Bridge and we look down there … I think it is basically well planned … I think Ebenezer Howard's ideas were good, that there should be plenty of gardens whether private or municipal … well they're [the gardens] a bit smaller now because of other reasons. And having the industry on one side of the railway line … well some people don't like that or didn't like it. There were people who didn't like it because they said it made a division. I don't hear people say that so much now, partly because there are more houses.[533]

Post-war expansion under the Development Corporation, the Commission for New Towns and the Urban District Council had all combined to make WGC a larger, more heavily populated place. As this quote and some others also demonstrate, however, many still cherish the garden city character that has been preserved. Long may that continue, but it will be up to the citizens of WGC and the local interest groups to ensure it retains its qualities.

As a final comment, therefore, it is interesting to note that the Facebook public group Welwyn Garden City News has more than 14,000 members, considerably more than a quarter of the town's population of 51,000 (2017 figures). The content demonstrates a still strong commitment by many local residents to preserving the beauties of WGC, encouraging sociability in neighbourhood and town-wide events, and in reporting incidents of crime, petty vandalism, litter-dropping and graffiti, as well as public-spirited acts regarding lost animals or lost property. There is still a great deal of local pride of place, and a high degree of participation, in WGC, demonstrating that Howard's vision for an active citizenry is still alive.

# BIBLIOGRAPHY AND SOURCES

## Archival Sources

HALS/DE/FJO/B113: 'British Visitors Entertained Here as Guest of Palmers', *Atlanta Journal*, 20 May 1960

HALS/DE/FJO/K1552a: Letter to the Chairman and Directors, WGCL, 19 March 1928, from FJO *et al*

HALS/DE/FJO/K147/7: Letter from Osborn and Reiss to *Welwyn Times*, 25 June 1951

HALS/DE/FJO/K330: Letter from Osborn to Frank Schaffer, 'Social Provision in New Towns', 10 October 1958

HALS/DE/FJO/B113: Letter from Osborn to Viscount Astor, 5 December 1944

HALS/DE/FJO/K147/7: Letters between Chambers and FJO, 19 March 1928; 21 March, 23 March 1928

HALS/DE/FJO/K442: Pallister, Minnie *Seeing the Garden* (Welwyn: Knight, Frank and Rutley, 1930s)

HALS/DE/FJO/B113: Palmer, Charles Forrest, 'What British Planning May Mean to America', 18 November 1948

HALS/DE/FJO/K61: 'The Personalities of Welwyn Garden City', 17 November 1916

HALS/DE/FJO/K468: *Welwyn Garden City Pioneers Party Souvenir and Programme*, Parkway Restaurant, 6 May 1946

HALS/DE/FJO/K332: Welwyn Garden City Ltd, *Houses in Charming Surroundings at Welwyn Garden City* (Welwyn: Welwyn Garden City Ltd; not dated but 1920s)

HALS/DE/FJO/K250: Welwyn Garden City Research Committee, *Living and Working in Welwyn Garden City* (WGC, 1940) [see also Jaqueline Tyrwhitt]

HALS/DE/FJO/K: H1–H14; H17–H33 [FJO travels overseas]

National Archives (US), College Park: The President's Special Housing Mission to Great Britain, *Biddle Diary*, 10 March 1962

# Published Printed Sources

Addison, Christopher, *The Betrayal of the Slums* (London: H. Jenkins, 1922)

Aldridge, Meryl, *The British New Towns: A Programme Without a Policy* (Abingdon: Routledge and Kegan Paul, 1979)

Alexander, Anthony, *Britain's New Towns: Garden Cities to Sustainable Communities* (Abingdon: Routledge, 2009)

Anon, 'Over £221 million spent on fifteen new towns', *Guardian,* 26 March 1960

Bayley, Stephen, *The Garden City* (Milton Keynes: Open University Press, 1975)

Beevers, Robert, 'Ebenezer Howard: The Man and His Message', in Allen, William Beevers, Robert, Hebbert, Michael, Miller, Mervyn and Onslow, John *Garden Cities and New Towns: Five Lectures* (Hertford: Hertfordshire Publications, 1990)

Beevers, Robert, *The Garden City Utopia: A Critical Biography of Ebenezer Howard* (Basingstoke: Macmillan, 1988)

Bloom, Nicholas, Dagen, *Suburban Alchemy: 1960s New Towns and the Transformation of the American Dream* (Columbus: Ohio State University Press, 2001)

Boyce and Everett, *SOE: The Scientific Secrets* (Stroud: Sutton, 2003)

*British Medical Journal,* 'Ten years of Welwyn Garden City', *British Medical Journal*, 1:3265, 1930

Brown, Colin, 'The Industry of the New Towns in the London Region', in Martin, J.E. *Greater London: An Industrial Geography* (London: G. Bell and Sons, 1966)

Brun-Rovet, Marianne and Timmins, Nicholas, 'Ageing New Towns in need of rapid update', *Financial Times,* 4 July, 2002

Buchanan, Colin, on behalf of the Steering Group and Working Group appointed by the Minister of Transport, *Traffic in Towns: A Study of the Long-Term Problems of Traffic in Urban Areas* (London: HMSO, 1963)

Buder, Howard, *Visionaries and Planners: The Garden City Movement and the Modern Community* (Oxford: Oxford University Press, 1990)

Burnett, John, *A Social History of Housing 1815–1985* (London: Routledge, 1991)

Butterfield, R.J., 'The Shredded Wheat Factory at Welwyn Garden City', in Goodman, David (ed.) *The European Cities and Technology Reader: Industrial to Post-Industrial City* (London and New York: Routledge, 1999)

Catterall, Peter *Labour and the Churches, 1918–1939: Radicalism, Righteousness and Religion* (London: Bloomsbury, 2018)

Chave, S. and Taylor, Lord *Mental Health and Environment* (London: Longmans, 1964)

Cherry, G.E., *The Evolution of British Town Planning* (Leighton Buzzard: Leonard Hill Books, 1974)

Cherry, G.E., *Town Planning in Britain since 1945* (Oxford: Blackwell, 1996)

Clapson, Mark, *Anglo-American Crossroads: Urban Planning and Research in Britain, 1940–2010* (London: Bloomsbury, 2013)

Clapson, Mark, *Britain in the Twentieth Century* (Abingdon: Routledge, 2009)

Clapson, Mark, 'Destruction and Dispersal: The Blitz and the "Break-Up" of Working-Class London', in Clapson, Mark and Larkham, P.J. (eds.), *The Blitz and its Legacy: Wartime Destruction to Post-war Reconstruction* (Farnham: Ashgate, 2013)

Clapson, Mark, 'From Garden City to New Town: Social Change, Politics and Town Planners at Welwyn, 1920–1948' in Meller, Helen and Porfyriou, Helen, *Planting New*

*Towns in Europe in the Inter-war Years* (Cambridge: Cambridge Scholars Press, 2016)

Clapson, Mark, 'Localism, the London Labour Party and the LCC between the Wars', in Saint, Andrew (ed.), *Politics and the People of London: A Centenary History of the London County Council* (London: Hambledon, 1989)

Clapson, Mark, *The Blitz Companion: Aerial Warfare, Civilians and the City since 1911* (University of Westminster Press, 2019)

Clapson, Mark, *Working-Class Suburb: Social Change on an English Council Estate, 1930–2010* (Manchester: Manchester University Press, 2012)

Clarke, Peter, *Hope and Glory: Britain 1900–1990* (London: Penguin, 1996)

Collings, Timothy, *Stevenage, 1946–1986: Images of the First New Town* (Stevenage: SPA Books, 1987)

Commission for the New Towns, *Annual Reports* (London: British Library, Parliamentary Papers Online)

Conkin, Paul, *Tomorrow a New World: The New Deal Community Programme* (Ithaca, New York: Cornell University Press, 1959)

Cullingworth, J.B., *Town and Country Planning in Britain* (London: George Allen and Unwin Ltd, 1974)

David, Gareth, 'New Town Sales Top £300m', *Observer*, 13 October 1985

Deakin, Nicholas and Ungerson, Claire, *Leaving London: Planned Mobility and the Inner City* (London: Centre for Environmental Studies, 1977)

de Soissons, Maurice, *Welwyn Garden City: A Town Designed For Healthy Living* (Welwyn and Hatfield: Publications for Companies, 1988)

Eserin, Angela, *The QEII: A Hospital's Story* (Welwyn: Angela Eserin, 2015)

Eserin, Angela and Hughes, Mike, *The Sir Frederic Osborn Archive: A Descriptive Catalogue* (Hertford: Hertfordshire Library Service, 1990)

Esher, Lionel, *A Broken Wave: The Rebuilding of England, 1940–1980* (Harmondsworth: Penguin, 1983)

Fishman, Robert, 'The American Garden City: Still Relevant?' in Ward, Stephen V. (ed.), *The Garden City: Past, Present and Future* (London: E. & F.N. Spon, 1992)

Freestone, Robert, *Model Communities: The Garden City Movement in Australia* (Melbourne: Thomas Nelson Australia, 1989)

Gadney, Reginald, 'Obituary: Viscount Esher', *Guardian*, 13 July 2014

Gummer, John, 'Those Four Million Houses', in Barnett, Anthony and Scruton, Roger, *Town and Country* (London: Vintage, 1999)

Hall, Peter and Ward, Colin, *Sociable Cities: The Legacy of Ebenezer Howard* (Chichester: John Wiley and Sons, 1998)

Hardy, Dennis, 'The Garden City Campaign: An Overview', in Ward, Stephen V. (ed.), *The Garden City: Past, Present and Future* (London: F&N Spon, 1992)

Harrison, Peter and Fraser, R.D.L., 'Alfred John Brown, 1993–1976', *Royal Australian Planning Institute Journal*, 15: 1977

Hebbert, Michael, 'A Hertfordshire Solution to London's Problems: Sir Frederic Osborn's Axioms Reconsidered', in William Allen, Robert Beevers, Michael Hebbert, Mervyn Miller and John Onslow, *Garden Cities and New Towns: Five Lectures* (Hertford: Hertfordshire Publications, 1990)

Hebbert, Michael, 'The British Garden City: Metamorphosis', in Ward, Stephen V. (ed.), *The Garden City: Past, Present and Future* (London: E&FN Spon, 1992)

Heraud, B.J., 'Social class and the new towns', *Urban Studies* 5:1 (1966)

Hill, Marion, *Welwyn Garden City* (Stroud: Sutton Publishing, 1999)

Howard, Ebenezer, *Garden Cities of Tomorrow*; edited with a preface by F.J. Osborn; introductory essay by Lewis Mumford (London: Faber and Faber, 1965)

Hughes, Michael, *The Letters of Lewis Mumford and Frederic J. Osborn: A Transatlantic Dialogue, 1938–1970* (Bath: Adams and Dart, 1971)

Jensen, Finn, *Modernist Semis and Terraces in England* (Farnham: Ashgate, 2012)

Kynaston, David, *A World to Build, 1945–48* (London: Bloomsbury, 2008)

Kynaston, David, *Austerity Britain: 1945–1951* (London: Bloomsbury, 2007)

Kynaston, David, *Family Britain: 1951–1957* (London: Bloomsbury, 2009)

Law, Michael John, *The Experience of Suburban Modernity: How Private Transport Changed Inter-war London* (Manchester: Manchester University Press, 2014)

Macfadyen, Dugald, *Sir Ebenezer Howard and the Town Planning Movement* (Manchester: Manchester University Press, 1933; 1970 reprint)

Mallinson, Richard, 'New towns: more success than failure', *Guardian*, 10 July 1969

Meacham, Standish, *Regaining Paradise: Englishness and the Early Garden City Movement* (New Haven and London: Yale University Press, 1999)

Miller, Mervyn, *English Garden Cities: An Introduction* (Swindon: English Heritage, 2010)

Morrison, Lord Morrison of Lambeth, *Herbert Morrison: An Autobiography* (London: The Hollen Street Press, 1960)

Mumford, Lewis, *The City in History: Its Origins, Its Transformations and Its Prospects* (Harmondsworth: Penguin, 1991)

Mumford, Lewis, 'The Garden City Idea'; introductory essay, in Howard, Ebenezer, *Garden Cities of Tomorrow*; edited with a preface by F.J. Osborn; introductory essay by Lewis Mumford (London: Faber and Faber, 1965)

Mumford, Lewis, *The Highway and the City* (New York: Harcourt Brace, 1963)

Nagy, Gergely and Szelényi, Károly, *The Garden Cities: The British Example* (Welwyn: Welwyn Garden City Heritage Trust, 2013)

Namorato, Michael V., *Rexford G. Tugwell: A Biography* (New York: Praeger, 1988)

Olechnowicz, Andrzej, *Working-Class Housing in England Between the Wars: The Becontree Estate* (Oxford: Oxford University Press, 1997)

Orwell, George, *The Road to Wigan Pier* (Harmondsworth: Penguin, 2001; first published by Victor Gollancz in 1937)

Osborn, F.J., *Genesis of Welwyn Garden City* (London: Faber and Faber, 1970)

Osborn, Frederic J., *New Towns After the War* (London: Dent, 1942)

Osborn, Frederic J., 'Preface' to Howard, Ebenezer, *Garden Cities of Tomorrow*; edited with a preface by F.J. Osborn; introductory essay by Lewis Mumford (London: Faber and Faber, 1965)

Osborn, Frederic J. and Whittick, Arnold, *New Towns: Their Origins and Achievements* (London: Leonard Hill, 1977)

Parsons. K.C., 'British and American Community Deisgn: Clarence Stein's Manhattan Transfer, 1924–1974', in Parsons K.C. and Schuyley, David (ed.), *From Garden City to Green City: The Legacy of Ebenezer Howard* (Baltimore: John Hopkins University Press, 2002)

Peel, Mark, *Good Times, Hard Times: The Past and the Future in Elizabeth* (Melbourne: Melbourne University Press, 1995)

Pevsner, Nikolaus, *The Buildings of England: Hertfordshire* (Harmondsworth: Penguin, 2002)

Pink, Louis H., *The New Day in Housing* (New York: John Day Company, 1928)

*Pilot, The,* 'Yes We Have No Shops', 1 February 1924

*Pilot, The,* 'The Conservative Party', 1 February 1924

Pomerantz Gary M., *Where Peachtree Meets Sweet Auburn: A Saga of Race and Family* (Harmondsworth: Penguin, 1997)

Pugh, Martin, *We Danced All Night: A Social History of Britain between the Wars* (London: Vintage, 2008)

Purdom, C.B., *Life over Again* (London: J.M. Dent, 1951)

Purdom, C.B., *The Building of Satellite Towns: A Contribution to the Study of Town Development and Regional Planning* (London: J.M. Dent, 1949)

Reeder, David, 'Representations of Metropolis: Descriptions of the Social Environment in *Life and Labour*', in Englander, David and O'Day, Rosemary (eds.) *Retrieved Riches: Social Investigation in Britain 1940 Life over Again 1914* (Aldershot: Scolar Press, 1995)

Reiss, Celia, *R.L. Reiss: A Memoir* (1968); available at: http://cashewnut.me.uk/WGCbooks/web-WGC-books-1965-1.php

Reston Foundation for Community Programmes, Inc., *Inside Reston, Virginia* (Reston: Reston Foundation for Community Programmes, Inc. 1974)

Roche Products Ltd, *Roche in Wartime, 1939 Life over Again 1945: The Record of a British Firm* (Welwyn Garden City: Roche products, 2008)

Rodgers, Daniel T., *Atlantic Crossings: Social Politics in a Progressive Age* (Cambridge, Massachusetts: Harvard University Press, 1998)

Rogers, Richard and Burdett, Richard, 'Let's Cram More Into the City', *New Statesman*, 22 May 2000

Saint, Andrew, '"Spread the People": The LCC's Dispersal Policy, 1889 Garling 1965', in Saint, Andrew (ed.), *Politics and the People of London: A Centenary History of the London County Council* (London: Hambledon, 1989)

Schaffer, Frank, *The New Town Story* (London: Paladin, 1972)

Shapely, Peter, *The Politics of Housing: Power, Consumers and Urban Culture* (Manchester: Manchester Press, 2007)

Shoskes, Ellen, *Jaqueline Tyrwhitt: A Transnational Life in Urban Planning and Design* (Farnham: Ashgate, 2013)

Sault, J.W. and Garling, *Who's What in Welwyn Garden City: What Town Planners Ought to Know*; volumes 1 and 2 (Welwyn: Alcuin Press, 1938)

Stern, R.M. and Massengale, J.M., *The Anglo-American Suburb* (London: Architectural Design Profile, 1981)

Tyrwhitt, Jaqueline, *Living and Working in Welwyn Garden City* (WGC, 1940)

Vaughan, Laura, *Mapping Society: The Spatial Dimensions of Social Cartography* (London UCL Press, 2018)

Ward, Dora, *Digswell from Domesday to Garden City* (Welwyn: Welwyn and District Regional Survey Association, 1953)

Ward, Stephen V., 'Ebenezer Howard: His Life and Times', in Parsons, K.C. and Schuyler, David (eds.), *From Garden City to New Town: The Legacy of Ebenezer Howard* (Baltimore: The John Hopkins Press, 2002)

Ward, Stephen V., *Planning and Urban Change* (London: Sage, 2004)

Ward, Stephen V., *The Peaceful Path: Building Garden Cities and New Towns* (Hatfield: University of Hertfordshire Press, 2016)

Watanabe, Shunichi, 'Garden City Japanese Style: the Case of Den-en Toshi Company Ltd, 1918–1928', in Cherry, Gordon (ed.), *Shaping an Urban World* (London: Mansell, 1980)

Welwyn Garden City Development Corporation *Annual Reports* (London, HMSO, 1948 et seq)

Welwyn Garden City Heritage Trust (hereafter WGCHT), *Memories-MP3-Recordings: Pre-November, 2010*

WGCHT, *Memories-MP3-Recordings: WDYTYL-Transcripts*: *Where Do You Think We Lived*
[Please note: there is no question mark in the unpublished, unindexed collections of
testimonies]

WGCHT, *Where Do You Think We Played? A Look at Leisure in WGC, 1920s–1970s*
(Welwyn: Welwyn Garden City Heritage Trust, 2017)

WGCHT, *Where Do You Think We Worked? A Timeline of WGC Industries, 1920–1960*
(Welwyn: Welwyn Garden City Heritage Trust, 2015)

WGCHT, *Where Do You Think We Lived?*: recordings and transcripts

WGCHT, *Where Do You Think We Played?*: recordings and transcripts

Welwyn Garden City Urban District Council, *Tenth Report from January 1st to
December 31st 1936 of the Medical Officer of Health and the Sanitary Inspector* (Welwyn:
WGCUDC, 1937)

Welwyn Garden City Urban District Council, *Eleventh Report from January 1st to
December 31st 1937 of the Medical Officer of Health and the Sanitary Inspector* (Welwyn:
WGCUDC, 1938)

Welwyn Garden City Urban District Council, *Welwyn Garden City: The Official Guide*
(Welwyn: WGCUDS, 1970)

Welwyn Hatfield District Council, *Welwyn Hatfield District Plan: Written Statement, April
1982* (Welwyn Hatfield: WHDC, 1982)

*Welwyn and Hatfield Times*, 16 July 2012, 'Census 2011: Welwyn Hatfield Population Tops
100,000'

*Welwyn and Hatfield Times*, 19 September 1990, 'Ex-refugees "repay a debt", by Kathryn
Giblin

*Welwyn Times*, 6 June 1929, 'Conservative Hertfordshire: Col. F.E. Fremantle Returned'

*Welwyn Times*, 8 January 1931, 'Fretherne Road and Segregation of Workers: A Socialist's
Accusation'

*Welwyn Times*, 20 January 1944, 'Housing After the War. Some of the Problems Reviewed'

*Welwyn Times*, 29 October 1931, 'Huge Poll for Fremantle; Lord Knebworth's Big
Majority'

*Welwyn Times*, 8 October 1931, 'Straight Fight Likely: Local Political Parties Ready'

*Welwyn Times*, 16 May 1929, 'The City's Permanent Hospital'

*Welwyn Times*, 6 April 1944, 'The Council in War Time. The Grave Housing Shortage'

*Welwyn Times*, 30 November 1944 'Town's Housing Problem. Ministry Allocated 50
Temporary Bungalows'

*Welwyn Times*, 2 March 1944, 'Praise for Radio Workers. A-A Chief Visits Home Counties
Factory'

*Welwyn Times*, 2 May 1929, 'Welwyn Garden City Health Association'

## Online Resources

adb.anu.edu.au/biography/brown-alfred-john-9596 (accessed June 2019)

www.bedfordpark.org.uk/suburb/short-history-of-the-suburb/ (accessed September 2019)

http://blogs.lse.ac.uk/lsehistory/2017/08/30/sydney-mary-bushell-1880-1959/__
(accessed January 2019)

www.cannockchase.gov.uk: Commuting_patterns_based_on_Annual_Population_Survey_
data_2008_tcm97-90449%20(5).pdf (accessed August 2015)

http://cashewnut.me.uk/WGCbooks/web-WGC-books-1965-1.php (accessed at various times; there is much useful information and many downloaded sources here)

www.jewishgen.org/jcr-uk/Community/welwyn/index.htm (accessed September 2019)

www.nationaltrust.org.uk/shaws-corner (accessed June 2019)

https://newtownherts.weebly.com/blog/the-houses-of-welwyn-garden-city#_(accessed March 2019)

www.ourwelwyngardencity.org.uk/content/people/c-b-purdom/c_b_purdom (accessed January 2019)

www.ourwelwyngardencity.org.uk/content/people/dinah-sheridan (accessed March 2019)

www.ourwelwyngardencity.org.uk/content/topics/wartime/wwii/jewish-refugees-come-to-welwyn-garden-city (accessed January 2019)

www.oxforddnb.com/view/10.1093/ref:odnb/9780198614128.001.0001/odnb-9780198614128-e-31520 (accessed January 2019)

www.oxforddnb.com/view/10.1093/ref:odnb/9780198614128.001.0001/odnb-9780198614128-e-31672 (accessed December 2018)

www.oxforddnb.com/view/10.1093/ref:odnb/9780198614128.001.0001/odnb-9780198614128-e-63130?docPos=1 (accessed December 2018)

www.oxforddnb.com/view/10.1093/ref:odnb/9780198614128.001.0001/odnb-9780198614128-e-38328 (accessed July 2019)

www.parliament.uk/biographies/commons/grant-shapps/1582 (accessed April 2019)

www.rent-offices.com/property/shire-park-welwyn-garden-city-al7-1tw/ (accessed June 2019);

https://suite.endole.co.uk/explorer/postcode/al7-1tw (accessed June 2019)

www.thomas-spence-society.co.uk_(accessed January 2019)

www.welhat.gov.uk/media/9345/Demographic-profile-of-Welwyn-Hatfield/pdf/Demographic_Profile_-_2018.pdf?m=636749457850500000 (accessed September 2019)

http://welwynhatfield.co.uk/wgc_society/?page_id=33 (accessed February 2019)

http://welwynhatfield.co.uk/wgc_society/?page_id=2402 (accessed June 2019)

www.whtimes.co.uk/news/welwyn-hatfield-council-local-plan-new-sites-added-1-6037348 (accessed September 2019)

www.welwyngarden-heritage.org

www.welwyngarden-heritage.org/oral-memories/qeii-hospital (accessed October 2019)

https://welwyngarden-heritage.org/photo-gallery (accessed June 2019)

www.whoshallivotefor.com/constituencies/w/welwyn-hatfield_(accessed April 2019)

https://en.wikipedia.org/wiki/Welwyn_Hatfield (UK_Parliament_constituency)_ (accessed April 2019)

www.youtube.com/watch?v=GMq-IRWbYlY

# NOTES

1   Nagy and Szelényi, *Garden Cities*, *passim*
2   Nagy and Szelényi, *Garden Cities*, p. 11
3   www.bedfordpark.org.uk/suburb/short-history-of-the-suburb (accessed September 2019)
4   Bayley, *Garden City*, p. 17
5   Bayley, *Garden City*, p. 17
6   Bayley, *Garden City*, p. 17
7   Burnett, *Social History of Housing*, pp. 159–166
8   Nagy and Szelényi, *Garden Cities*, pp. 49–52
9   Mumford, 'Garden City Idea', p. 30
10  www.thomas-spence-society.co.uk (accessed January 2019)
11  Mumford, 'Garden City Idea', p. 29
12  Bayley, *Garden City*, p. 9
13  Howard, *Garden Cities of Tomorrow*, p. 136
14  Howard, *Garden Cities of Tomorrow*, p. 139
15  Beevers, *Garden City Utopia*, p. 17
16  Ward, 'Ebenezer Howard', pp. 18–19
17  Mumford, *Highway and the City*, p. 63
18  Stern and Massengale, *Anglo-American Suburb*, p. 25
19  Ward, 'Ebenezer Howard', p. 18
20  Roberts and Taylor, *Garden City Movement*, p. 12
21  Bayley, *Garden City*, p. 4
22  Howard, *Garden Cities of Tomorrow*
23  Osborn, 'Preface', p. 18
24  Miller, *English Garden Cities*, p. 4
25  WGCHT, *Memories-MP3-Recording: WDYTYL-Transcripts: Where Do You Think We Lived?* (hereafter *WDYTWL*): Alexander D.
26  Saint, 'Spread the people', p. 216
27  Beevers, *Garden City Utopia*, p. 73
28  Beevers, *Garden City Utopia*, p. 78
29  Vaughan, *Mapping Society*, pp. 61–92
30  Reeder, 'Representations of metropolis', pp. 328–330
31  Saint, Andrew, 'Spread the people', pp. 214–236
32  Rodgers, *Atlantic Crossings*, pp. 396–397

33    Howard, *Garden Cities of Tomorrow*, pp. 151–160
34    de Soissons, *Welwyn Garden City*, p. 33
35    Roberts and Taylor, *Garden City Movement*, p. 14
36    Clapson, *Working-Class Suburb*, p. 28
37    Morrison, *Herbert Morrison*, p. 65
38    Clapson, 'Garden City to New Town', p. 17
39    Clarke, *Hope and Glory*, p. 90
40    Addison, *Betrayal of the Slums*, *passim*
41    Howard, *Garden Cities of Tomorrow*, p. 139
42    Macfadyen, *Sir Ebenezer Howard*, p. 121
43    Ward, *Peaceful Path*, p. 88
44    de Soissons, *Welwyn Garden City*, p. 21
45    Cited in Macfadyen, *Sir Ebenezer Howard*, p. 121
46    Roberts and Taylor, *Garden City Movement*, p. 9
47    de Soissons, *Welwyn Garden City*, p. 22
48    Osborn, *Genesis*, p. 20
49    Purdom, *The Garden City*, *passim*
50    Roberts and Taylor, *Garden City Movement*, p. 39
51    Reiss, *A Memoir*, p. 11
52    Reiss, *A Memoir*, p. 8
53    Reiss, *A Memoir*, p. 11
54    Reiss, *A Memoir*, p. 16
55    Roberts and Taylor, *Garden City Movement*, p. 37
56    de Soissons, *Welwyn Garden City*, p. 36
57    Reiss, *Welwyn Garden City, 1920–1959*, pp. 13–14; in WGCDC, *Welwyn Garden City: Official Handbook and Directory* (Welwyn Garden City: *Welwyn Garden City: Official Handbook and Directory*, 1960); see also WGCHT, *Keeping Up Appearances* DVD
58    Reiss, *Welwyn Garden City, 1920–1959*, pp. 13–14
59    Osborn, *Genesis*, p. 20
60    Osborn, *Genesis*, p. 20
61    Reiss, *Welwyn Garden City, 1920–1959*, pp. 16–17
62    Reiss, *Welwyn Garden City, 1920–1959*, p. 27
63    *The Pilot*, 'Conservative Party'
64    Welwyn Garden City Ltd, *Welwyn Garden Citizen's Handbook*, p. 9
65    Cited in Altman and Chambers, *Culture and Environment*, p. 271
66    Hill, *Welwyn Garden City*, pp. 56–67
67    WGCHT, *Memories-MP3-Recordings-Trancripts-WDYTYL*: Kit L.
68    Reiss, *Welwyn Garden City, 1920–1959*, p. 14; Lady Churchill Biog.
69    Osborn, *Genesis*, p. 15
70    Osborn and Whittick, *New Towns*, illustrations between pp. 80–81
71    Reiss, *Welwyn Garden City, 1920–1959*, p. 17
72    Purdon, *Satellite Towns*, p. 24
73    Shapely, *Politics of Housing*, *passim*; Olechnowicz, *Working-Class Housing*, *passim*
74    Purdom, *Satellite Towns*, pp. 24–25
75    Welwyn Garden City Ltd, *Houses in Charming Surroundings*
76    HALS/DE/FJO/K442: Pallister, *Seeing the Garden*, no page numbers.
77    WGCHT, *Memories-Pre-November-2010*: Joyce F.
78    Meacham, *Regaining Paradise*, p. 181

79   Mumford, *City in History*, p. 590

80   WGCHT, *Keeping Up Appearances* DVD

81   Jensen, *Modernist Semis*, p. 51

82   Harrison and Fraser 'Alfred John Brown', p. 48; see also http://adb.anu.edu.au/biography/brown-alfred-john-9596 (accessed June 2019)

83   WGCHT, *Keeping Up Appearances* DVD

84   Purdom, 'Introduction', p. 5

85   Purdom, 'Introduction', p. 6

86   Purdom, 'Introduction' pp. 6–7

87   Pevsner, *Buildings of England*, pp. 398–399

88   WGCHT, *Keeping Up Appearances* DVD

89   Pevsner, *Buildings of England*, p. 398

90   Planning Exchange, *New Towns Record CD Rom*, 'David Irving'

91   Esher, *Broken Wave*, p. 247

92   Cited in Esher, *Broken Wave*, p. 247

93   Clapson, *Invincible Green Suburbs*, pp. 62–115

94   HALS/DE/FJO/K468: *Welwyn Garden City Pioneers Party Souvenir*

95   WGCHT, *Memories-MP3-Recordings-Trancripts-WDYTYL*: John H.

96   Osborn, 'The Personalities'

97   Sault and Garling, *Who's What*, no page numbers

98   Purdom, *Life over Again*, p. 136

99   http://blogs.lse.ac.uk/lsehistory/2017/08/30/sydney-mary-bushell-1880-1959 (accessed January 2019)

100  Clapson, *Britain in the Twentieth Century*, p. 348

101  Beevers, 'Ebenezer Howard', p. 30

102  This section on places of worship owes much to Welwyn Publications Ltd, *Welwyn Garden Citizen's Handbook*, pp. 15–21

103  Welwyn Publications Ltd, *Welwyn Garden Citizen's Handbook*, p. 17

104  WGCHT, *Memories-MP3-Recording: WDYTYL-Transcripts*: Mary A.

105  WGCHT, *Memories-MP3-Recording: WDYTYL-Transcripts*: Clifford B.

106  Welwyn Publications Ltd, *Welwyn Garden Citizen's Handbook*, p. 17

107  Welwyn Publications Ltd, *Welwyn Garden Citizen's Handbook*, p. 21

108  WGCHT, *WDYTWW?*, pp. 1–9

109  Alexander, *Britain's New Towns*, p. 64

110  *The Pilot*, 'Yes We Have No Shops'

111  WGCHT, *WDYTWW-Memories-MP3-Audio*: Marion W.

112  Hall, *Welwyn Garden City*, pp. 56–71

113  WGCHT, AE, *Industries in WGC 1920s and 1930s* (notes)

114  Butterfield, 'Shredded Wheat Factory', pp. 128–130

115  WGCHT, *Memories-WDYTWL*: Marion T.

116  WGCHT, AE, *Industries in WGC 1920s and 1930s* (notes)

117  WGCHT, *WDYTWW?*, 9; *Welwyn Hatfield Times*, 4 February 2010

118  WGCHT, *Memories-WDYTWL*: Barcley Corsets

119  Welwyn Garden City Development Corporation, *Official Handbook and Directory* (1960), p. 17

120  WGCHT, *Memories-MP3-Recordings-Pre-November 2010-transcripts*: Queenie M.

121  WGCHT, *WDYTWW-Memories-MP3-Audio*: Marion W.

122  WGCHT, *Memories-MP3-Recordings-Pre-November 2010-transcripts*: Queenie M.

123   WGCHT, AE, *Industries in WGC 1920s and 1930s* (notes)

124   WGCHT, *WDYTWW?*, p. 26

125   WGCHT, *Memories-MP3-Recordings-WDYTYL-transcripts*: Bernard C.

126   WGCHT, *WDYTWW?*, pp. 78–79

127   WGCHT, *Memories-MP3-Recordings-WDYTYL-transcripts*: A.F. and M.S.

128   Clapson, *Britain in the Twentieth Century*, p. 302

129   WGCHT, *Memories-MP3-Recordings-WDYTYL-transcripts*: Aiken F. and Massey S. WGC Film Society

130   WGCHT, AE, *Industries in WGC 1920s and 1930s* (notes)

131   https://www.bbc.co.uk/news/uk-england-nottinghamshire-23574665 (accessed January, 2020)

132   WGCHT, *Memories-MP3-Recordings-WDYTYL-transcripts*: John R.

133   Law, *Suburban Modernity*, p. 154

134   WGCHT, *Memories-MP3-Recordings-WDYTYL-transcripts*: Anthony T.

135   This section on the interwar economy owes much to WGCHT, *WDYTWW?*, *passim*

136   WGCHT, *Memories-MP3-Recordings-WDYTYL-Transcripts:* Marion H. (2). See also: www.ourwelwyngardencity.org.uk/content/people/dinah-sheridan (accessed March 2019)

137   WGCHT, *Memories-MP3-Recordings-WDYTYL-Transcripts:* Joy Reid

138   WGCHT, WGCHT, AE, *Industries in WGC 1920s and 1930s* (notes)

139   WGCHT, *WDYTWW?*, p. 57

140   WGCHT, *WDYTWW- Neosid-Pemetzrieder-GmbH+Co-Written Note*

141   WGCHT, *WDYTWW-*Maurice F.

142   Pevsner, *Buildings of England*, p. 396

143   Clapson, 'Garden City to New Town', p. 8

144   HALS/DE/FJO/K1552a: letter to the Chairman and Directors, WGCL, 19 March 1928, from FJO *et al*

145   HALS/DE/FJO/K147/7: Letters between Chambers and FJO, 19 March 1928; 21 March, 23 March 1928

146   This section on the Purdom Crisis is closely based on Clapson, 'Garden city to new town', pp. 8–10

147   HALS/DE/FJO/K147/7: letter from FJO and Reiss to *Welwyn Times*, 25 June 1951

148   Gill, *C.B. Purdom*: www.ourwelwyngardencity.org.uk/content/people/c-b-purdom/c_b_purdom (accessed January 2019)

149   Hughes, *Osborn, Sir Frederic James*: www.oxforddnb.com/view/10.1093/ref:odnb/9780198614128.001.0001/odnb-9780198614128-e-31520 (accessed January 2019)

150   de Soissons, *Welwyn Garden City*, pp. 83–84

151   Cherry, *Evolution of British Town Planning*, p. 111

152   Cherry, *Evolution of British Town Planning*, p. 111; Clapson, 'Localism, the London Labour Party', pp. 127–129

153   de Soissons, *Welwyn Garden City*, p. 65

154   Orwell, *Road to Wigan Pier*, pp. 195–196

155   de Soissons, *Welwyn Garden City*, p. 93

156   WGCHT, *Memories-MP3-Recording: WDYTYL-Transcripts*: Eric B.

157   WGCHT, *WDYTWP?*, pp. 1–33

158   *Welwyn Garden City News*, 28 October 1921

159 WGCHT, *WDYTWP-Excerpts made from Play Audio Summary Sheet*
160 WGCHT, *WDYTWP?*, p. 3
161 WGCHT, *WDYTWP-Football-WGC-1920s-70s-Roy Williams-Transcript*
162 WGCHT, *WDYTWP?*, pp. 94–98
163 WGCHT, *WDYTWP-Memories-MP3-Audio*: Alistair B.
164 Pugh, *We Danced All Night*, pp. 284–285
165 WGCHT, *WDYTWP?*, p. 144
166 WGCHT, *WDYTWP?*, pp. 85–87, 123–126
167 Pugh, *We Danced All Night*, pp. 284–285
168 WGCHT, *WDYTWP?*, pp. 155–158
169 *Welwyn Times Festival Supplement*, 4 July 1929; on golf and class see Pugh, *We Danced All Night*, pp. 284–285
170 WGCHT, *WDYTWP?*, p. 115
171 WGCHT, *WDYTWP?*, pp. 86–87, 152–153
172 WGCHT, *WDYTWP-Excerpts made from Play Audio Summary Sheet*
173 WGCHT, *WDYTWP?*, pp. 42–43
174 Purdom, *Life over Again*, p. 175
175 Purdom, *Life over Again*, p. 179
176 WGCHT, *Memories-MP3-Audio: WDYTYL-Transcripts*: Richard M.
177 WGCHT, *WDYTWP?*, p. 39
178 WGCHT, *WDYTWP?*, p. 39
179 WGCHT, *WDYTWP?*, p. 127
180 WGCHT, *WDYTWP?*, pp. 162–163
181 WGCHT, *WDYTWP?*, pp. 127–128; see also *WDYTWP-Transcripts:* Judith C. on Old Time Music Hall; Steve D. and Derek G. on the WGC Band; Tony Skottowe on Welwyn Opera, etc.
182 WGCHT, *WDYTWP-Transcripts*: Ladies Luncheon Club
183 WGCHT, *WDYTWP?*, p. 57
184 WGCHT, *WDYTWP-Notes-Childhood-Childhood Play;* WGCHT, *WDYTWP-Notes-Childhood-Teenagers*; see also WGCHT, *WDYTWP?*, pp. 57–64
185 Vaughan, *Mapping Society*, p. 77
186 Pink, *New Day in Housing*, pp. 75–76
187 *Welwyn Times*, 8 January 1931 'Fretherne Road'
188 HALS/DE/FJO/K250: Welwyn Garden City Research Committee (1937), *passim*
189 Tyrwhitt et al (1940), 'Preface'
190 Shoskes, *Jacqueline Tyrwhitt*, p. 36
191 Shoskes, *Jacqueline Tyrwhitt*, p. 70, 118–120
192 Tyrwhitt et al, *Life and Work*, p. 3
193 Tyrwhitt et al, *Life and Work*, pp. 79–80
194 Tyrwhitt et al, *Life and Work*, p. 80
195 Tyrwhitt et al, *Life and Work*, pp. 79–80
196 Tyrwhitt et al, *Life and Work*, pp. 79–80
197 WGCHT, *Memories-MP3-Recording: WDYTYL-Transcripts*: Kit L.
198 WGCHT, *Memories-MP3-Recording: WDYTYL-Transcripts*: Gordon A.
199 WGCHT, *Memories-MP3-Recording: WDYTYL-Transcripts*: Joan S.
200 WGCHT, *Memories-MP3-Recording: WDYTYL-Transcripts*: Michael A.
201 Young, D.F., Leslie Mitchell: www.oxforddnb.com/view/10.1093/ref:odnb/9780198614128.001.0001/odnb-9780198614128-e-38328 (accessed July 2019)

202  Ward, *Peaceful Path*, pp. 114–115
203  Ward, *Peaceful Path*, p. 115
204  Buder, *Visionaries and Planners*, p. 126
205  *Welwyn Times*, 10 October 1940
206  *Welwyn Times*, 10 October 1940
207  Eserin, *The QEII*, pp. 7–8
208  *British Medical Journal*, 'Ten years of Welwyn', p. 1184
209  Anon, *Health*, New Towns CD Rom
210  *Welwyn Times*, 2 May 1929, 'Welwyn Garden City Health Association'; *Welwyn Times*, 18 April 1929, 'Council's Chairman and Vice Chairman'
211  *Welwyn Times*, 16 May 1929, 'The City's Permanent Hospital'
212  WGCHT, *Memories-MP3-Recordings-Trancripts-WDYTYL*: Clifford B.
213  Welwyn Garden City Urban District Council, *Tenth Annual Report of Medical Office of Health*, p. 6
214  Welwyn Garden City Urban District Council, *Eleventh Annual Report of Medical Office of Health*, p. 5
215  Eserin, *The QEII*, p. 10
216  Eserin, *The QEII*, p. 10
217  Eserin, *The QEII*, p. 10
218  Welwyn Publications Ltd, *Welwyn Garden Citizen's Handbook*, p. 47
219  Welwyn Garden City Ltd, *Welwyn Garden City Directory* (1938), p. 83
220  Welwyn Publications Ltd, *Welwyn Garden Citizen's Handbook*, p. 47
221  *Welwyn Times*, 29 October 1931,' Huge poll for Fremantle'
222  *Welwyn Times*, 8 October 1931, 'Straight fight likely'
223  Catterall, *Labour and the Free Churches*, p. 60
224  Catterall, *Labour and the Free Churches*, pp. 151–178
225  WGCHT, *Memories-MP3-Recording: WDYTYL-Transcripts*: Pat L.
226  WGCHT, *Memories-MP3-Recordings-Pre-November 2010*: Elizabeth D.
227  Clapson, *Blitz Companion*, p. 35
228  *Welwyn and Hatfield Times*, 'Ex-refugees repay a debt'
229  WGCHT, *WDYTWW?*, p. 41
230  Shoskes, *Jaqueline Tyrwhitt*, pp. 70, 118–120
231  WGCHT, *Memories-MP3-Recordings-Trancripts-WDYTYL*: Freddie G.
232  WGCHT, *Memories-MP3-Recordings-Pre-November 2010*: Sam O.
233  www.ourwelwyngardencity.org.uk/content/topics/wartime/wwii/jewish-refugees-come-to-welwyn-garden-city (accessed January 2019)
234  WGCHT, *WDYTWP-Research-Transcript*: Jewish + Zionist Clubs
235  WGCHT, *Memories-MP3-Recording: WDYTYL-Transcripts*: Chris B.
236  WGCDC, *Official Handbook and Directory* (1960), pp. 19–20
237  WGCHT, *Memories-MP3-Recording: WDYTYL-Transcripts*: Gordon A.
238  de Soissons, *Welwyn Garden City*, p. 97
239  WGCHT, *Memories-MP3-Recording: WDYTYL-Transcripts*: Mary H.
240  WGCHT, *Memories-Excerpts-Transcripts: WDYTYL*: Sarah L.
241  de Soissons, *Welwyn Garden City*, pp. 98–101
242  WGCHT, *Memories-MP3-Recordings Pre-November 2010*: Queenie M.
243  WGCHT, *Memories-MP3-Recordings-WDYTYL-Transcripts*: Ena W.
244  de Soissons, *Welwyn Garden City*
245  WGCHT, *Memories-Excerpts-Transcripts- WDYTWP*: Les B.

246   WGCHT, *Memories-Excerpts-Transcripts-WDYTWP*: Brian D.

247   WGCHT, *Memories-Excerpts-Transcripts*-WDYTWP: Shirley S.

248   de Soissons, *Welwyn Garden City*, pp. 99–100

249   de Soissons, *Welwyn Garden City*, pp. 101–102

250   de Soissons, *Welwyn Garden City*, p. 99

251   de Soissons, *Welwyn Garden City*, pp. 99–102

252   Boyce and Everett, *SOE,* pp. 266, 269

253   Boyce and Everett, *SOE,* pp. 266–279

254   Boyce and Everett, *SOE*, pp. 275–279

255   *Welwyn Times*, 2 March 1944, 'Praise for Radio Workers'

256   WGCHT, *Memories-MP3-Recordings-Trancripts-WDYTYL*: Freddie G.

257   WGCHT, *WDYTWW?*, p. 57

258   WGCHT, *WDYTWW?*, p. 57

259   WGCHT, *WDYTWW?*, pp. 59–61

260   Roche Products, *Roche in Wartime*, *passim*

261   Roche Products, *Roche in Wartime*, pp. 28–29

262   Roche Products, *Roche in Wartime*, p. 24

263   de Soissons, *Welwyn Garden City*, p. 99

264   de Soissons, *Welwyn Garden City*, pp. 105–106

265   WGCHT, *Memories-Pre-Nov2010*: Queenie M.

266   de Soissons, *Welwyn Garden City*, p. 98

267   de Soissons, *Welwyn Garden City*, p. 98

268   WGCHT, *Memories-WDYTWL*: Shirley S.

269   WGCHT, *Memories-WDYTWL*: Marion T.

270   WGCHT, *WDYTWW?*, p. 68

271   de Soissons, *Welwyn Garden City*, pp. 100–101

272   de Soissons, *Welwyn Garden City*, p. 106

273   Clapson, *Britain in the Twentieth Century*, p. 107

274   *Welwyn Times*, 20 January 1944, 'Housing After the War. Some of the Problems Reviewed'

275   *Welwyn Times*, 6 April 1944, 'The Council in War Time; The Grave Housing Shortage

276   *Welwyn Times*, 30 November 1944, 'Town's Housing Problem'

277   Kynaston, *Austerity Britain*, p. 102

278   Cherry, *Town Planning in Britain*, pp. 87–112; Ward, *Planning and Change*, pp. 74–78

279   Hughes, *Osborn, Fredric James*

280   *Welwyn Times*, 19 December 1940

281   Osborn, *New Towns After the War*, p. 13

282   Hall and Ward, *Sociable Cities*, pp. 45–47

283   Hall and Ward, *Sociable Cities*, pp. 45–47

284   Clapson, *Destruction and Dispersal*, pp. 103–104

285   Osborn and Whittick, *New Towns*, pp. 49–51, 180

286   Kynaston, *A World to Build*, pp. 160–162

287   Kynaston, *A World to Build*, p. 32

288   Ward, *Peaceful Path*, pp. 170–172

289   Saint, '"Spread the People"', p. 229

290   National Archives (US), College Park: Special Housing Mission, Biddle Diary, 10 March 1962

291  HALS/DE/FJO/B11: Letter from Osborn to Viscount Astor, 5 December 1944
292  Cited in Esher, *Broken Wave*, pp. 28–29
293  Walker, 'Elizabeth Denby': www.oxforddnb.com/view/10.1093/ ref:odnb/9780198614128.001.0001/odnb-9780198614128-e-63130?docPos=1 (accessed December 2018)
294  Ward, *Peaceful Path*, p. 173
295  Saint '"Spread the People"', pp. 226–227
296  *Welwyn Times*, 11 January 1945
297  *Welwyn Times*, 21 December 1944
298  GB Instructional Films/BAF, *Development of the English Town*, www.youtube.com/ watch?v=GMq-IRWbYlY
299  de Soissons, *Welwyn Garden City*, p. 107
300  Collings, *Stevenage*, p. 11
301  Collings, *Stevenage*, p. 15
302  de Soissons, *Welwyn Garden City*, p. 110
303  Reiss, *Welwyn Garden City, 1920–1959*, p. 20
304  *Welwyn Times*, 2 November 1944
305  *Welwyn Times*, 8 March 1945
306  de Soissons, *Welwyn Garden City*, p. 102
307  HALS/DE/FJO/K261/1; letter from Chambers to FJO, 25 July 1944
308  Quoted in Hall and Ward, *Sociable Cities*, p. 53
309  Alexander, *Britain's New Towns*, p. 137
310  Osborn and Whittick, *New Towns*, p. 18
311  *Parliamentary Debates, House of Commons (Hansard), Fifth Series*, Vol. 422, 1945–1946, columns 1089-90
312  Hebbert, 'Hertfordshire Solution', p. 43
313  Quoted in de Soissons, *Welwyn Garden City*, p. 117
314  de Soissons, *Welwyn Garden City*, p. 117
315  de Soissons, *Welwyn Garden City*, p. 117
316  WGCHT, *Memories-MP3-Recordings-Trancripts-WDYTYL*: Elizabeth F.
317  Collings, *Stevenage, 1946–1986*, p. 11
318  Clapson, 'Destruction and Dispersal', p. 99
319  WGCL, *Statement to the Shareholders*, pp. 13–14
320  WGCL, *Statement to the Shareholders*, pp. 15–19
321  Purdom, *Life over Again*, pp. 87–88
322  *Welwyn Times*, 30 January 1948
323  Ibid; see also *Welwyn Times*, 27 February 1948
324  *Welwyn Times*, 25 March 1948; 14 May 1948
325  Schaffer, *New Towns Story*; see also A.W.K. 'Financial notes', *The Spectator*, 7 July 1923
326  *Welwyn Times*, 25 March 1948; Welwyn Garden City Ltd (1948)
327  Welwyn Garden City Ltd (1948), pp. 10–11
328  *Welwyn Times*, 25 March 1948
329  *Welwyn Times*, 30 January 1948; 12 March 1948; 25 March 1948
330  Welwyn Garden City Ltd (1948), p. 2
331  *Welwyn Times*, 12 March, 1948; 25 March 1948
332  *Welwyn Times*, 2 April 1948
333  *Welwyn Times*, 27 February 1948; *Welwyn Times*, 2 April 1948

334  *Welwyn Times*, 27 February 1948

335  *Welwyn Times*, 28 May 1948

336  WGCL, *Statement to the Shareholders*, p. 25

337  WGCL, *Statement to the Shareholders*, pp. 25–26

338  de Soissons, *Welwyn Garden City*, p. 122

339  de Soissons, *Welwyn Garden City*, pp. 122–123

340  Gadney, 'Viscount Esher'

341  Welwyn Garden City Development Corporation, *First Annual Report*, 1948–1949, p. 151

342  Welwyn Garden City Development Corporation, *First Annual Report*, 1948–1949, p. 151

343  Hatfield Development Corporation, *First Annual Report, 1948–1949*, p. 83

344  Hatfield Development Corporation, *First Annual Report, 1948–1949*, p. 83

345  *The Times*, 3 January 1948; *Welwyn Times*, 9 January 1948; *Welwyn Times*, 14 May 1948

346  Theakston, 'Sharp, Evelyn Adelaide'

347  Osborn (1970); 'Foreword' by Baroness Sharp, p. 4

348  Ward, *Digswell from Domesday*, p. 5

349  Deakin and Ungerson, *Leaving London*, pp. 41–60; Heraud (1968), pp. 38–40

350  www.cannockchase.gov.uk:Commuting_patterns_based_on_Annual_Population_Survey_data_2008_tcm97-90449%20(5).pdf (accessed August 2015)

351  Hebbert, 'Hertfordshire Solution', p. 43

352  Kynaston, *Austerity Britain*, pp. 159–163

353  de Soissons, *Welwyn Garden City*, pp. 124–125

354  WGCHT, *Cresta Silks-Crysede, Graces Guide* (notes)

355  'The Eylure Story' (no page numbers; typescript in possession of the WGCHT); WGCHT, *Memories-MP3-Recordings-Pre-November 2010*: Eric A.

356  Mallinson, 'New Towns'

357  Brown, 'Industry of the new towns', in Martin, *Greater London*, p. 240

358  Brown, 'Industry of the new towns', in Martin, *Greater London*, pp. 240–243

359  WGCHT, *WDYTWW?*, p. 46

360  WGCHT, *WDYTWW?*, pp. 70–72

361  https://welwyngarden-heritage.org/photo-gallery accessed June 2019; see also WGCHT, *WDYTWW?*, *passim*

362  WGCHT, *WDYTWW-Memories-MP3-Audio*: Marion W.

363  de Soissons, *Welwyn Garden City*, p. 206

364  de Soissons, *Welwyn Garden City*, p. 206

365  www.rent-offices.com/property/shire-park-welwyn-garden-city-al7-1tw (accessed June 2019); https://suite.endole.co.uk/explorer/postcode/al7-1tw (accessed June 2019)

366  Hall, *Welwyn Garden City*, pp. 56–67; https://newtownherts.weebly.com/blog/the-houses-of-welwyn-garden-city#_(accessed March 2019)

367  Anon, *Underlying Principles*, New Towns Record CD Rom

368  Anon, *Underlying Principles*, New Towns Record CD Rom

369  Eserin, email to this writer, June 2019

370  Mallinson, 'New Towns'

371  de Soissons, *Welwyn Garden City*, p. 234

372  *Welwyn Times*, 18 January 1952

373  WGCHT, *WDYTWP?*, p. 88

374  Welwyn Garden City Development Corporation, *Eighth Annual Report* (1956), p. 410

375   Welwyn Garden City Development Corporation, *Eighth Annual Report* (1956), pp. 410–411

376   Clapson, *Invincible Green Suburbs*, pp. 140–142

377   WGCHT, *Memories-WDYTWL*: Francesca H.

378   WGCHT, *Memories-Pre-November 2010*: Gillian L.

379   WGCHT, *Memories-Pre-November 2010*: Gillian L.

380   Clapson, *Suburban Century*, pp. 128–129

381   Chave and Taylor, *Mental Health* (London: Longmans, 1964);
      www.welwyngarden-heritage.org/oral-memories/qeii-hospital
      (accessed October 2019)

382   WGCHT, *Memories-Excerpts-Transcripts- WDYTWP*: Hazel B.

383   WGCHT, *WDYTWP-Research-Transcripts*: Philip G.; Gosling Sports Park-Start

384   Osborn and Whittick, *New Towns*, 236; WGCDC *Annual Reports*

385   WGCHT, *Memories-Pre-November 2010*: Gillian Lewis

386   Clapson, *Working-Class Suburb*, pp. 42–43

387   Clapson, *Invincible Green Suburbs*, p. 39

388   Hughes, *The Letters*, pp. 203–204

389   Clapson, *Social History of Milton Keynes*, pp. 40–42

390   Clapson, *Invincible Green Suburbs*, pp. 160–162

391   Clapson, *Invincible Green Suburbs*, p. 162

392   WGCHT, *WDYTWP?*, p. 48

393   WGCHT, *WDYTWP-Research-Transcripts*: Philip G.; Gosling Sports Park-Start

394   de Soissons, *Welwyn Garden City*, p. 233; WGCHT, *WDYTWP-Club-Histories-Sports-WGC Cricket: Transcript Excerpts: Chris M. Welwyn Wheelers;* WGCHT, *WDYTWP?*, pp. 42–45; 80–84

395   WGCHT, *WDYTWP-Club Histories-Sports-WGC Cricket Club: Additional Notes* WGCHT, *WDYTWP-Club-Histories-Sports-WGC Cricket: Transcript Excerpts Alistair and Dennis*

396   Kynaston, *Family Britain*, pp. 547–558

397   WGCDC, *Eighth Annual Report* (1956), p. 410

398   WGCHT, *WDYTWP-Transcripts*: Margaret C.

399   WGCHT, *Memories-WDYTWL*: Francesca H.

400   HALS/DE/FJO/K330: Osborn, 'Social Provision in New Towns'

401   WGCHT, *WDYTWP?*, pp. 34–36

402   WGCHT, *WDYTWP-Transcripts*: 65 Club

403   WGCHT, *WDYTWP-Transcripts*: WGC Campus Club

404   WGCHT, *WDYTWP-Transcripts*: WGC Campus Club

405   Welwyn Publications Ltd, *Welwyn Garden Citizen's Handbook*, p. 11

406   *Welwyn Times*, 27 July, 'Dumpleton is New MP' (1945)

407   Clapson, 'Rise and fall', *passim*

408   Alexander, *Britain's New Towns*, p.137

409   Hebbert, *Metamorphosis*, p. 173

410   Hebbert, *British Garden City: Metamorphosis*, p. 173

411   Hardy, 'Garden City Campaign', pp. 181–188

412   Hardy, 'Garden City Campaign', p. 191

413   Cullingworth, *Town and Country Planning*, pp. 245–246

414   Welwyn Garden City Development Corporation, *Eleventh Annual Report* (1959), p. 405

415   Anon, 'Over £221m. spent', *passim*
416   David, 'New town sales', *passim*
417   Brun-Rovet, Timmins, 'Ageing New Towns', *passim*
418   Schaffer, *New Town Story*, pp. 237–238
419   Osborn and Whittick, *New Towns*, p. 237
420   Cullingworth, *Town and Country Planning*, p. 245
421   Alexander, *Britain's New Towns*, p. 138
422   Aldridge, *British New Towns*, p. 90
423   Commission for the New Towns, *Fifth Annual Report*, p. 2
424   Commission for the New Towns, *Fifth Annual Report*, p. 3
425   Eserin, *QEII*, p. 11
426   Thanks to Angela Eserin for this information; see also WGCHT, *WDYTWP?*, p. 49
427   de Soissons, *Welwyn Garden City*, p. 174
428   WGCHT, *WDYTWP-Memories-Excerpts-Transcripts*: John S.
429   de Soissons, *Welwyn Garden City*, p. 175
430   Ward, *Planning and Urban Change*, p. 142
431   Clapson, *Britain in the Twentieth Century*, p. 47, 253–254
432   Ministry of Transport, *Traffic in Towns*, p. 11
433   Ministry of Transport, *Traffic in Towns*, p. 165
434   de Soissons, *Welwyn Garden City*, p. 129
435   de Soissons, *Welwyn Garden City*, pp. 165–66; 171
436   de Soissons, *Welwyn Garden City*, p. 234, 235
437   de Soissons, Welwyn Garden City, p. 234
438   WHDC, *Welwyn Hatfield District Plan*, p. 1
439   WHDC, *Welwyn Hatfield District Plan*, pp. 20–30
440   WHDC, *Welwyn Hatfield District Plan*, p. 28
441   WHDC, *Welwyn Hatfield District Plan*, p. 28
442   WHDC, *Welwyn Hatfield District Plan*, pp. 28–29
443   WHDC, *Welwyn Hatfield District Plan*, p. 89
444   WHDC, *Welwyn Hatfield District Plan*, pp. 10–19
445   WHDC, *Welwyn Hatfield District Plan*, pp. 31–32
446   WHDC, *Welwyn Hatfield District Plan*, p. 33
447   WHDC, *Welwyn Hatfield District Plan*, pp. 33–34
448   WGCHT, *WDYTWP-Club Histories-Transcripts*: Save the Woods Campaign; information from Bev T.
449   WGCHT, *WDYTWP-Club Histories-Transcripts*: Mid-Herts Footpath Society
450   www.nationaltrust.org.uk/shaws-corner (accessed June 2019)
451   WHDC, *Welwyn Hatfield District Plan*, p. 66
452   WHDC, *Welwyn Hatfield District Plan*, pp. 66–71
453   Pevsner, *Buildings of England: Hertfordshire*, p. 398
454   https://en.wikipedia.org/wiki/Welwyn_Hatfield (UK Parliament constituency); www.whoshallivotefor.com/constituencies/w/welwyn-hatfield (both accessed April 2019)
455   www.parliament.uk/biographies/commons/grant-shapps/1582 (accessed April 2019)
456   www.whtimes.co.uk/news/over-70-of-welwyn-hatfield-residents-would-vote-to-remain-in-eu-1-5551442 (accessed March 2019)
457   www.citypopulation.de/php/uk-england-eastofengland.php?cityid=E35001153 (accessed March 2019)

458   *Welwyn Hatfield Times*, 16 July 2012 'Census, 2011'
459   www.citypopulation.de/php/uk-england-eastofengland.php?cityid=E35001153 (accessed June 2019)
460   www.welhat.gov.uk/media/9345/Demographic-profile-of-Welwyn-Hatfield/pdf/ Demographic_Profile_-_2018.pdf?m=636749457850500000 (accessed September 2019)
461   www.jewishgen.org/jcr-uk/Community/welwyn/index.htm (accessed September 2019)
462   www.welhat.gov.uk/media/9345/Demographic-profile-of-Welwyn-Hatfield/pdf/ Demographic_Profile_-_2018.pdf?m=636749457850500000 (accessed September 2019)
463   http://welwynhatfield.co.uk/wgc_society/?page_id=33 (accessed February 2019)
464   Reiss, *Welwyn Garden city, 1920–1959*, p. 14
465   HALS/DE/FJO/H17–H33
466   HALS/DE/FJO/H1–H14
467   HALS/DE/FJO/H26–H32
468   Corden, *Planned Cities*, pp. 35–42
469   Corden, *Planned Cities*, pp. 44–48
470   Pink, *New Day in Housing*, p. 75
471   Parsons, 'British and American', p. 131
472   Bloom, *Suburban Alchemy*, p. 19
473   Fishman, 'American Garden City', p. 149
474   Conkin, *Tomorrow a New World*, p. 305
475   Namorato, *Rexford G. Tugwell*, pp. 114–115
476   Pomerantz, *Where Peachtree Meets*, pp. 141–248
477   Palmer, *Adventures*, p. 173
478   Palmer, *Adventures*, p. 174
479   Palmer, *Adventures*, p. 175
480   Reiss, *A Memoir*, p. 30
481   Reiss, *A Memoir*, pp. 30–34
482   Palmer, *Adventures*, p. 231
483   Palmer, *Adventures*, pp. 231–232
484   HALS/DE/FJO/B113: Palmer 'What British Planning', *passim*
485   HALS/DE/FJO/B11: 'British Visitors'
486   Clapson, *Anglo-American Crossroads*, pp. 103–105
487   Clapson, *Anglo-American Crossroads*, p. 106
488   Clapson, *Anglo-American Crossroads*, p. 108
489   Clapson, *Anglo-American Crossroads*, p. 105
490   Reston Foundation for Community Programmes, Inc., *Inside Reston, Virginia*, no page numbers
491   Hughes, *The Letters*, p. 371
492   Hughes, *The Letters*, pp. 462–463
493   HALS/DE/FJO/B113: Letter from Palmer to Osborn, 5 July 1967
494   Cited in Clapson, *Anglo-American Crossroads*, p. 111
495   Clapson, *Anglo-American Crossroads*, p. 113
496   Clapson, *Anglo-American Crossroads*, pp. 116–117; Corden, *Planned Cities*, pp. 118–119
497   HALS/DE/FJO/B113: Letter from Osborn to Palmer, 16 September 1963

498  Ward, *Peaceful Path*, pp. 287–340
499  Ward, *Peaceful Path*, pp. 321–322
500  Ward, *Peaceful Path*, pp. 318–320
501  Ward, *Peaceful Path*, p. 322
502  Ward, *Peaceful Path*, p. 323
503  Watanabe, 'Garden City Japanese Style', pp. 129–143
504  Clapson, *Blitz Companion*, pp. 137–142
505  Osborn and Whittick, *The New Towns*, p. 159
506  Osborn and Whittick, *The New Towns*, p. 54
507  Hughes, *The Letters*, p. 404
508  Hughes, *The Letters*, p. 404
509  Ward, *Peaceful Path*, pp. 328–329
510  Based on this writer's visits to Japanese new towns in 2006, 2011, 2017.
511  Peel, *Good Times, Hard Times*, p. 23
512  Peel, *Good Times, Hard Times*, pp. 43–44
513  Ward, *Peaceful Path*, p. 329
514  Commission for the New Towns, *Eighth Annual Report*, p. 25
515  Hughes, *The Letters*, p. 471
516  Commission for the New Towns, *Eighth Annual Report*, p. 1
517  Hughes, *The Letters*, p. 476
518  Freestone, *Model Communities*, p. 4
519  Clapson, *Anglo-American Crossroads*, pp. 149–152
520  Rogers and Burdett, 'Let's cram more', p. 25
521  Urban Task Force, *Towards an Urban Renaissance*, p. 26
522  Gummer, 'Those Four Million Houses', p. 185
523  Gummer, 'Those Four Million Houses', p. 185
524  Clapson, *Social History of Milton Keynes*, *passim*
525  http://welwynhatfield.co.uk/wgc_society/?page_id=2402 (accessed June 2019)
526  www.mortgagestrategy.co.uk/government-details-plans-for-25000-new-homes/
     (accessed March 2019); www.whtimes.co.uk/news/welwyn-hatfield-council-local-
     plan-new-sites-added-1-6037348 (accessed September 2019)
527  WGCHT, *Memories-MP3-Recordings-WDYTYL-transcripts:* Jenny S.
528  WGCHT, *Memories-MP3-Recordings-WDYTYL-transcripts*: Gladys A.
529  WGCHT, *Memories-MP3-Recording: WDYTYL-Transcripts*: Gordon A.
530  WGCHT, *Memories-MP3-Recordings-WDYTYL*: Anne W.; see also WGCHT,
     *Memories-MP3-Recordings-WDTYL*: Nora P.
531  WGCHT, *Memories-MP3-Recordings-Pre-November 2010*: Elizabeth D.
532  WGCHT, *Memories-MP3-Recordings-Pre-November 2010*: Elizabeth D.
533  WGCHT, *Memories-MP3-Recordings-Pre-November 2010*: Mary A.

# INDEX

Note: page references in *italics* indicate illustrations; WWI and WWII stand for World War I and World War II.